# FREEDOM
# TO
# DIFFER

The Shaping of the Gay and Lesbian
Struggle for Civil Rights

## DIANE HELENE MILLER

NEW YORK UNIVERSITY PRESS

*New York and London*

NEW YORK UNIVERSITY PRESS
New York and London

Library of Congress Cataloging-in-Publication Data
Miller, Diane Helene, 1966–
Freedom to differ : the shaping of the gay and lesbian struggle
for civil rights / Diane Helene Miller.
    p.    cm.
Includes bibliographical references and index.
ISBN 0-8147-5595-X (cloth : alk. paper). — ISBN 0-8147-5596-8
(pbk. : alk. paper)
1. Gay rights—United States—History. 2. Lesbians—Legal status,
laws, etc.—United States. 3. Women's rights—United States—History.
4. Lesbian feminism—United States. 5. Achtenberg, Roberta.
6. Cammermeyer, Margarethe, 1942– . I. Title.
HQ76.8.U5M55    1988
306.76'6'0973—dc21      98-13816
                              CIP

Manufactured in the United States of America

10 9 8 7 6 5 4 3 2 1

# FREEDOM
## TO
# DIFFER

For Anne and Anon,
with love

Freedom to differ is not limited to things that do not matter much. That would be a mere shadow of freedom. The test of its substance is the right to differ as to things that touch the heart of the existing order.

—Supreme Court Justice Harry Blackmun,
from his dissent to *Bowers v. Hardwick*

# CONTENTS

# ACKNOWLEDGMENTS

The occasion of completing a book provides one of the rare moments in life in which one is compelled to cease one's ongoing work, at least momentarily, and take stock of one's emotional and intellectual debts: to give thanks where thanks are due. Doing so dispels the myth of the isolated writer, for while the process of writing can be a lonely one, a truer representation of scholarly work is one that casts a wider net to encompass a community of others who have influenced, directly or indirectly, that scholar's work.

To begin at the beginning, I wish to thank my parents, Jay and Lois Miller, for instilling in me at an early age a love of learning, an understanding of the value of an education, and a strong work ethic to help me achieve it. They have endowed me with the intellectual and financial means, as well as the self-discipline, to pursue an excellent and extensive education. I am grateful for their generosity and the freedom and privilege they have given me to pursue my chosen career path. I also thank my sister, Elaine Miller; my brother, Ira Miller; and my sister-in-law, Ann Kowel Miller, for their love and support.

I am fortunate to be a feminist scholar at a time and in a place where my role models have been feminist women. My awakening as both a scholar and a feminist began at Trinity University as a student of Vicki Aarons, professor of English, who is without question the finest teacher I have ever known. She introduced me to the excitement of the life of the mind and to the importance and joys of feminist scholarship. My admiration for her, the knowledge and skills I acquired in her classroom, and the guidance she provided shaped my undergraduate years as well as my future career. Trinity itself will always be a second home to me, and so much of who I am has been influenced by the people and ideas I first encountered there.

My feminist education has been furthered by other strong women who have been my teachers, either formally or unofficially. In the former group,

Cindy Jenefsky, Celeste Condit, Ramona Liera-Schwichtenberg, and Evelyn Fox Keller taught me much of what I know about feminist theory and criticism, for which I am deeply grateful. In the latter group, Coleen Grissom, Peg Layton, and Ann Knoebel have inspired me with their intellect, wisdom, and humor. Their faith in my abilities has encouraged me to greater belief in myself.

Many individuals have helped me along the way since this project began. This book is based on a dissertation I completed at the University of Georgia. Several faculty members were particularly supportive during my search to find a topic that would be meaningful to me and to shape a research agenda that would have an impact on a wider community. For their support and guidance I thank, again, Celeste and Cindy. I am grateful to Tricia Lootens, whose enthusiastic response to my project inspired me during moments of doubt. Her thoughtful insights and suggestions considerably improved the final version of this book. I also express my gratitude to Cal Logue, not only for his assistance on this project but also for the innumerable things I have learned from him through our collaborative work. Our association has been in all ways a joy to me.

I thank my editor at New York University Press, Jennifer Hammer, for her guidance, her patience in answering the innumerable questions of a first-time author, and her belief in the book and its possibilities. I also express my appreciation to copy editor Joanna Lee Mullins, whose remarkable attention to detail greatly enhanced the book's readability and consistency. I am grateful to Mary Newcombe, one of Grethe Cammermeyer's lawyers, for providing me with transcripts and other documents I could not find elsewhere and for patiently explaining some of the legal intricacies of the case. In addition, I wish to acknowledge the two courageous women whose stories stand at the heart of this book. Roberta Achtenberg and Grethe Cammermeyer inspire us all with their courage to be who they are, openly and proudly. In standing up for themselves and their own beliefs, they set a standard of integrity to which we can all aspire.

I am indebted to several readers who generously volunteered their time to read and comment on drafts of this manuscript. Among these are J. A. Bergerson, Marsha Black, Celeste Condit, Pam Lannutti, Anne Layton, and Tricia Lootens. I am also deeply grateful for the insights, ideas, and phenomenal editing of a friend who, sadly, must remain unnamed here. Her work as a public school teacher and the well-being of her children forces her to remain anonymous, lest she endanger the people and the livelihood she cherishes. Her contributions to the clarity of my thought and my writing in this book are immeasurable. With her quiet pride, she stands as a reminder both of the very real dangers that continue to confront gays and lesbians every day and of the tremendous but often hidden contributions that anonymous members of our communities make to our cause. I thank her with all my heart. I hope that someday her anonymity will no longer be necessary.

I am incredibly fortunate to be surrounded by a family of friends who are, blessedly, too numerous to name but who I trust will know who they are. First and foremost, I thank the members of the Athens Area Lesbian Social Group for their encouragement, support, generosity, humor, and love. This book is in so many ways a tribute to you all. For friendship over the years, I am grateful to Kelly Bender, J. A. Bergerson, Sammie Foss, Elizabeth Holman, Chris Kesler, Caroline Carriker, Julie Chapman, Jeff Hebert, Donna Stachowiak, and David Tuttle. I am so thankful to share my life with my adored and (intermittently) faithful cat companion, Butterscotch, who is a constant source of joy to me. Finally, I express my gratitude and love to Anne Layton, whose encouragement, support, patience, and understanding sustained me throughout the writing of this book. Her love reminds me, day after day, of the reasons we must continue to struggle for full liberation, and of why we ultimately must triumph.

# PREFACE

I am the child from down the street.
Now I've grown into someone you might never meet.
                            —Tret Fure, "Something Blue"

Eve Kosofsky Sedgwick, a well-known scholar in the field of gay and lesbian studies, opened her book *Tendencies* by writing, "I think everyone who
does gay and lesbian studies is haunted by the suicides of adolescents" (1993,
1). The statistics on suicide among gay and lesbian teens are dramatic and
horrifying.[1] They are also far too close to home to have a purely academic
ring to them. Only a few years ago, these statistics touched my own university community when a lesbian undergraduate committed suicide, apparently for reasons connected with the oppression she faced or expected to
face due to her sexual orientation. In her memory, her family endowed a
lecture series at the university to bring in speakers in the field of gay and lesbian studies. They hoped that educating young lesbians and gay men would
help them find alternatives to a final escape from a society that makes them
feel rejected and unwanted.

   This book is not about suicide, nor about adolescence, so perhaps the relevance of this preface will not immediately be apparent. Yet Sedgwick's
observation, the life of the young woman who committed suicide in my
own community, and the subsequent actions of her family bring home the
motivation and the impulse for this kind of work with a clarity and an
urgency that no theoretical justification can capture. Obviously, there are
academic motives for undertaking such a study. Yet there is also something
more: a faith that language plays a central role in shaping our internal and
external worlds; a belief that scholarly pursuits are intimately connected to

the achievement of social change; and a hope that the visibility of the written word has the potential to reach people within and beyond academia in a way that appeals to more than detached intellectual interest, a way that actualizes "humanistic" study in its profoundest sense.

Any inquiry into issues of gay or lesbian representations must be circumscribed by the recognition of real lives in peril, by the urgency of achieving social change that ensures the safety of those lives and makes them livable. Human beings are constantly subject to powerful, if constructed, categories, and those categories have concrete consequences that affect happiness, health, opportunity, safety, even life and death. In reality, most of these outcomes remain untouched by even the most dazzling of our theoretical insights. There are obvious limitations to approaching social change through academic means, undeniable drawbacks to the slow timetable and the indirect effects of scholarly pursuits. Arguably, such writing may never save an adolescent life, may never arrive in time, may never reach those whose lives we dream of changing. The specter of adolescent suicide, and of other physical and emotional violence inflicted on lesbians and gay men by themselves and others, is a constant reminder of how many lives have been and remain beyond our reach.

Yet there are also possibilities here, opportunities for reaching out in the hope that our work will mean something to someone, with the belief that it can make a difference. Scholarship of this sort, like the inauguration of a lecture series, is not simply a memorial to what has been, not only a means of recognizing what is past. It is also a statement of hope, a belief that despite the tragedies we have not been able to prevent, there are some that perhaps we can. It is, above all, a commitment to creating another kind of future. In a sense, this may be what all of us—as scholars, writers, and simply human beings—in our highest aspirations seek to achieve.

# CONSTRUCTIONS AND DECONSTRUCTIONS
## Gay Politics, Lesbian Feminism, and Civil Rights

Whatever is unnamed, undepicted in images, whatever is omitted from biography, censored in collections of letters, whatever is misnamed as something else, made difficult-to-come-by, whatever is buried in the memory by the collapse of meaning under an inadequate or lying language—this will become, not merely unspoken, but *unspeakable*.
—Adrienne Rich (1979, 199)

## PROLOGUE

In the winter of 1993, shortly after his inauguration, President Bill Clinton nominated longtime supporter Roberta Achtenberg for the position of assistant director of Housing and Urban Development (HUD). Achtenberg, an openly lesbian lawyer and lesbian rights advocate, had served on the Board of Supervisors of San Francisco from 1991 to 1993. Her selection to a position in the president's cabinet required the approval of the Senate, making her the first openly gay or lesbian nominee ever to face the Senate confirmation process. Because she made no secret of her sexual orientation, Achtenberg and her supporters anticipated some resistance to her candidacy from conservative senators. However, the battle began sooner and more brutally than expected, with Senator Jesse Helms's statement to the *Washington Post* that the Senate should refuse to confirm "a damn lesbian." Many of Helms's colleagues condemned his outright bigotry, yet the issue of Achtenberg's sexual orientation became a key point of attack for her mostly Republican opponents.

Colonel Margarethe (Grethe) Cammermeyer had been a highly respected nurse in the United States National Guard for twenty-seven years when she began preparing to apply for the War College to enable her to compete for the position of chief nurse of the National Guard in 1989. During the routine questioning required for top secret security clearance, Cammermeyer revealed that she was a lesbian. As a result of the military board hearing that followed, and despite a flawless record of service, in 1992 she was not only refused the promotion but was also separated from the National Guard, stripped of her rank, and denied a number of the benefits of her long tenure. Cammermeyer subsequently filed a civil discrimination suit against the military and was reinstated by a district court judge in 1994.[1] Nevertheless, the battle left its scars. Cammermeyer was denied her lifelong dream of attaining the rank of general, serving as chief nurse of the National Guard, and retiring with full military honors. Instead, she spent the culminating years of her distinguished career embroiled in legal battles against the institution to which she had dedicated her life, fighting against the people and the country she had defended and loved.

## INTRODUCTION

Since the 1970s, the feminist and lesbian/gay rights movements have made substantial progress in advancing their struggles for equality.[2] At times, the two movements' goals have coincided, and they have joined together to pursue mutually beneficial ends. These include challenging gender stereotypes, broadening narrow gender roles for women and men, and affirming the right of all individuals to control their own bodies. On other occasions, the two groups have worked with a complete disregard for each other or even at cross-purposes. At such moments, each has been insensitive to the oppression experienced by the other and to the ways in which each has participated in and benefited from the other's oppression. Caught in the middle are those women who belong in, yet are frequently marginalized by, both movements: gay women, or lesbians, whose existence has often been disregarded or concealed by the leaders of both social movements.

To examine the status of lesbians within and between these movements is to engage feminist theory, gay studies, and public discourse at a powerful and controversial crosscurrent. The feminist movement continues to raise many of the major ongoing debates of our time, forcing public confrontation of issues as broad-ranging as rape, domestic violence, abortion, sexual harassment, and the feminization of poverty. Anyone who doubts the dissent that still rages around feminism need only observe the broad-based support for the current conservative Republican Congress or the vast radio and television audiences who avidly follow Rush Limbaugh's diatribes. As the right-wing backlash continues to spread, the perceived feminist attack on "family values" is overshadowed by a group seen as even more threatening: gays and lesbians. The gay and lesbian claim to equal rights has produced one of the most explosive public debates in progress today.

The arguments surrounding gay and lesbian rights constitute crucial *public* debates, not only because they are conducted through public channels and institutions but also because they directly engage questions about the relationship between public discourse and minority identities. As the military's current "Don't Ask, Don't Tell" policy attests, the very formation of identities is based in part on their assertion: who we are depends in part on how we represent ourselves, and on how others represent us, through language and visual images (Shotter and Gergen 1989, ix). The point is not simply that giving the name to gay or lesbian individuals and communities affirms our existence. More broadly, by highlighting certain facets of gay and lesbian lives and obscuring others, the discussions produced by gay and lesbian rights controversies help *constitute* identities. They do so by providing particular frameworks within which gays and lesbians may be seen and understood, by ourselves and by others.

In relation to these frameworks, lesbians occupy a tenuous position that places us both within and outside the feminist and lesbian/gay rights movements. We are multiply silenced, our existence doubly erased. First, we are negated by a dominant culture for whom we are emphatically "Other" by virtue of being neither men nor heterosexual. Second, we are often forgotten or ignored by groups of gay men and heterosexual women, for whom we are neither wholly insiders nor outsiders. For lesbians who are also marginalized with respect to race, class, age, physical ability, or other elements of identity, experiences of exclusion are further intensified through a dynamic that has been called "multiple jeopardy" (King 1988).[3] Perhaps because of this multiple marginality, even those scholars who specifically set out to reclaim silenced or "lost" public voices have frequently neglected the study of lesbians.

Among scholars who study communication, for example, attention to women's speech or "women's issues" has gradually grown more prevalent and more accepted, although this change has occurred at a painfully slow pace. Nonetheless, these scholars by and large continue to ignore the prodigious public discourse on gay and lesbian rights generated in this country in recent years. While the American public and the mass media in particular widely debate the implications of gay and lesbian rights struggles, those who study public discourse have remained unusually silent on the subject.[4] Such neglect is striking in relation to an issue that currently constitutes one of the most widespread topics of public debate in this country and is likely to become even more contentious in the coming years.

If communication scholars have been reluctant to address gay issues generally, however, they have been hesitant to the point of nearly unbroken silence to broach the specific issues of lesbian speech or lesbian rights struggles. Those wishing to research any facet of communication about lesbians often find themselves scanning the indexes of books with *gay*, *feminist*, or *women* in the title, hoping to find an entry for lesbians. Frequently, they find none. In fact, those wishing to do lesbian scholarship are immediately confronted with a number of obstacles. First is the fear of discrimination and prejudice against one's work or oneself when one pursues a research project about lesbians, regardless of one's own sexual orientation. Second, materials are often not easily accessible, as much of the writing that does exist is published by alternative presses or small journals that are unavailable even in the libraries of large research institutions. Finally, the considerations of publishing and academic job security discourage scholars from writing about lesbians. As both a marginalized and a stigmatized minority, lesbians are considered at best a "special interest group" and at worst a threat to family values and the American social fabric.

The neglect of lesbian issues within speech communication has persisted despite growing bodies of lesbian feminist work in related areas such as literary studies, cultural studies, history, and psychology.[5] Because these fields have led the way in developing lesbian studies, their disciplinary perspectives predominate in this emerging field. The result has been a relative flourishing of scholarship that focuses on fictional accounts, personal narratives, and other artistic and cultural endeavors, highlighting self-expression and the sharing of personal experience. Still needed, however, is another framework, crucial to any movement for social change: a method for examining public expression as communication, representations as political strategies, and messages in terms of their effects.

Such a framework would highlight self-identification as a distinct mode of communication. Declarations of identity serve several functions: they are at once powerful individual expressions, reinforcing one's sense of belonging to a particular group; communicative messages, conveying that identification to others; and representations, offering particular portrayals of the individual and his or her group to the public. Statements of self-identity can modify public understandings and portrayals of a group, while a group's public representations can influence individual and collective self-identities. This mutual interaction of language and identity may either extend or abridge the available range of identities for a given group (Shotter and Gergen 1989, ix). Such consequences may be particularly striking for lesbians and gays, who are, as a group, "consciously involved in creating [their] own identity and purpose," and whose public representations remain hotly contested (Fejes and Petrich 1993, 397).

To understand how various uses of language expand or restrict gay and lesbian identities, access to rhetorical approaches becomes vital. The word *rhetoric* is often used disparagingly to refer to language that is all ornament and little substance (Foss 1996). However, the term also refers to the art of using language effectively and persuasively. More broadly, *rhetoric* refers to the use of symbols, such as language and visual images, for the purpose of communication. Those who study rhetoric examine how speakers and writers use such symbols not only to *represent* reality but to *create* it. "Rhetoric is not simply the translation of some knowledge that we acquired somewhere else into a communicable form. It is the process by which our reality or our world comes into being; reality or knowledge of what is in the world is the result of communicating about it" (Foss 1996, 6).

From a rhetorical perspective, investigating the effects of language is a crucial form of inquiry because "what we count as 'real' or as 'knowledge' about the world depends on how we choose to label and talk about things" (Foss 1996, 6). The term *rhetorical criticism* describes the process of analyzing persuasive symbols and their effects in a given situation or context. Rhetorical critics analyze how persuasive appeals are constructed to create particular understandings of the world and to affect a given audience in a specific way. Such critics are therefore able to suggest how certain kinds of "knowledge" and versions of "reality" come to be widely accepted, and how others come to be devalued or erased, through the strategic use of symbols. Rhetorical approaches focus on how language and images function in concrete situations. They thereby enhance our ability to become more thoughtful, discerning, and critical consumers of public discourse.

Although those who study rhetoric have not granted the issue of gay and lesbian rights the attention it deserves, given its social significance, a rhetorical approach does have a valuable and needed perspective to add to those that are contributed by other disciplinary and interdisciplinary standpoints. Rhetorical perspectives can make a dual contribution to the analysis of lesbian and gay rights initiatives. First, they take as their texts persuasive, nonfictional public discourse, which enables them to analyze representations that proliferate in some of today's most widespread and influential discussions. Second, they illuminate not only the *intentions* that motivate such discourse but also the *consequences* of particular uses of language for various audiences. Rhetorical analysis allows us to set aside questions of "positive" or "negative" images. It allows us to examine, instead, how particular language and images function in a given context and for a designated audience.

This book investigates the representations of lesbians produced in two primary arenas of civil rights struggle: the United States political and military systems. It focuses on two case studies of discrimination against lesbians, examining how the language and images employed by advocates and opponents in each case shape available understandings of lesbian (and often gay) lives. More specifically, it examines how a focus on equal rights arguments, also referred to as civil rights strategies, constrains lesbian and gay identities and self-definitions; how such an approach regulates future liberatory endeavors; and how it prescribes a particular set of lesbian and gay public images that excludes certain individuals and communities. This book identifies those possibilities we create and those we exclude through an emphasis on civil rights strategies. It examines, finally, the role rhetoric can play in illuminating the heterosexual nature of institutions, both military and political, and in revealing the inherent inequalities on which such institutions are founded.

More broadly, this book points to the ways in which *all* categories of sexuality are shaped and delimited by language and in which sexual and other minority classifications may be produced by the very discourses that seek to regulate or protect them. These discourses at once assume the existence of such categories and create their parameters. In the process of constructing minority identities, dominant identities are also established and legitimated. Their boundaries are strengthened by the force of the binary opposition at work, and by the marginalization of the out-group. This process of group definition and differentiation solidifies distinctions between heterosexuality and homosexuality. The dividing line between categories is thereby strengthened, and sexual self-definition is limited on both sides. This process is thoroughly rhetorical and of the utmost importance. It influences at an intimate level the ways in which we are able to conceive of ourselves and others, touching on our most deeply held convictions about our own identities and the identities of those around us.

I begin this book by highlighting the exclusion of lesbians from much of feminist scholarship and gay studies. I offer a brief introduction to the mainstream lesbian/gay rights movement and its guiding civil rights agenda, examining how the specific oppression of lesbians challenges a number of this movement's goals. A lesbian feminist analysis of lesbian/gay rights discourse enables us to consider both the advantages and the risks of two of the movement's guiding objectives: voice and visibility. Voice refers to political participation and cultural influence, while visibility represents the right to acknowledge openly a gay or lesbian identity. To explore the complexity that is introduced into these concepts when lesbian specificity is taken into account, I examine the cases of Roberta Achtenberg and Grethe Cammermeyer. Their stories illustrate some of the ways in which lesbians have been represented in recent years through particular institutional discourses. I focus on the language and images used to characterize these women and to establish their relationship to the category "lesbian." I also suggest how these representations might influence broader public understandings of lesbians as individuals and as a group.

I argue that when some level of lesbian and gay voice or visibility is achieved, as in these high-profile cases, another level of institutional oppression is imposed to maintain the dominant culture's control over the images and language that proliferate around a controversial issue.[6] Images and language are continually subject to the threat of misinterpretation or assimilation, and the gains associated with greater visibility are balanced with some attendant losses. Rhetorical criticism examines not only the value of expressing one's identity but also the consequences of public discussions of identity. In this book, I analyze such discussions for their potential to extend or limit opportunities for self-definition and the formation of individual and group identities. Metaphors of visibility and voice convey the importance of self-expression as a form of individual empowerment, independent of its public consequences. However, social movements must concern themselves not only with individual self-realization but also with identifying broadly effective political strategies and creating coherent visions for liberation. These imperatives call for a rhetorical perspective, grounded in textual analysis, to examine how various discursive strategies produce particular outcomes. Rhetorical analysis, drawing on the theoretical insights of feminist, gay, and lesbian studies, can bring these insights to bear on the concrete circumstances that directly affect the lives of millions of gays and lesbians every day.

As I begin this investigation, a few qualifications will help clarify my terminology, my intentions, and the scope of my analysis. Throughout this book I refer to a "dominant" American culture, an identifiable "mainstream," and "dominant" groups of people whose views have shaped traditional institutions. Yet it is important to recognize that such references are inevitably problematic and oversimplified. Our identification as insiders or outsiders in relation to a "dominant" culture is constantly shifting, so that nearly all of us feel included based on some elements of identity and excluded based on others. We may be privileged by our gender, race, age, education, physical ability, religion, or social class, to name but a few variables; we may also be excluded based on any of these characteristics. Very few of us can identify consistently as either mainstream or marginalized, when all social stratifications are accounted for.

Thus, while I want to account for the effects of oppression on marginalized individuals and groups, I do not want to perpetuate the fiction that we can identify a single, powerful group of individuals who constitute a societal mainstream (Clausen 1997). I am not suggesting that a particular individual or group can be identified either as omnipotent or as entirely without power. Nor do I wish to homogenize individuals based on their group identification, and so fail to acknowledge, for example, feminist men, anti-racist whites, gay- and lesbian-friendly heterosexuals, and others for whom privilege has not blunted social consciousness.

Likewise, by identifying the political strategies favored by a powerful or "dominant" group of mostly white, middle-class or affluent gay men within the lesbian/gay rights movement, I do not wish to deny or discount the presence of more radical gay men. Groups of gay men such as the Radical Faeries or Black and White Men Together are often denied the publicity granted to those in the movement who present more mainstream or "acceptable" media images. I do not wish to minimize, either, the presence and influence of outspoken lesbian feminists throughout the history of the movement. Even my use of the phrase "lesbian and gay rights movement" represents a distortion. Rather than having one cohesive political center, the movement has always been a divided, contested site. Conflicts have occurred within the movement both historically and currently. Thus, although the themes of assimilation and equality have predominated, they have never been exclusive themes. My use of this phrase, while necessary, nevertheless obscures and artificially unifies a multitude of perspectives, priorities, identities, and strategies for the purposes of clarity and convenience. At the same time, it obscures the vital contributions of numerous bisexual, transsexual, and transgender men and women to the movement. I use this distortion consciously, although reluctantly, because of the danger of portraying the movement as monolithic and obscuring the rich diversity that is one of its greatest strengths. I hesitate, moreover, to represent our movement as a straw person that is easily attacked, wishing instead to provide a thoughtful and nuanced critique of the movement in all its complexity.[7]

Finally, I acknowledge the limitations of choosing to focus on these particular case studies. Both Roberta Achtenberg and Grethe Cammermeyer are white, professional lesbians, privileged by race and class (although Achtenberg is Jewish, another marginalizing factor). Because they are members of the dominant race and class, these features of their identities go unmarked, and unremarked upon, in the context of these debates. As a result, within their struggles "questions of discrimination based on race or class, and the interconnectedness of these forms of oppression with homophobia, are bracketed" (Phelan 1994, 117). The hiddenness of race and class in these discussions may tempt us to neglect or discount their impact. Nevertheless, such factors are always implicitly present, interwoven throughout these debates with conceptions of gender and sexual orientation.

Even the movement's focus on silencing as a hallmark of lesbian oppression is deficient when it fails to account for the varying configurations of silence and voice available to women in different ethnic communities. Thus, whereas lesbians are silenced in the wider societal context "as lesbians," this silencing may vary in form and intensity among different groups of lesbians. For example, in contrast to the historical division of public and private spheres that has denied white, middle-class women a public voice, "the distinct division between male and female spheres of activity . . . has never been prevalent in black speech communities." Perhaps as a result, "black women have been described as generally outspoken and self-assertive speakers. . . . There is a fundamental tendency toward male-female communicative parity in black culture which starkly contrasts to the tendency toward communicative asymmetry which scholars emphasize for white women and men" (Stanback 1985, 181, 182; see also Collins 1991). The constraints on African American women's speech must therefore be distinguished from those that affect white women. "In black communities (and diverse ethnic communities), women have not been silent. Their voices can be heard. Certainly for black women, our struggle has not been to emerge from silence into speech but to change the nature and direction of our speech, to make a speech that compels listeners, one that is heard" (hooks 1989, 6).

In light of such differences, I am mindful of the ways in which choosing to focus on the cases of two white, professional women risks homogenizing gays and lesbians by portraying "a false unity among what is in fact a tremendously diverse collectivity" (Phelan 1994, 117). Examining the stories of such women is an indispensable part of assessing the overall consequences of civil rights-based approaches. However, these women should not be viewed as representative of gays or lesbians as a group, nor should the importance of their relative privilege be overlooked. Their stories are significant, provocative, and inspiring. Yet they must also serve as a constant reminder of the vast number and endless variety of stories we have yet to hear. This book is only a beginning.

## BACKGROUND AND SIGNIFICANCE OF THE BOOK

On June 28, 1969, in an event that had become commonplace in New York's Greenwich Village, police raided a popular gay bar known as the Stonewall Inn. What distinguished this raid from hundreds of other raids of gay bars was that on this night the patrons responded not only with resistance but with confrontation, turning a routine police action into a two-day riot. Gay men, lesbians, and transvestites, some patrons of the bar and others who came to support their fight, battled physically and psychologically with police to defend their right to the same freedom of assembly enjoyed by heterosexuals. While these men and women were not the first to argue for their right to fair and equal treatment, what has come to be known as the Stonewall Rebellion remains a landmark event in the fight for lesbian and gay liberation. This event is often identified as the official beginning of the social movement for gay and lesbian rights.[8]

The Stonewall Rebellion marked a new kind of visibility for gays and lesbians, whose everyday lives were otherwise defined by a careful monitoring of self-expression. What erupted during the riots at Stonewall was, certainly, a claim for equal rights. However, it was also something more: the beginning of a movement not just for equality but also for liberation and social change. The participants in this movement aimed to intervene not only in police procedure and the legal system but also in the public and private discourses that regulated their identities and circumscribed their lives. On that night, and through the days and nights that followed, many gays and lesbians refused to remain hidden any longer in deference to these constraints, insisting on being seen and heard in ways they had not previously demanded. Rather than disguise who they were to avoid social ostracism and police persecution, they "came out"—out of their individual and collective "closets" as well as literally out of the bar and into the streets—to demand acknowledgment of their existence and humanity. In their move from private to public space, this small group stood up for itself and, in the process, spoke out for many others who had lived for too long behind shrouds of invisibility, silence, and shame.

The contemporary lesbian and gay rights movement has come a long way in the nearly thirty years since Stonewall, bringing about political change and social acceptance for gays and lesbians that was unimagined, and unimaginable, just a short time ago. Gay men and lesbians are, as both our supporters and opponents are eager to note, more visible than ever before. "Out" gays and lesbians occupy positions of power in a variety of fields, including the entertainment industry, journalism, sports, politics, and even religion. Debates over gay and lesbian rights consume many pages of local and national publications, appearing on the covers of magazines with widespread circulation and popular appeal, such as *Time, Newsweek, U.S. News and World Report*, and the *New Republic*. In addition, a burgeoning industry of gay- and lesbian-produced mass media has emerged, with a proliferation of local and national newsletters, newspapers, magazines, journals, films, and television programs produced specifically by and for gay and lesbian audiences.

Within the legal realm, domestic partner benefits for cohabiting gay and lesbian couples have become available in some cities. Such benefits are also offered by an increasing number of businesses, including universities such as Emory and Northwestern and major corporations such as IBM, Apple Computer, Microsoft, Bank of America, Walt Disney, and the San Francisco 49ers. The legalization of same-sex marriage is being pursued in Hawaii's courts, with some light of success. The Supreme Court overturned Colorado's Amendment 2, an anti-gay rights initiative passed by state voters, stemming the tide of anti-gay initiatives on ballots across the country. The Clinton presidency, though fraught with disappointments for lesbian and gay rights activists, has nonetheless brought questions of gay and lesbian rights to the forefront of American consciousness, as the hotly debated "Don't Ask, Don't Tell" policy forced military personnel and civilians of all sexual orientations to examine their views on a formerly taboo subject.

Yet, while the gains of the lesbian and gay rights movement have been substantial, a right-wing backlash has emerged, predictably, to swing the pendulum back. In response to efforts to legalize same-sex marriage in Hawaii, state legislatures across the country have rushed to outlaw same-sex marriage in their states. The Defense of Marriage Act (DOMA), which limits the definition of marriage to a union between a man and a woman, was easily passed by Congress in 1996. In the midst of what has been nicknamed the "lesbian baby boom," legislatures have taken steps to prevent gays and lesbians from becoming foster parents or adopting children, while gay and lesbian parents are being denied custody of their biological children at an alarming rate. The military has stepped up its dismissal of gays and lesbians despite the implementation of the "Don't Ask, Don't Tell" policy. The Employment Non-Discrimination Act (ENDA), a federal bill that would have prohibited discrimination against lesbians and gays in the workplace, was narrowly defeated by Congress in 1996. In addition, violence against gay men and lesbians continues at an alarming rate, in incidents ranging from the fatal beating of naval officer Allen Schindler by his shipmates in 1992, to attacks on lesbian and gay high school students by their peers, to the bombing of a lesbian bar in Atlanta in February 1997 (which remains, to date, unsolved).

The resurgence of right-wing efforts to halt and reverse social change, the persistence of anti-gay violence, and ongoing discrimination against gays and lesbians in areas such as housing, employment, child custody, and military service have all galvanized the lesbian and gay rights movement to renewed social and political struggle in the 1990s. Partly as a result of the movement's battles, victories, and defeats, media coverage of gay and lesbian issues has proliferated. American public discourse has returned again and again to discussions of homosexuality: what "causes" it; what should be "done" about it; and to what degree it should be accepted or tolerated in families, schools, communities, the arts, religious institutions, and the military. As a result, "in place of the silence that once encased the lives of homosexuals, there is now a loud argument" (Sullivan 1993, 24).

Lesbian and gay rights are undoubtedly among the most contentious and widely debated issues of our time. These debates reach into the heart of individual and community values, raising questions about gender roles, love, sexuality, and the family. Inevitably, then, the discussions generated around such issues have been numerous, heartfelt, and heated. Gay and lesbian issues, like gays and lesbians themselves, continue to grow both more central to and more controversial within American public discourse. How we talk about such issues, and how we hear others talk about them, influences our sense of self, our perceptions of one another, and our vision of the society we want to live in, now and in the future. Just as various views of women have influenced the fate of women's rights throughout history, so today competing portrayals of gays and lesbians call for different political strategies and produce varied social consequences. The public discourse generated today around gay and lesbian issues will have lasting effects on how we see ourselves, sexually and otherwise, well into the next century.

At one level, what is at issue for gays and lesbians today is whether and where we will "fit" in a heterosexist, patriarchal society, as evidenced by the struggle for control over laws and other forms of public influence. Yet beneath this level of struggle lie issues of representation and self-definition, crucial questions about who we are, how we want to be perceived, and how much we are willing to sacrifice as the price of "tolerance." The interaction of public and private discourse in debates over gay and lesbian rights may encourage, erase, liberate, or regulate gay and lesbian identities. In doing so, such speech may enrich or impoverish the range of available opportunities for gay and lesbian lives. It can present us with possibilities we had not previously imagined, or conversely, it can construct barriers that limit the potential we see in our lives. These questions thus involve not only the present but also the future of the gay and lesbian movement.

Given the importance of language in influencing the strategies and success of the movement, as well as the quality of gay and lesbian lives, my investigation seeks to answer two broad questions. First, what kinds of lesbian representations emerge from the competing discourses in each of these case studies? How are "lesbians" and "lesbianism" constructed, represented, and understood within these contexts of American public life? The second and related question examines the effects of these representations. How do the strategies of supporters and opponents broaden the possibilities for lesbian self-definition and enable a wider range of lesbian identities and politics? How do these rhetorical choices constrict or eliminate such possibilities?

This book investigates the construction of the category "lesbians" in political and military discourse. The relationship between language and identity in lesbian representations is of particular interest because homosexuality represents a "limit case" of the range of invisibility experienced by marginalized groups. Members of nondominant groups experience varying degrees of invisibility in relation to the dominant group (Sedgwick 1990). Some minority individuals are literally "visible" to others, due to characteristics such as gender, skin pigmentation, facial features, or physical disability. However, these individuals may nevertheless be ignored by members of the dominant culture, treated individually or collectively as though they cannot be seen or do not exist. Others may be able to "pass" as members of the dominant culture in some situations, as they may or may not be recognized as members of a marginalized group; examples include many Jews, light-skinned African Americans, and those who are physically disabled in ways that are not apparent in all situations. Still other marginalized individuals and groups are rarely or never identifiable by outward characteristics. For them, visibility requires an act of will, and invisibility may become a strategy for survival. Members of these groups, whose nonconformity to the assumptions of the dominant culture is not visually marked, are constantly misrecognized unless they take steps to counter such assumptions (Taylor 1995).

It is in this last category that lesbian identity is most often located, because despite popular stereotypes, lesbians are not reliably recognizable from external features (particularly to nonlesbians). Lesbian identity is most often invisible unless specifically acknowledged by the lesbian herself. Such a revelation is referred to as "coming out of the closet," or simply "coming out." Coming out is the act of making one's sexual identity known to oneself and others. Because of the prevailing assumption of heterosexuality, revealing one's lesbian identity frequently requires a deliberate act of verbal or nonverbal communication. Moreover, the paucity of lesbian representations in the mass media and the lack of role models in the experience of most lesbians mean that creating a lesbian identity depends heavily on the transmission of experiences either interpersonally or from available books and other resources (Lynch 1990; Plummer 1995; Trebilcot 1994).

Coming out by publicly identifying oneself as a lesbian has long been, and remains today, an important means of combating both sexism and heterosexism.[9] Although much has changed in the discourses of gay rights and lesbian feminism since the 1970s, the importance of reclaiming a marginalized identity remains fundamental to many gays and lesbians. Where our identities have been used as weapons against us, many believe, we are empowered by reclaiming those identities and organizing around them to produce social change. Such a view has been continually asserted by many in the lesbian/gay rights movement, as well as by members of other social movements. Affirming one's love for a member of the same sex in the context of a homophobic society is such a radical and transformational act that it has generally been viewed as a cornerstone of gay and lesbian liberation.

The act of coming out, for this highly invisible group, is not a one-time occurrence but an ongoing concern. In every situation and with each new person encountered, the choice must be made whether or not to acknowledge one's minority identity (Sedgwick 1990; Zimmerman 1982). Hiddenness and visibility are rarely absolute, so that for most of us, secrecy and openness coexist, in various combinations and with differing degrees of comfort or unease. Most of us are out to someone significant in our lives: a friend, a family member, a counselor, or another lesbian or gay man. Yet, because of the stigma and the material disadvantages imposed on gays and lesbians, "there are remarkably few of even the most openly gay people who are not deliberately in the closet with someone personally or economically or institutionally important to them" (Sedgwick 1990, 67–68).

Moreover, given "the deadly elasticity of heterosexist presumption," even gays and lesbians who make a concerted effort to be out in all situations "find new walls springing up around them even as they drowse." Each day requires a renewed commitment to self-disclosure, for "every encounter with a new classful of students, to say nothing of a new boss, social worker, loan officer, landlord, [or] doctor, erects new closets" (Sedgwick 1990, 68). Like communication itself, the act of coming out is a continual process. It occurs in an endless variety of contexts, and its effects depend on numerous situational variables. Though little studied, the coming-out process may represent a central mode of interpersonal and public communication in contemporary societies, where multiple differences abound but dominant cultural assumptions remain entrenched.

The figure of the closet and its attendant rebellion of coming out originated in the lesbian and gay community. However, it has been borrowed by other marginalized groups to refer to any act of acknowledging or revealing a marginalized identity, regardless of its degree of visibility. For example, one can come out as a Jew (Bennett 1982; Sedgwick 1990), but one can also come out with pride as a fat woman (Sedgwick 1990). Thus the rhetorical processes that produce lesbian and gay identities do not exist in a vacuum but are related to the processes that shape other minority identities. For this reason, the study of lesbian representations may help us understand how metaphors of voice and visibility influence the self-identities of other marginalized groups.

The lesbian and gay rights movement that has evolved over the past three decades shares some characteristics with lesbian feminism, while differing in other respects. The predominance of metaphors of visibility and voice and the emphasis on a close connection between being seen and being heard are shared by many minority groups. Yet strategies for addressing these issues often differ. For example, some lesbian feminists are committed to developing and valuing a space along the margins of society from which to challenge patriarchal institutions and develop a culture of their own. Such efforts may be located on a spectrum of possibilities, bounded on one end by absolute separatism and on the other by the goal of complete assimilation. The mainstream lesbian and gay rights movement often falls nearer the latter end, striving to attain equality within existing institutions. Patterned implicitly and often explicitly after the model of change established by the black Civil Rights movement of the 1960s, the movement for lesbian and gay rights argues for the recognition of its members as constituting a "suspect class" as defined by law and thereby entitled to the protections granted to other minority classes based on characteristics such as race, religion, or disability (Robson 1992).

Lesbian legal theorist Ruthann Robson provides a helpful definition of the concept of suspect class status as it relates to sexual orientation:

> The hallmarks of a suspect class are ... derived from legal notions of race. Traditionally, a suspect class must be a social minority that has been historically discriminated against and continues to be relatively politically powerless, and its members must possess immutable characteristics that are identifiable. Although these criteria are certainly not absolute, arguments that lesbians are within a suspect class based on sexual orientation must work within the traditional hallmarks. The most troublesome factor is the immutable identifiable characteristic. Discussions of the applicability of this factor lead to debates whether lesbianism is an identity or an activity. For legal protection, it must be an identity, and a relatively unchanging one. (1992, 82)

By appealing to the still-controversial claim of an innate and immutable lesbian or gay identity, the argument for suspect class status places issues of identity in the forefront of gay and lesbian civil rights efforts.

More broadly, "suspect classifications" are defined by law as "acts of classification that are suspicious under equal protection doctrine" (Halley 1991, 354). The establishment of a group as belonging to a suspect classification is the first step in protecting its members under this doctrine. Equal protection laws scrutinize government acts that appear to disadvantage a group based on an irrelevant characteristic of their identity. For example, it is legal for the government to distinguish between classes of individuals according to their annual income, and to tax them at different rates based on this distinction, without violating the equal protection clause. It is illegal, however, for the government to impose different rates of taxation on individuals of different races who earn the same annual income, because race constitutes a suspect classification and therefore is not an appropriate basis for such distinctions (Wolinsky and Sherrill 1993). The suspect classification designation is intended to protect all citizens against decision making based on certain protected characteristics.

This emphasis on decision making or "acts of classification," rather than on minority individuals themselves, highlights a frequently misunderstood element of anti-discrimination laws. In relation to racial discrimination, for example, "the fact that most race-based suits are brought by people of color does not change the fact that anti-discrimination provisions protect all citizens of all races" (Fajer 1996, 211). The scope of such laws is therefore not limited to protecting the members of minority groups. "A landlord does not violate the Fair Housing Act by refusing to rent to an African-American, but rather by refusing to rent to anyone on the basis of their race." This distinction is important because an individual who is not a member of such a group but who is discriminated against because he or she is *perceived* as belonging to that group is still protected under such laws. Thus "firing someone because you incorrectly believe them to be Jewish ought to be illegal, even if the person is not a member of the 'protected class' of Jews" (Fajer 1996, 210). This clarification suggests that gaining protections based on sexual orientation is not just an issue of concern to gays and lesbians. Such a change in the law would benefit not only self-identified gays and lesbians but also a much broader range of men and women whose appearance or behavior does not conform to traditional gender roles. Because they may be perceived as gay or lesbian, they, too, are at high risk for discrimination. Heterosexuals would also be protected under such laws from decision making that would exclude them from privileges based on their *hetero*sexuality, if such protection were needed.

The reality of the need for civil rights is unavoidable in the face of rampant institutionalized discrimination against lesbians. Like gay men, lesbians can still be legally harassed in the workplace, fired from jobs, discharged from military service, evicted from homes, and denied custody of children on the basis of sexual orientation alone (Phelan 1994). The question, then, is not *whether* lesbians should engage in civil rights initiatives but, rather, what is gained and what is lost in specific examples of such endeavors. This book focuses that question on the potential for lesbian self-definition and representation, examining how these possibilities are shaped by the language of civil rights arguments. This approach shifts the question of civil rights away from wearying debates about the nature or "origins" of homosexuality. It concentrates instead on how "lesbianism" and homosexuality in general are constructed through language in two interconnected arenas of civil rights struggle.

The cases of Roberta Achtenberg and Grethe Cammermeyer illustrate various dimensions of the public debate over lesbian civil rights. These women's stories are unusual in that both received national media coverage rarely accorded to gay rights cases generally, and to lesbian rights cases especially. Such high-profile cases are particularly significant because they make visible the struggle for control over meanings of lesbianism as it occurs within some of the most influential realms of American public life. At the same time, the cases thrust these particular lesbians into the limelight "as lesbians" and thus establish them, with or without the blessing of gay and lesbian communities, as representatives of a much larger but far less visible constituency.

This work adds to a growing body of scholarship on lesbians that has been largely concentrated in the fields of literature and history. Lesbian fiction and poetry have been the subject of an increasing number of articles and books, yet virtually no scholarship outside of law reviews looks at the nonfictional discourse surrounding lesbian issues. Even though Achtenberg and Cammermeyer are nationally known figures whose words and actions place them at the forefront of the public debate over lesbian and gay rights, to date no scholarly work (other than law articles) has been published about either woman. Yet what is said about them and the language used to portray them—whether by supporters or opponents, whether in a Senate chamber, military board hearing, or court of law—will have profound effects on public perceptions and understandings of lesbians. Of equal, if not greater, significance is the fact that because many lesbians themselves lack representations or role models, what we come to know and understand about these public figures through the discourse that surrounds them may deeply affect lesbians' self-images and identities. These include, importantly, the self-images of young women just beginning to identify themselves as lesbians. For these reasons, it is vital to examine the rhetorical strategies employed in these debates and the key terms of voice and visibility, highlighting both the emancipatory and the regulatory potential of these strategies.

At a time when American politics have shifted abruptly to the right and conservative groups have succeeded in reversing the civil rights gains of other minorities, there is an urgent need to assess the direction of the lesbian and gay rights movement (Vaid 1995). The juxtaposition of lesbian visibility—witness the capitalist production of "lesbian chic"—with the evident power of the religious right forces us to examine existing representations in order to ascertain whether all increases in visibility mark progress. If not, we need to ask whether and when the aims of lesbians and gay men are undermined by the achievement of minor concessions and provisional tolerance that stave off larger demands. Likewise, we need to examine these representations with an eye to discovering what the newfound and widely hailed "inclusion" of gays and lesbians in the mainstream represents. We need to determine whether, in fact, it is only the "whitest and brightest" who are accepted or, more likely, tolerated, while those who are unable to pass for all but sexually straight are excluded. The mainstreaming of a few powerful figures at the expense of, rather than for the benefit of, other gays and lesbians should be a matter of concern for all of us (Hollibaugh 1993; Smith 1993).

From a legal standpoint, we must assess the limits of existing institutional frameworks for the purposes of lesbian liberation. The fragility of civil rights gains has been demonstrated by the crumbling of affirmative action initiatives in the mid-1990s, and some observers have argued that the Civil Rights movement never accomplished for African Americans all that it was credited with achieving (Bumiller 1988). The legal system, along with other mainstream institutions, may be inherently unable to advance minority rights precisely because it is founded on the very principles of exclusion and hierarchy that those who desire such rights seek to overturn (Becker 1995; Robson 1992; Smart 1989; Wilson 1995). If inequality is built into the system itself, those who seek parity within its framework will be forced to adapt themselves and amend their objectives in relation to it. In doing so, they inadvertently reinforce its authority, hierarchies, and injustices.

Recognizing these limitations invites a shift of focus from looking at lesbian identities as a puzzle or problem to examining homophobic social institutions as the problem. It encourages us to ask how the discourse of these institutions constructs lesbians in a way that deems us both "sick" and "scandalous" (Phelan 1993, 775). By viewing institutional structures as problematic and contestable, we are reminded that gains and losses, victories and defeats, are rarely unambiguous in relation to such systems. In examining the consequences that ensue when we do and when we do not achieve our ends, we must consider not only the gains of victory and the losses of defeat. We must also consider the possibility of advancement through our apparent losses, as well as the failures that may accompany even our most celebrated victories. We need to take a broader, macroscopic view of the political landscape, examining how our strategies contribute to an overall vision of a more egalitarian society. Only then can we identify which strategies we need to rethink, refine, or reject in response to counterattacks or attempts at assimilation.

Finally, we must examine the liberal discourse through which civil rights initiatives are expressed, looking carefully at what it says and does for us. What kinds of self-definitions and self-understandings does liberal discourse construct for lesbians? What happens to lesbian voices under the aegis of liberal politics? What roles are available and what kinds of visibility and empowerment can lesbians access within a liberal framework? Equally important, to whom is this visibility and empowerment available within lesbian communities? If we choose to work within existing institutions, we must examine the kinds of identities available to us through the language of these institutions and the degree to which we can successfully challenge and broaden institutional limits. Otherwise, our efforts to confront institutions and demand inclusivity may inadvertently validate the legitimacy and authority of these structures, reestablishing the dominance of homophobic thought and language in the larger social structure.

Issues of lesbian representation, like other lesbian issues, have rarely been addressed in scholarly literature as valid questions in their own right, to the great detriment of lesbian studies. "As soon as the lesbian is lumped in—for better or for worse—with her male homosexual counterpart, the singularity of her experience (sexual and otherwise) tends to become obscured. We 'forget' about the lesbian by focusing instead on gay men" (Castle 1993, 12). The experiences of lesbians differentiate us in important ways from both heterosexual women and gay men. Yet these differences are unaccounted for in analyses of feminist or gay discourse (Wolfe and Penelope 1993). While issues of lesbian identity clearly overlap with questions of heterosexual female and gay male identities, then, lesbian identities exceed the bounds of both. They therefore deserve and demand independent consideration (Zimmerman 1992).

A comprehensive understanding of the discourse surrounding lesbian oppression and lesbian rights remains some distance in the future. Scholarship about lesbians is still scarce, and the need for research is pressing. It can be overwhelming to consider how little is known about these and other marginalized women and to recognize the degree to which we are impoverished by our lack of knowledge about such groups. Speech communication is but one academic discipline that suffers from its inattention to the discourse of gay and lesbian rights. This book is intended to help fill this gap in our knowledge, and to bring us nearer to that encompassing understanding in the future.

## Theoretical Contexts for This Work

Lesbian studies is an interdisciplinary perspective located at the intersection of women's studies and gay studies. Recently, it has also been influenced to varying degrees by "queer theory," an approach that seeks to destabilize our taken-for-granted assumptions about sexuality and categories of sexual orientation. Each of these perspectives informs the analysis and critique undertaken by this book. A brief explanation of each field of study follows.

## Gay Studies

Gay scholarship would seem an obvious place to start looking for work on lesbians. The term *gay*, like the more clinical designation *homosexual*, ostensibly refers to both men and women with an erotic or affectional orientation toward members of their own sex, while *gay liberation* refers to the attainment of freedom and equality for all such individuals. However, many books that claim to focus on "gay" issues in fact concern themselves solely with men or incorporate only a passing claim to inclusivity, with no real attention to lesbian specificity. With few exceptions (see Altman 1982), books written by gay men have been singularly inattentive to the experiences and problems of lesbians (Edwards 1994).[10] In other minority cultures whose men and women establish primary, intimate relationships, the writing of men often abounds with images of their female counterparts, however stereotyped, objectified, or idealistic. In contrast, the writing of gay men is at times devoid of any awareness of, or reference to, lesbians and their lives. Thus, while the writing of other groups of men is prone to objectifying or fetishizing women in a manner that highlights their "Otherness," the writing of gay men is often guilty of precisely the opposite offense: the erasure of lesbian specificity or difference, brought about by the mistaken belief that lesbians suffer from forms of oppression and, consequently, have needs and objectives that are identical to those of gay men.

On the one hand, therefore, gay scholarship is largely unhelpful in offering insight into the lives, experiences, and concerns of lesbians, including concerns surrounding identity and representation. On the other hand, such work cannot simply be dismissed. Many of the issues of discrimination faced by gay men and lesbians *are* similar, and the lesbian and gay rights movement has attempted at some levels to coordinate efforts among gay men and lesbians for common gains. Moreover, and perhaps most important, gay men and lesbians often remain undifferentiated in public discussions. This is true for many supporters as well as for those who would perpetrate violence against us (Phelan 1993). For these reasons, it is crucial that we acknowledge the ways in which gay male perspectives have shaped and continue to shape the lesbian and gay rights movement and in which gay male interests and images have reached the dominant culture, to a much greater extent than have lesbian concerns or representations.

Investigating lesbian representations provides an avenue for exploring the role of voice and visibility for gay men as well. Men who transgress traditional masculine gender expectations are often subject to greater censure than are women who are perceived as imitating men. For example, it is relatively acceptable and even stylish for a woman to dress in men's clothing, including such traditional male apparel as a suit and tie. In contrast, men who dress in women's clothing are swiftly and strongly reproached. The hatred of gay men is a fear of men who behave "as women." Such men are seen as subjecting themselves sexually to another man, allowing themselves to be objectified, penetrated, and thus possessed by a man in the way that is expected of women. Where lesbians are hated for their strength, gay men are hated for their perceived weakness. Where lesbians are feared for their power, gay men are despised for occupying a position of powerlessness and thereby raising the possibility that any man might occupy such a position. Analysis of lesbian representations provides a much-needed link between feminist theory and gay studies, between two groups who too often fail to recognize the resemblance between their situations, either theoretically or materially.

## Lesbians in Feminism

Historically, within much of feminist theory, gender has provided the primary (if not sole) lens through which to analyze structures of oppression. In response to the historical silencing of women's voices, some feminist critics have sought out the lives and words of women who were neglected by traditional scholarship, at the same time developing approaches that value women's contemporary experience and facilitate the telling of women's stories. By emphasizing the distinctiveness of women's ways of knowing, reasoning, speaking, and writing, these scholars often highlight differences between men and women and constitute women as a group with important shared characteristics (Belenky et al. 1986; Gilligan 1982; Showalter 1985).

In recent years, however, numerous writers have challenged the presumption that women's interests are best served by representing themselves as a group defined by their resemblance to one another and their differences from men. Women of color, Third World women, Jewish women, working-class women, and lesbians of all backgrounds have argued that their needs have been discounted by feminist critical approaches that ignore the differences among women in favor of a group identity. "Not all women experience sexism in the same way" (Anzaldúa 1990a, 219). Thus it is vital that we attend to the manner in which "class, culture, race, and sex intersect in various ways to produce different kinds of women, lesbians, and lesbian communities" (Sandoval 1982, 242).

Such an awareness suggests that the differences among women are of a significance equal to, if not greater than, our commonalities, and that the predominance of white, middle-class, heterosexual perspectives in the feminist movement has often silenced other women's voices by glossing over such differences in the name of sisterhood. What is lost in succumbing to such illusory unity is the precision and incisiveness that enables a persuasive critique of oppression. As Cherríe Moraga cautions, "*The danger lies in failing to acknowledge the specificity of the oppression*" (1983, 29). Responding to the call for specificity, women who are multiply marginalized have begun to develop their own critical methods to explore texts from more complex and particular perspectives of race, class, and gender (see Anzaldúa 1990b; Collins 1991; Flores 1994; Lugones 1990; Minh-ha 1990; Rebolledo 1990).

The emphasis on articulating specific configurations of oppression has led to a form of lesbian politics grounded in reclaiming and celebrating marginalized elements of identity. Such a perspective identifies the multiple, hidden, and contrary positions as insiders and outsiders that characterize lesbian experience, resulting in the fragmentation of the self into various, sometimes conflicting compartments of identity (Anzaldúa 1990b; Frye 1983; Grahn 1984; Rich 1979). As Audre Lorde explains, "I find I am constantly being encouraged to pluck out some one aspect of myself and present this as the meaningful whole, eclipsing or denying the other parts of self. But this is a destructive and fragmenting way to live" (1984, 120). One way to counter this effect is to unite with others who are subject to the same forms of oppression, pursuing a politics that addresses multiple sources of marginalization and enables its adherents to be "all of who we are" (Beck 1982, xxx). In this way, the assertion of identity provides a crucial link between individual survival and political empowerment.

What such a politics of identity works against most clearly is assimilation, a loss of specificity that occurs when difference is diluted into the sameness of the dominant culture. A politics based on identity influences understandings of lesbian identity for both lesbians and nonlesbians. The question of how to conceive of identity is at once a compelling theoretical issue and a deeply personal one, marking a key tension in feminist, and especially lesbian feminist, theorizing. Understandings of identity provide the ground on which politics are organized and alliances forged, but they also shape most profoundly our sense of self, influencing our lives from our most private interactions to our most public acts. A politics based on identity often emphasizes the influence of characteristics rooted deep within us, identifying this inner depth as the source of the true selves and authentic voices that must be reclaimed, revealed, and celebrated.

Although white, middle-class lesbians have responded to mainstream feminism with much the same feeling of exclusion as have women marginalized by race or class, their situation differs in notable ways. Most centrally, whereas other groups of women have been historically (and in most cases, continue to be) underrepresented in the feminist movement, lesbians have been central to feminism from its earliest days and have actively participated in all of its undertakings. They have not always been visible as lesbians in these roles, sometimes because of individual choice but other times because of general anti-lesbian sentiment among feminists (Douglas 1990) or because their visibility as lesbians was seen as detrimental to the feminist movement (Kaye/Kantrowitz 1992; Mennis 1982; Rich 1986).

Nevertheless, despite the failure of the feminist movement to acknowledge or address many of the problems that lesbians face, some of the most influential, respected, and visible feminist writers have been lesbians. The very homophobia of the early women's movement, as expressed by Betty Friedan's labeling of lesbians as a "lavender herring" and, later, a "lavender menace," testifies to the presence of large numbers of lesbians in the movement (Gomez 1995, 35). Thus a tension exists between the clear influence lesbians have had on feminist politics and theory and the feminist movement's history of dismissing as "special interests" the concerns of lesbians.

Too often, heterosexual feminists fail to recognize the connections between lesbian oppression and the oppression of all women.[11] Yet only when feminists have crystallized this connection can we recognize the importance of lesbian liberation for *all* women. Because "heterosexuality is a social organization of power . . . that enforces gender inequality between biological males and females" (Blasius 1994, 76), any female rejection of male dominance is often read as a refusal of heterosexuality as well. Thus the hatred and fear of lesbians and the social forces that make lesbianism stigmatized and invisible constitute a threat to *any* woman who fails to conform to a traditional "woman's role," whatever her sexual orientation. This includes the woman who, for any reason, chooses not to marry, not to bear or to raise children, or not to live in a situation of financial and emotional dependence on a man regardless of her marital status. It includes the woman who chooses a nontraditional career, who fails to dress or speak or behave in ways that are appropriately "feminine," who sleeps with many different men, or who refuses to sleep with a certain man or any men (regardless of her sexual orientation). It includes, as well, the woman who refuses to signal her possession by a man in even symbolic ways, as by choosing not to wear a wedding ring or by keeping her own last name after marriage.

Prejudice against lesbians is grounded in sexism and misogyny, as is prejudice against gay men (Bunch 1987; Kaye/Kantrowitz 1992; Koedt 1973; Pharr 1988). The mistrust of any woman who does not need a man signals a fear of women's strength and autonomy. It indicates as well a recognition of the threat posed to male power when women discover that, despite what we may have been taught, we possess the intelligence and strength to succeed without relying on a man. The derision directed at lesbians is, in fact, directed at all women who have the audacity to function independently of a man's support, whether or not they choose to relate sexually to men. Similarly, the hatred of gay men is grounded in the definition of women as those who are sexually available to men and the consequent perception that a man who is sexually available to other men puts himself in the despised position of a woman.

Many women who proclaim themselves feminists are accused of being lesbians, as are women who have short hair, participate in sports, don't wear makeup (or high heels, jewelry, or dresses), or whose appearance or behavior in any other way defies feminine stereotypes. A heterosexual woman who believes she is protected from homophobia need only proclaim audibly that she doesn't need a man to find out how quickly the label *lesbian* will be applied. We can recognize immediately the transgressive nature of her statement, and many listeners would become suspicious about the sexual orientation of a woman who made such a statement. This response suggests that the hatred directed toward women who acknowledge loving women is undergirded by the fear of women whose self-esteem does not depend on male approval and who find sources of power and means of survival other than dependence on a man.

Clarifying the connection between homophobia and misogyny demands a broader conceptual framework than a heterosexual feminist perspective provides. Thus although this discussion may seem to have strayed from its focus on lesbian identity, in fact it has returned to an issue that is central to the acknowledgment of such an identity. Coming out as a lesbian involves not only the choice to love other women but usually, though not necessarily, the choice *not* to be the intimate partner of a man.[12] While this may seem self-evident, it is significant because it marks the decision to live without material and other forms of privilege granted to heterosexual women who conform to society's standards of femininity. Acknowledging and accepting a lesbian identity represents both a personal gain and an accompanying loss of privilege, and it is the threat of this loss that imposes such widespread silence. Yet, if one is forced to hide from others and from oneself, this entails another kind of loss and another form of deprivation, a diminishing of self into the pain of invisibility.

## Voice and Visibility

Public voice and political visibility are seen as key goals in the struggle for lesbian and gay civil rights. Attention to voice often parallels concerns of visibility; lesbians, for example, are both silenced and invisible as lesbians. Indeed, invisibility implies a degree of silence, and lack of voice implies hiddenness. Yet, while these are not mutually exclusive processes, neither are they completely identical. For example, many women have historically been denied a public voice, forbidden to speak publicly or to claim political influence or representation. Nevertheless, they have been far from invisible, either historically or currently. For centuries, women have been looked upon and treated as objects or possessions. Through portrayals in art, literature, law, and even scientific treatises (see Keller 1985), some groups of women have been denigrated as sex objects, while others have been idealized and put on pedestals. In both cases, they have been granted visibility yet denied an empowering voice. Certain classes of women, like children, have long been admonished to be seen and not heard. This directive communicates clearly the possibility that visibility and lack of voice can and should coexist and may even be prescribed. This juxtaposition of visibility with silence has long characterized the oppression of such women, as ubiquitous images portray them as objects to be admired and possessed rather than as human beings to be respected and valued.[13]

Conversely, women have long worked behind the scenes to contribute to important, ostensibly male accomplishments. In this way, women's influential voices permeate our entire history, even where women themselves remain invisible. Many of women's assigned domestic tasks, like many functions carried out by poor and working class men, are relegated to the background in a manner that obscures recognition of who has done them. Such concealment not only masks the identity or the existence of the worker; it often prevents even the awareness that work has been done.[14] Women may have a voice in household decisions. They may influence or actively participate in their husband's or boss's career. They may participate in numerous other endeavors where they make key contributions to a variety of fields. However, their work and influence have remained largely unseen, virtually invisible. Such contributions, like the everyday work of raising children or running a household, show how women's influence may be abundantly present while women themselves remain concealed. History abounds with examples of extraordinary women whose intellectual and artistic contributions have been and continue to be widely misidentified as the work of men. This pattern of voice without visibility signifies participation without recognition or acknowledgment, reaffirming women's second-class status by denying their claim to their own accomplishments. In this way, voice without visibility, like visibility without voice, can be more oppressive than liberating.

This same hiddenness characterizes gay and lesbian achievements. The influence of lesbians and gay men has always been pervasive throughout our culture. Yet such participation has come at the price of our visibility. To have our voices heard, we have been forced to remain closeted as gays and lesbians. When we do achieve public visibility, we are often subjected to misrepresentations that deny our humanity, distort our words and images, and denigrate our lives and love. Both configurations—voice without visibility and visibility without voice—are characteristic forms of oppression. They are familiar attributes of prejudice based on class, race, and gender as well as on sexual orientation. When we contribute our ideas and skills while being denied recognition or credit, or when we achieve visibility only to be exploited as objects, we confront the double bind that is oppression's most telltale sign (Frye 1983).

In emphasizing voice or visibility as a key strategy for our movement, we necessarily adopt the clusters of meaning, both literal and metaphorical, associated with each choice. Visibility directs our attention to what can and what cannot be seen. The centering of vision necessarily raises the question of what is inaccessible to vision, returning us to questions of secrecy and taboo, of what must not be seen: sexual secrets. This metaphor directs our attention to bodies, to physicality, and to sexuality. A concern with visibility draws attention to questions of behavior or conduct—from political activism to "appropriately" gendered activity or dress to sexual practice itself. Emphasizing physical presence can be a strategy of resistance when large numbers of people visibly support an oppositional cause. Groups can influence the political process by demonstrating a voting bloc or by challenging oppressive institutions or practices, in ways ranging from peaceful demonstration to outright violence. Nevertheless, focusing on physical presence can also be a technique of the oppressor. Dominant groups may exaggerate the numbers of or the threat posed by a marginalized group, in order to provoke fear and hatred of its members. An emphasis on the body may be used to debase a group, by reducing it to its physical being. Oppressors thereby portray minority group members as animals, subject to physical drives unchecked by morality or reason. This strategy has been effective in many campaigns of hatred, most notably in the discourses of Nazi Germany and U.S. slavery.

Whereas visibility directs our attention to the corporeal, to bodies and actions, metaphors of voice emphasize ideology and identity, the power of ideas and stories. Our voices are instruments through which we challenge dominant beliefs when we speak of our lives in ways that contradict dominant representations. Historically, many groups of women, along with groups of minority men, have been denied the right to speak publicly. Women who are multiply marginalized are likewise multiply silenced. Even the power of self-naming has been withheld, as the dominant culture imposes gender, racial, and sexual identities without regard to the self-identification of individuals. Because of this disregard for subjective identity and the sweeping imposition of silence, voice serves as a powerful metaphor for resisting oppression. This is true not only in the field of speech communication, where an emphasis on voice would seem inevitable, but also in feminist, lesbian, and gay studies across the disciplines. The importance of finding one's own voice and making that voice heard is widely acknowledged as a means of personal and collective empowerment among many minority groups.

Nevertheless, the value of voice remains equivocal because of its reliance on language, a tool that most often operates in the service of the dominant ideology. The categories of language are generated and given meaning within a system of patriarchal belief, and even a rebellious application of language represents an engagement with and reliance on a sexist and heterosexist conceptual framework.[15] While voice is often viewed unproblematically as a liberatory concept, we must remember the ways in which our use of language may be complicit with dominant interests. Using language as a mode of resistance is a double-edged sword, because it means adopting categories and terminology that are often inherently at odds with our own experiences or beliefs. The French philosopher Jean-François Lyotard cautioned that "being in opposition is one of the modes of participation within a system" (Phelan 1993, 776). Indeed, to rebel against a stigmatized identity, groups are often forced to organize around that identity, defining themselves through the linguistic categories imposed by the very ideology they wish to undermine (Epstein 1987).

In identifying either voice or visibility as our key concern, we prioritize one of two senses, hearing or seeing, and we select a particular framework within which to perceive the project of liberation. Feminists as well as lesbian and gay rights advocates employ both concepts to some extent. For example, the Gay and Lesbian Alliance Against Defamation (GLAAD) has used the phrase "Equality through Visibility in the Media." The AIDS Coalition to Unleash Power (ACT-UP), one of the most radical groups of AIDS activists, employs the slogan "Silence = Death," which draws on Audre Lorde's admonition that "your silence will not protect you" (Segrest 1995).

Opponents of lesbian and gay rights often fail to distinguish between these concepts at all. The military's "Don't Ask, Don't Tell" policy, for example, stubbornly equates voice with visibility. It seeks to uphold its ban on gays and lesbians and to maintain the appearance of uniform heterosexuality by imposing a smothering silence that maintains invisibility. This prevents the military from having to acknowledge the many gays and lesbians who have served and currently serve in its ranks, and who include some of its most decorated soldiers. The military's effort to equate voice, visibility, and identity—what we cannot see and do not say does not exist—illustrates the power of language to create or suppress what we come to think of simply as "reality." It testifies, as well, to the influence of public representations on the ability of minority group members to name and define themselves. As Adrienne Rich has written, "Invisibility is not just a matter of being told to keep your private life private; it's the attempt to fragment you, to prevent you from integrating love and work and feelings and ideas, with the empowerment that that can bring" (1986 199-200). Such effects are only intensified for those whose history has been largely hidden not only from outsiders but even from themselves.

## The Ambivalence of the Closet

The achievement of voice and visibility is crystallized in the act of coming out, marking the shift from confusion or hiddenness to awareness or acknowledgment, a move from private to public identity. "Coming out" has a dual meaning, referring both to an individual's self-awareness of being gay or lesbian and to the decision to share this information with others. In a context in which heterosexuality is presumed, heterosexuals generally do not need to state their sexual orientation to have it accurately perceived.[16] In the same context, a gay man or lesbian who does not explicitly come out as such is often misperceived as heterosexual. The presumption of heterosexuality is so deeply rooted in our culture that any declaration of lesbian identity is momentous. On a national level, where representations of lesbians are especially scarce, the identification of oneself as a lesbian represents a particularly bold and courageous act.

A key element of the silence imposed on gays and lesbians is that we are required to display a certain "discretion" in public settings. Even when one's gay or lesbian sexual orientation is known to others, secrecy is often expected or demanded by admonitions not to "flaunt" our sexuality (see Sedgwick 1990). Those few nationally known figures whose gay or lesbian identity is a matter of public record are nevertheless expected to minimize its visibility or discount its effect on their public lives. Quite often, this has been the road taken by (mostly male) gay politicians, who see in this strategy the means of least resistance in attaining access to political power.

The act of coming out on the national level, like coming out to family and friends, is subject to multiple interpretations and possesses a multitude of possible consequences for gays and lesbians, politically and otherwise. For example, in one sense there is a clear victory for lesbians and gays in the appointment of a lesbian to the president's cabinet or in the reinstatement of a lesbian colonel to her military post. Nevertheless, these events also have a price and may not send as unequivocal a message as we first suppose. The assertion and affirmation of identity categories, even oppositional categories such as "lesbian" and "gay," is not an unquestionable good, for "identity categories tend to be instruments of regulatory regimes." As a result, "the invocation of identity is always a risk" (Butler 1993, 308). Specifically, the rhetoric that is used to achieve these victories and the ways in which lesbians are portrayed through this discourse may have lasting effects on how the public sees lesbians and how lesbians see themselves. The act of coming out and the figure of the closet associated with it are themselves problematic and fraught with tension. While movement leaders often present the refusal to be closeted, and the greater exposure coming out affords, as an uncontested good, political strategy demands a more careful examination of the various consequences of "outness." "The discourse of 'coming out' has clearly served its purposes, but what are its risks?" (Butler 1993, 308). Or, more colloquially put: "The good news is, we finally exist to people other than ourselves. The bad news is, on what terms?" (Hollibaugh 1993, 27).

The question is a provocative one, for lesbians and gays have often realized that whereas hiddenness or "closetedness" has its liabilities, it also bestows a certain freedom from regulation, along with opportunities for self-naming and self-preservation, that would be impossible under conditions of visibility. "Becoming visible means being forced into categories that do not fit, that are premised on the denial of our reality" (Becker 1995, 147). Thus, although the closet may be seen as a structure that excludes and confines gays and lesbians, from another perspective it can be viewed as a shelter that shields us from the dangers "outside." The closet offers a measure of protection for lesbians and gays even as it insulates heterosexuality from the potential challenge of our presence. Voluntarily coming out (as opposed to being involuntarily "outed") signals a relinquishing of the closet's protection along with an escape from confinement. Coming out marks both one's subjection to public stereotypes of homosexuality and one's readiness to challenge these dominant misunderstandings. The act of coming out, then, is inevitably characterized by contradictions and trade-offs in terms of safety and freedom. "Freedom from" is sacrificed to the pursuit of "freedom to," as we forgo what feels like the safety of silence and invisibility in order to stand up for our rights and liberties.

In the discourse of coming out, the assertion of an "outside" always reaffirms the existence of a closet. "Being 'out' always depends to some extent on being 'in'; it gains its meaning only within that polarity. Hence, being 'out' must produce the closet again and again in order to maintain itself as 'out.'" The continual reinscription of this binary opposition prompts the question "We are out of the closet, but into what?" (Butler 1993, 309). This "outside" is always, first, a disappointment, as it inevitably fails to provide the anticipated freedom of total disclosure. Within this system of meaning, another impenetrable space always exists beyond the closet. "The closet produces the promise of a disclosure that can, by definition, never come" (Butler 1993, 309). Thus the act of coming out involves at best a reconfiguration of boundaries that places us inside yet another set of walls. In these terms, being "out" is always something of a letdown. Yet, this partial and unsatisfactory disclosure nevertheless renders lesbians and gay men more exposed and highly vulnerable. What is visible is subject to discrimination, regulation, appropriation; that which can be seen and recognized by the dominant culture may also be labeled and defined by it. "As more homosexuals come out, new stereotypes are created; the assertion of homosexuality has in turn created new forms of homophobia" (Altman 1982, 22). In this way, the act of coming out, as an act of making visible, is inherently subject to reinterpretation and appropriation.

Moreover, as minority groups are well aware, any representation is not necessarily better than no representation at all. While our public invisibility gives us at least some opportunity to define our own self-image, when lesbians and gays are portrayed by and for the mass media, the images may be at best unflattering, at worst inflammatory. These images may incite hatred and even violence against us. Portrayals of lesbians and gays in television and film, when they have existed, have historically been grossly stereotypical. They have presented ridiculous characters who are frequently objects of scorn. Only recently have mainstream movies and television shows begun to incorporate gay and lesbian characters who are multidimensional and sympathetic, rather than solely laughable or narrowly sexual beings. Although such portrayals are increasing in both television and film, they remain rare enough to be notable, as evidenced by the furor over Ellen DeGeneres's character coming out on her television show, *Ellen*. Because we have so few images of lesbians or gay men, those that exist take on representative status. This situation is exacerbated by the hiddenness of the variety and diversity among lesbians and gay men in many communities. Because of their significance, the few representations we do have must be scrutinized for the understandings they create and the possibilities they obscure. This is equally, if not more, true for the representations created through public language, during debates over policy and within the context of legal decisions.

Coming out, then, is a mixed blessing, not only for individuals but on a societal level as well. For this reason, we must look at the "success" of the Achtenberg nomination and the Cammermeyer court battle in terms of both their liberating and their limiting potentials. We must examine the impact that such high-level debates may have on broader cultural constructions of homosexuality; for lesbianism in particular has, arguably, benefited from its lack of visibility. Our cultural constructions of sexuality deny that sex is possible without the presence of a penis, and so sex or signs of affection between women are often not strongly condemned or regulated partly because they are not believed, because intimacy between women is inconceivable or nonexistent in our binary system of gender and our definition of sexuality (Faderman 1981; Wittig 1992). "Lesbianism is not explicitly prohibited in part because it has not even made its way into the thinkable, the imaginable, that grid of cultural intelligibility that regulates the real and the nameable" (Butler 1993, 312). Bringing lesbianism to light in the public manner of a Senate debate or a civil court hearing thus introduces both an opportunity and a threat to the self-definition of lesbians and of lesbian and gay communities.

## Queer Theory

A final context of scholarship, queer theory, has emerged in recent years from earlier scholarship on sexuality. This perspective encompasses theories by and about gays, lesbians, bisexuals, transsexuals, and transgendered people (see Wiegman 1994, 17n. 1). Taking its inspiration, its direction, and much of its content from the writings of the late French philosopher Michel Foucault, queer theory argues that categories of sexual identity and understandings of sexuality are not timeless or naturally occurring. Instead, they are social constructions, created and maintained through mechanisms of power and varying across different social, historical, and political contexts. Denying a view of sexual drives and scripts as innate or even as clearly classifiable, queer theory reveals the instabilities underlying the seemingly rigid and unchanging categories of sexuality. Its technique is sometimes referred to as "queering" existing categories, an act of challenging and destabilizing, or "making strange," the fundamental assumptions that uphold such classifications.

In place of stability and permanence, queer theory offers a view of sexual identity categories as socially constructed and rigorously policed. Queer theorists attempt to undermine or "deconstruct" the hierarchical arrangements that reduce complex, multiple differences to simplistic binary oppositions (Butler 1993; de Lauretis 1993; Sedgwick 1990; Wittig 1993). Yet, rather than proposing additional categories, queer theorists question the feasibility of identity categories per se, challenging claims of a shared identity within groups classified by sexual orientation ("gays," "lesbians," etc.). Instead, they identify the classification of people based on sexual orientation as a recent and historically specific phenomenon, designed to serve the interests of those in power by creating deviant and marginalized categories of *people* rather than simply types of behaviors. With this rationale, some queer theorists challenge the personal and political utility of coming out, which represents in their view a misguided acceptance and embracing of the labels imposed on us by an oppressive dominant culture (Butler 1993).

In contrast to a politics that embraces identity categories, queer theory criticizes the easy acceptance of such labels. It contends that identity categories do not dwell within individuals but instead are culturally constructed and assigned to us. Because our identities are constructed in and through powerful social institutions, we internalize these categories as part of our fundamental sense of self. Thus, despite their external origins, such classifications come to *feel* as though they emanate from deep within us. Such a view rejects the assumption that categories of identity are "natural" or "innate," that is, that they exist prior to or outside of language and other relations of power. It argues instead that such categories are not real or internal but display an "apparent 'interiority' and 'reality'" that is actually "an illusion produced by our internalization of what is, in fact, a highly politicized and public discourse" (Bennett 1993, 96). Far from reflecting our inner selves, such categories compel us, with varying degrees of success, to conform to their boundaries. When we acquiesce, the categories appear unshakable. When we refuse, we reveal their instability. Within this view, the ways in which we conceive of individual subjects and stratify those subjects by gender, race, class, and sexuality are historically and discursively constructed, maintained entirely through language and other power relations. These relations construct and enforce the appearance of continuous, stable identities. They police the boundaries of those identities and arrange them hierarchically.

The notion that language and reality construct each other, that what we think of as "reality" is itself constructed through language, is grounded in the sociological tradition of social constructionism. Social constructionism argues that what we may accept as given or natural "facts" are actually constructed and reinforced by the very language and behaviors through which they are expressed. From this perspective, the struggle to integrate various categories of identity is illusory, misleading, and dangerous insofar as it represents the acceptance and internalization of externally imposed labels. Categories of difference, or identities, are seen as sources of oppression that we must vigorously reject, not embrace. Whereas a politics of identity advocates the construction or assembly of identity against the forces that impose fragmentation from without, this contrasting view urges the continual rejection of apparently uniform and stable categories. It decries the "regulatory imperatives" that stealthily inhabit consciousness, imposing an illusory sense of difference that exerts control not only from without but also from within (Butler 1993, 309).

This challenge to categories of difference reminds us that what is politically strategic in the short run may have negative consequences in the long run, as any external labels we accept can still be manipulated by others and used against us. This perspective also cautions against mistaking strategy for "truth" when we allow legal concepts to replace our own lesbian self-definitions (Robson 1992).[17] We must be wary of the dangers of naturalizing myths that disguise social constructions as biological givens; they can mislead us into viewing categories of difference as historically invariable and our second-class status as therefore unchangeable. Such accounts uphold oppression by reaffirming heterosexuality's primacy and naturalness and by leaving the notion of fixed sexual categories intact. As long as we continue to organize people into two "opposite" categories of heterosexuals and homosexuals, the latter will always remain subordinate "Others," the lower rung in a hierarchical relationship.

From this perspective, acceptance, much less celebration, of externally imposed categories as authentic differences reinforces rather than undoes identity-based oppression. Where a politics of identity resists oppression by reclaiming marginalized identities, queer theory pursues the same objective by rejecting identity categories altogether. It identifies heterosexuality and homosexuality as equally constructed (as opposed to "natural," or biologically rooted in individuals), each dependent on the other and on structures of power and language for its meaning. In this view, no individual or group is either "inside" or "outside" systems of power. Instead, all identities and their meanings are constituted through the very operation of such systems, all equally subject to regulation and, potentially, transformation.[18]

The case studies I present here represent historical instances in which various sides struggle for authority over the meanings of contested language and images. Such moments provide rare opportunities to watch the process of meaning making at work. These examples, like other "contests for the production of sexual meanings . . . provide important opportunities to challenge, if not renegotiate, the public limits on how human (erotic) pleasures can be both embodied and represented" (E. Cohen 1993, 212). The debates on the Senate floor and in the courtroom may be examined as the sites of precisely these kinds of contests. In these battles, the victor is determined by more than the outcome of the confirmation vote or the judge's decision, and the stakes are higher than one woman's political or military career. If coming out is always a risky proposition, then political and legal discussions of lesbian and gay issues offer no guarantee "that the instrumental uses of 'identity' do not become regulatory imperatives" (Butler 1993, 309).

In fact, establishing one woman as the only visible lesbian in the upper echelon of government and another as the only visible lesbian in the upper levels of the military has caused these high-profile individuals to attain in the public eye a representative status for all lesbians. The entire question, so highly controversial in the lesbian and gay movement, of "which version of lesbian or gay ought to be rendered visible" (Butler 1993, 311) is sidestepped by the presence of such a highly placed politician and a National Guard colonel. Moreover, the movement's true diversity—the differences of race, class, and other characteristics among lesbians and gay men—is replaced by a homogenizing image of white, professional lesbians. These particular representations become the ground on which gay and lesbian activists must do battle, whether or not they have or would have chosen it.

It is possible to see in the Achtenberg and Cammermeyer debates a microcosm of the anti-gay and "pro-gay" arguments and to analyze both the value and the limitations of these arguments for achieving their respective political goals.[19] Such issues as whether homosexuality is a choice or is biologically given, the separation of public and private realms, the historical and contemporary discourses of perversion, the threat lesbianism poses to male dominance and ideals of masculinity, and the controversy over "family values" are all addressed in these discussions. Each issue provides a link between political or military competence and the discourse of sexuality. Such pairings have become increasingly familiar in the political climate of the 1990s, most notably since the Anita Hill/Clarence Thomas hearings and the advent of "Don't Ask, Don't Tell." Centrally, and underlying these other disputes, rests the issue of whether homosexuality refers primarily to a category of human beings or to a particular sort of behavior. The ways in which this question is addressed, on the Senate floor and in the courtroom, both reflect and create a narrow, limited, and limiting conception of homosexuality in general and lesbianism in particular. Bringing to bear the understandings gleaned from a variety of theoretical contexts allows us to examine such representations and to analyze their advantages and drawbacks for the project of lesbian and gay liberation.

Informed by the literature of feminist, lesbian, gay, and queer studies, this book investigates how struggles over the meanings of lesbian identity manifest themselves within particular, concrete battles. It examines, as well, how lesbian specificity may be sacrificed within the broader struggle for gay and lesbian rights. My analysis draws on the stories of two women who, despite their very different backgrounds and objectives, shared a willingness to stand up for their beliefs and a refusal to hide or deny who they were. Their freedom to differ was met with hostile opposition, from Congress and from the military. It is as a result of their integrity and courage in facing these challenges that their personal stories became visible to a nation.

## CONCLUSION

In a context of gay civil rights and lesbian feminism, right-wing backlash and "lesbian chic," this book examines the political and social construction of "the lesbian" in the 1990s. By analyzing the discourse surrounding the struggles of two lesbians whose stories attracted national media attention, I explore the kinds of lesbian representations that emerge from debates within military and political institutions. In a broader frame, I investigate the complexity of notions of visibility and voice in assertions of lesbian identity, as well as the promise and the threats that accompany the highlighting of these metaphors as liberatory strategies.

This study will contribute to scholarship in rhetorical, feminist, and gay and lesbian studies, all of which intersect in instances of lesbian representation. Lesbian oppression is accomplished in part through rhetorical means, particularly the suppression of language and the denial of representations. However, when such suppression is no longer entirely effective, new language and representations, whether generated by opponents or proponents, can themselves further the cause of oppression. In addition, the language and images a group employs to portray its own struggle shape both the manner in which the group envisions its liberation and the ways in which its detractors formulate their opposition. By focusing on a marginalized group that has only recently begun to generate images and language that reach a public audience, this study reveals how choices about representation shape the possibilities for individual identity, group identity, and a liberatory vision. Those choices, at the same time, help define how a group articulates its struggles, its defeats, and its triumphs.

# ᚹ 2 ᚹ

## CLINTON'S "DAMN LESBIAN"
### Politics and Visibility in the Achtenberg Debate

> The price of increasing power is increasing opposition.
> —from *The I Ching* (in Lorde 1984, 158)

## INTRODUCTION

In May 1993, a debate raged for three days in the U.S. Senate chamber, marking what its participants proclaimed a "historic" event. With Bill Clinton's choice of Roberta Achtenberg for the position of assistant secretary for Housing and Urban Development (HUD), Achtenberg became the first "out" lesbian in history to be nominated for a United States cabinet post. During the nomination hearing held before the Committee on Banking, Housing, and Urban Affairs on April 29[1] and the subsequent Senate filibuster that continued for nine and a half hours on May 19 and 20 and concluded with more discussion and a vote on May 24, Achtenberg's professional qualifications for the post became intimately tied in debate to her identification as a lesbian, despite the efforts of her supporters to keep her sexual orientation in the background. In its candid discussion of the relevance of Achtenberg's "homosexual lifestyle" to her personal and political competence, the Senate debate offers a rare glimpse of the political and social construction of homosexuality in general, and lesbianism in particular, in process.

As the first openly gay or lesbian person ever nominated for the president's cabinet, Achtenberg faced hostility and severe censure from conservative members of the Senate, most notably Senator Jesse Helms and other

39

conservative Republicans. During the acrimonious debate on the Senate floor over Achtenberg's nomination, Helms and others expressed their opposition to confirming someone whom Helms had referred to in a newspaper interview as a "damn lesbian."[2] Thus the issue of sexual orientation and its relationship to politics was raised even before the official debate began, setting the tone and framework for the discussion and positioning the "lesbian issue" at the forefront of the debate. The language and meanings that shaped the debate, as well as the outcome of the confirmation proceedings, reflect existing cultural meanings of lesbianism and produce new ones.

In this way, Achtenberg's ultimate confirmation tells only part of the story. The discussion surrounding a presidential nomination, while ostensibly centering on the nominee herself, also conveys the senators' approval or disapproval of broader policy matters. "Without a doubt, the Senate interprets its role in the confirmation process as not simply screening the personal qualities of the nominees but is instead using the confirmation process to highlight its policy differences with the administration" (King and Riddlesperger 1991, 197).[3] Indeed, an article in the *New York Times* relates that "Republican strategists have noted that President Clinton has suffered political damage from his support for gay rights, and the campaign to defeat Ms. Achtenberg appeared to be part of a strategy to underscore differences between the two parties" (Krauss 1993, A12). Such observations are particularly meaningful in light of the fact that Achtenberg's nomination was announced during the controversy over lifting the ban on gays in the military, at a time when Clinton was faced with "fierce resistance" from both "top military officers and some lawmakers" (Reuters 1993). At the time of the Achtenberg confirmation proceedings, the Senate Armed Services Committee was in the process of holding hearings on lifting the military ban.[4] Because "the confirmation process provides the Senate with a forum to express its opinions on the president's policies" (King and Riddlesperger 1991, 192), the Achtenberg debate must be viewed in the context of a larger struggle for political control.

In this understanding of the political process, the Achtenberg confirmation proceedings, like the nomination itself, were at once remarkable and quite predictable in their reassertion of heterosexuality as the unmarked norm, in relation to which homosexuality exists only as a deviant "Other." What bear examination here are the somewhat surprising ways in which Achtenberg's supporters, as much as or more than her opponents, attempted to limit the understanding of lesbianism to its narrowest possible definition, all the while congratulating themselves for their progressiveness. In framing her sexual orientation as a private and (therefore) irrelevant matter, Achtenberg's supporters de-emphasized or erased implications of challenge and change that her nomination presented to the deeply ingrained heterosexism and homophobia of politics as usual. At the same time, her most vitriolic opponent, Jesse Helms, was the first, and seemingly the only, member of the Senate to acknowledge (and often, indeed, to exaggerate) the extent of the challenge her confirmation posed.

The discourse of the Achtenberg debate presents a persuasive and appealing, but at times contradictory and self-defeating, argument in support of gay and lesbian rights. The predominant strategy of Achtenberg's Senate supporters employs a civil rights perspective, calling on the familiar argument of liberal tolerance that often takes center stage in the rhetoric of lesbian and gay rights. A gay and lesbian civil rights argument implicitly draws on, at the same time that it creates, an essentialized understanding of gays and lesbians as constituting a distinct and identifiable class of people. It then deploys this understanding as a means of seeking "suspect class" status and of gaining legal protections for gays and lesbians based on equal protection laws.

Within this argument lies an ambiguous and often troubling relationship between "identity" and "behavior." One goal of civil rights appeals is precisely to establish homosexuality as an *identity*. Such appeals seek to gain suspect class status for gays and lesbians in order to associate them with other, more "established" minority groups based on identity features such as race.[5] Being gay or lesbian, this argument runs, is much like being Asian or African American. It is a distinct, apparently "biological" characteristic that designates one decisively as a member of a particular group. From this perspective, being gay or lesbian is a characteristic that refers to a state of being, describing "who one is" apart from any particular actions one might take.

However, civil rights initiatives also seek protection for *behaviors*, in this case sexual behaviors, under the right-to-privacy laws. Such an argument was made unsuccessfully in the infamous Supreme Court case of *Bowers v. Hardwick*.[6] As this case made clear, the government is unwilling to extend the right to privacy to gay or lesbian sexual acts, just as it is unwilling, as yet, to endow homosexuals with suspect class status. Despite this hostile context, arguments for gay and lesbian civil rights have continued to proceed on both the identity and the behavior fronts simultaneously. The result is an oddly ambivalent and, at times, indecipherable relationship between identity and behavior, in which the two are presented as neither clearly connected to nor decisively separable from each other. Nor, therefore, is either framing of the issue clearly predominant during the debate on the Senate floor.

Achtenberg's most ardent and vocal Senate supporters employ such civil rights strategies to insist that her political experience and qualifications are the only appropriate matters for discussion at her confirmation hearing. They argue not only that sexual orientation is irrelevant in judging a candidate's ability to perform a job well but also that the addition of Achtenberg and other out gays and lesbians to the political system makes no difference, that ultimately it neither challenges nor changes that system. This argument reassures skeptical senators that only "good" gays and lesbians, that is, those who will not agitate for change, will be considered acceptable candidates for government posts. It thus establishes early the limits of tolerance, not only for Achtenberg but for gays and lesbians generally: public participation comes at a cost, and that cost, ironically, is the inability to advocate for change for a broader constituency. Although the senators ultimately confirmed Achtenberg, their discussion reveals that the admission of a lesbian into the president's cabinet marks the beginning and the end of the changes they are willing to contemplate. Responding to these limits, Achtenberg supporters hasten to reassure their colleagues that this apparent change is really no change at all.

At the same time, and perhaps paradoxically, supporters frame Achtenberg's nomination as an occasion for celebration. "This is a nomination that is heroic . . . this nomination is important, because it really is a challenge," asserts Senator Carol Moseley-Braun (S6214).[7] Supporters portray the nomination as a significant change in policy that marks the beginning of a new political era of equality and the end of a long history of intolerance and discrimination. Such a framework is particularly resonant in the context of this particular nomination, because the position Achtenberg has been nominated for, assistant secretary of HUD, would place her in the role of arbiter of fairness and justice by implementing anti-discrimination and equal opportunity laws in housing. The backdrop for this discussion, therefore, is the role of HUD as an organization specifically designed to fight discrimination and guarantee equal access to fair housing, particularly for racial minorities, low-income families, and families with children.

Importantly, however, while the laws enforced by HUD are designed to prevent discrimination, they do not include protection for gays and lesbians. Currently, discrimination based on sexual orientation is still permissible in all arenas under the law. This situation explains the seemingly paradoxical need for Achtenberg's supporters to celebrate the breaking down of barriers that her nomination represents while simultaneously insisting on the irrelevance of her sexual orientation to any of the "real" issues under discussion. The apparent contradiction is unscrambled if we examine the rhetorical consequences of this juxtaposition. The effective message is that sexual orientation is private, therefore irrelevant, therefore insignificant to the discussion. What is significant, according to supporters, is that after centuries of discrimination, the Senate has recognized that sexual orientation is, after all, a private matter. As such, it is unrelated to the affairs of the government and so provides no justification for excluding gays and lesbians from holding high political office. In other words, Achtenberg's supporters frame her nomination as a progressive policy change that will bring about, finally, no structural change at all.

The Senate debate offers a specific instance of the broader rhetorical structure of gay and lesbian civil rights discourse, bringing forth many of the most familiar arguments of a liberal lesbian/gay rights position. As such a representative instance, it allows us to examine the effects of various rhetorical strategies employed in making the liberal case for "tolerance." These effects include the particular understandings of lesbian identity that such strategies produce; their impact on the possibilities of voice and visibility for this underrepresented group; and the overall gains and losses associated with the use of such strategies for the lesbian/gay rights movement. It is important to remember that those who speak on behalf of Roberta Achtenberg in this forum are speaking neither as representatives nor as advocates of gay and lesbian rights per se; they may or may not support such rights. Nevertheless, their arguments are valuable here precisely because they adopt the most prevalent discourses generated by the lesbian/gay rights movement as a means of defending Achtenberg's right to serve in this government post. The arguments of these lawmakers may have a tremendous influence on the creation of public policy and in the setting of precedents for the Senate's handling of future gay and lesbian nominees.

This chapter analyzes the texts of the two formal discussions of Achtenberg's nomination: the Banking Committee's nomination hearing (hereafter referred to in references as *Nominations*) and the subsequent debate on the Senate floor, as recorded in the *Congressional Record*. I examine how the language used in the hearing and in the debate establishes Roberta Achtenberg as a visible, highly placed role model, whose achievement marks a shining moment in the struggle for gay and lesbian civil rights. I also examine how the language employed in the Senate chamber, in particular the metaphor of "crossing the line," used repeatedly to describe the accomplishment of Achtenberg (and, by extension, the gay and lesbian community), becomes a means for both supporters and opponents to establish a narrow definition of lesbian identity that restricts the possibilities for voice and visibility as components of an acceptable lesbian existence.

## ASSIMILATING DIFFERENCE

Of particular interest in this case is what happens in the wake of the increased and increasing visibility of gays and lesbians, a group whose historical oppression has been based in part on our invisibility. No one on either side of the debate contests the fact that gay and lesbian visibility has increased markedly in the 1990s. Tom Stoddard, writing in the *Advocate*, a leading gay and lesbian magazine, put it most clearly when he dubbed 1993 "the Year of Visibility" (1993, 45). In an article naming Achtenberg the *Advocate*'s 1993 Woman of the Year, Stoddard announced, "This was the year we conquered our heritage of invisibility. We seemed to be everywhere—demanding an end to the Pentagon's policy of discrimination, marching on Washington, boycotting Colorado, and generally causing political trouble."

The recent increase in the visibility and outspokenness of many gays and lesbians goes a long way toward combating long-held prejudices against us. As that which is unknown becomes more often seen and heard, and thus better known, it has the potential to dismantle stereotypes and prejudice. When that which was once frightening, alien, or unfamiliar becomes commonplace, those who were "Other" are more likely to be perceived in all their human complexity, instead of through the single lens of their difference. When a group becomes visible and audible, its members can more readily be judged by their character, skills, and abilities, by their minds and spirits, instead of by false images and prejudice. Negative stereotypes dissociate gays and lesbians from the values extolled by much of middle America: values of love, caring, and family. Gaining visibility and voice enables gays and lesbians to express our own allegiance to such values, even if the forms of this love and caring and the structure of these families may differ. When people begin to discover, across chasms of apparent difference, that we all share the same fundamental needs for food, shelter, safety, and love; when the recognition of common humanity leads not to assimilation and the annihilation of difference but to the ability to communicate with and learn from one another while respecting our differences; when those in positions of power and privilege genuinely desire such understanding and begin to recognize what has been lost for everyone through the marginalization of entire communities; when these elements are in place, the "Othering" process that maintains prejudice and discrimination can begin to be dismantled.[8]

Equally crucial for the goal of social transformation is the impact of voice and visibility on gays' and lesbians' own empowerment. The power to speak for oneself and the right to be oneself openly are crucial components in the process of overcoming internalized oppression. "Internalized oppression" refers to "the incorporation and acceptance by individuals within an oppressed group of the prejudices against them within the dominant society ...the mechanism within an oppressive system for perpetuating domination not only by external control but also by building subservience into the minds of the oppressed groups." The consequences of such internalization may include "self-hatred, self-concealment, fear of violence and feelings of inferiority, resignation, isolation, powerlessness, and gratefulness for being allowed to survive" (Pheterson 1990, 35).

The overcoming of internalized oppression may represent an even greater threat to the status quo than does the altering of heterosexuals' attitudes. With visibility come pride and an unwillingness to remain hidden or to feel ashamed. This leads to greater numbers of gays and lesbians coming out and an ever-increasing gay and lesbian presence in all aspects of public and private life. Closeted gays in high-profile positions might therefore feel freer to come out, as has occurred in the entertainment industry with celebrities such as Ellen DeGeneres, k.d. lang, Melissa Etheridge, and Elton John and in the sports world with athletes such as Martina Navratilova, Muffin Spencer-Devlin, Rudy Galindo, and Greg Louganis. Just as important, when young gays and lesbians see that an out lesbian such as Achtenberg can be appointed to a high government post, they, too, might aspire to such positions, including those that would enable them to bring about changes in government policy regarding gays and lesbians. The argument about Achtenberg and the outcry against her activism, then, may be read as an argument not only about what she might do personally but also about what those who follow her might do. What is apparent to all present is that once Achtenberg has been confirmed, others *will* follow. Once the first step has been taken, there can be no grounds for excluding future candidates based on sexual orientation alone.[9]

The Achtenberg debate illuminates the quick and effective means by which a new level of rhetorical oppression can be implemented and can take hold when one level is challenged or undermined. In the war of words against Roberta Achtenberg and those she is seen to represent,[10] it becomes clear that when members of an oppressed group achieve a certain degree of visibility in spite of attempts to deny or erase their existence, alternate means of oppression are imposed. Some, which take the form of overt verbal or physical attacks, are all too familiar and recognizable to us. Yet other, more insidious forms also appear. These subtler, encoded forms may be equally destructive but more difficult to identify or decipher. The silencing and erasure of gays and lesbians have long been effective means of perpetuating negative stereotypes, promoting the prejudices of heterosexuals, and maintaining the internalized oppression of gays and lesbians themselves. By keeping so many lesbians and gay men hidden even from their families and friends, these forms of oppression ensure that vast numbers of those who live or work with gays or lesbians believe that they have never met a member of this group, that they share no common bonds, and that the lives of gays and lesbians are utterly alien to their own.

Even those senators who support Achtenberg's nomination employ language that reinscribes boundaries around the possibilities for tolerable or acceptable difference. As a result, the lesbian "Other" who is admitted into the ranks of the dominant group remains subject to their control, her difference constrained within permissible limits of heterosexual dominance. A civil rights argument is highly effective for achieving this objective. Accessing the rhetoric of civil rights means relying implicitly, and often explicitly, on an analogy with race. For the purposes of the liberal senators, this analogy serves well. It is, after all, a popular and well-rehearsed liberal argument that race is "simply" a difference in skin color, and that therefore racial minorities can and should achieve success within white institutions (although preferably not in overwhelming numbers). According to this argument, discriminatory policies prevent minority group members from fulfilling their potential, and once such policies are dropped and the playing field is, presumably, level, minorities will be equally able to compete and succeed within such institutions. The goal of progressive liberal institutions, within this framework, is to implement anti-discrimination policies as a means of integrating racial minorities into existing institutions.

Such a framing of the problem might be thought of as the "white light" metaphor for assimilation. In a society where difference was valued, all of the "colors" of American society would combine to produce a rainbow of color; that is, to create institutions that represent the values, beliefs, and practices of Americans of genuinely diverse racial backgrounds. Yet just as combining all the colors of light yields not a multicolored spectrum but white light, assimilation absorbs difference to uphold the continuing dominance of white institutions, along with their attendant values and practices. White light is thus a vivid metaphor for assimilation; only by refracting it, by breaking it apart, can we recapture the varied colors of the spectrum.

A similar anti-discrimination/assimilation approach is adopted in the Achtenberg debate. In this version, which is possible only in the case of a white woman whose race is rendered invisible, sexual orientation replaces race, and the rationale runs as follows: sexual orientation is only about whom one has sex with, but this difference in choice of sexual partners does not and should not affect public life. Thus gays and lesbians willing to fit into heterosexual institutions must be allowed to do so, but only insofar as their presence is not disruptive to heterosexual privilege, to the ways in which heterosexuality is enforced and assumed in American culture. Again, the civil rights paradox is at work: the presence of even out gays and lesbians can be tolerated only as long as compulsory heterosexuality, that is, heterosexuality as a presumption and a norm, remains firmly entrenched. The notion of liberal tolerance demands a trade-off: the marginalized group are rewarded for conforming to dominant values and behaviors, and the dominant group recognize the minority group on the condition that the latter aspire to be just like them, that they choose to assimilate. Within these parameters, something like tolerance is possible only for those who successfully mimic the dominant group's behaviors and values.

The advantages of this approach for members of the dominant group are manifold. Most immediately, it excuses them from the need to educate themselves about other groups or to seek a greater awareness and understanding of those who are unlike themselves. On a societal level, dominant institutions need not be questioned or challenged; they remain intact and unchanged, while minority individuals must adapt in order to fit into them. To the extent that marginalized group members can accommodate themselves to these institutions, they may gain the privileges (education, employment, political influence, etc.) such institutions bestow. While such an approach to equality necessitates a high degree of self-negation for members of a minority group, it requires the fewest genuine concessions from members of the dominant group while allowing them to maintain the appearance of concern for the oppressed. This strategy circumvents demands for the dominant group to engage in self-questioning or other self-reflection, as well as any need to sacrifice existing privileges or status. Even where diversity is ostensibly welcomed, it is simultaneously erased, becoming yet another band of color that disappears into white light.

The effort to maintain control over and assimilate difference while claiming respect for diversity produces a civil rights discourse that is riddled with contradictions. While civil rights arguments draw upon the assumption of an identity-based community, for instance, their guiding objective of assimilation undercuts the very principle of difference on which such a community is based. The discourse of Achtenberg's Senate supporters upholds, without acknowledging, this contradiction in her status. On the one hand, her supporters maintain the significance of the difference based on sexual orientation. They do so by positioning Achtenberg as a member and a representative of an identifiable gay and lesbian community and by presenting their acceptance of her as a reason for self-congratulation. On the other hand, they insist that although her sexual orientation does introduce difference, it is not a difference that makes a difference. By portraying Achtenberg as "mainstream" (S6208) and separating her from activism and social change, her supporters insist that sexual orientation is an inconsequential feature of identity—a characteristic that has acquired the veneer of importance only through its years of exclusion and discrimination by political bodies such as their own. Within this framework, homosexuality both does and does not need to be explained away, excused, or justified, because although it *is* a difference, it does not *make* a difference.

The root of this contradiction lies in the conflicting interpretations of sexual orientation as an activity or a fundamental element of identity, a behavior or a state of being. This issue underlies the discussion here as it does the broader argument of lesbian and gay civil rights, yet Achtenberg's supporters never explicitly address or resolve the issue. When supporters separate Achtenberg's "mainstream" politics from her presumably nonmainstream personal characteristics, they access a framework of identity as private, irrelevant, and insignificant, as the difference that makes no (real) difference.

This strategic choice makes sense given the legal and political context, for behaviors are precisely what are *not* protected here. While at least one court has ruled "that homosexual *persons*, as a particular kind of person, *are* entitled to Constitutional protections under the Equal Protection Clause," the Supreme Court has resolutely refused to offer the same sort of protection for homosexual *acts*. "The Supreme Court in *Bowers v. Hardwick* notoriously left the individual states free to prohibit any acts they wish to define as 'sodomy,' . . . with no fear at all of impinging on any rights, and particularly privacy rights, safeguarded by the Constitution" (Sedgwick 1993, 57). Such a ruling presents a potent opportunity for attacks based on homosexual behavior, broadly defined. This division of agent from act, and private from public, sets up a dichotomy in which one's protection as a lesbian or gay man, even if granted, nevertheless does not extend to any acts one might perform within the context of that identity—acts that include not only sexual activity but also political activism.

Achtenberg's opponents use the behavior/identity, or public/private, distinction as a means of expressing their disapproval of her based on her "lifestyle" (a term implying behavior and willful choice), while seemingly maintaining a sympathetic stance toward her minority identity. The strategy of splitting behavior from identity pays homage to the protections that have generally been granted to minority identity by the courts. While lesbian and gay identity is not legally protected, attacks on identity have largely fallen out of favor in public discourse. Civil rights/identity discourse calls on this trend and asks that it be extended, formally, to protect the rights of lesbians and gays. It justifies this application of equal protection law by claiming, implicitly if not explicitly, that sexual orientation provides the basis for defining a particular class of people as analogous to racial minorities.[11] Achtenberg's supporters use this comparison between gays and lesbians and more established or "legitimate" minorities to highlight her nomination as a progressive political moment, and to portray her opponents as steeped in old prejudices and outdated modes of discrimination.

## HOMOSEXUALITY AS A "NATURAL" CATEGORY

On the Senate floor, as elsewhere, "homosexuality" is frequently conceptualized as a "biological" category, similar to those of race and sex.[12] As in discussions of race or sex, the biological designation suggests a fixed and unchanging category, a "natural" and incontestable distinction, and therefore a means by which people can be classified and organized in a purely "objective" fashion. Biological categories are viewed as given, subject to neither social construction nor individual judgment. They are understood as entirely confined by identifiable and universally recognized boundaries, such that transgressing these boundaries may be described as "crossing a line." In the case of sexual orientation, the line divides heterosexuality and its attendant privilege clearly and absolutely from its ostensible and inferior opposite, homosexuality.

One implication of a biological category is that it refers to an attribute of an individual agent, a feature of identity rather than a description of behavior. This distinction accounts for a fundamental difference between the rhetoric of gay rights supporters and that of opponents. "Pro-gay" rhetoric often considers homosexuality to be innate and immutable, a characteristic of the individual that is not under his or her control. In contrast, anti-gay rhetoric locates homosexuality in particular sexual acts that are seen as freely chosen (Brummett 1979). In this way, gays and lesbians are portrayed by their detractors as *willfully* stepping outside the realm of constitutional protection and therefore accountable for what is viewed as voluntary nonconformity and rebellious, immoral behavior.

A parallel distinction characterizes the rhetoric of the Senate debate. Achtenberg's supporters hold firmly to a perspective that labels homosexuality a biological, and therefore private and protected, category of identity. Their position follows from a standard argument of lesbian and gay rights supporters. "An important theme in Pro[-gay] rhetoric compares the plight of gays with other, more 'established' minorities: blacks, Jews, Indians, etc. Pros thus argue that gays 'find themselves' in that condition, as do blacks, and must be accepted on those terms" (Brummett 1979, 254). This stance is articulated in the Senate discussion through the comparison between Achtenberg and Carol Moseley-Braun. Senator Don Riegle, chair of the Banking Committee, remarks to Achtenberg, "In a sense, you're crossing one of those invisible lines that we have in our society in terms of . . . sexual orientation," an accomplishment he compares to that of "Carol Moseley-Braun . . . [who] has been the first person in effect to cross the color line" (*Nominations* 1993, 30). Before the full Senate, he explicitly equates sexual orientation with other forms of discrimination, asserting, "If you are qualified and you step forward, you ought to be judged only on the basis of your qualification, not skin color, not ethnic background, not sexual orientation" (S6102). His comparison is given even greater authority by Moseley-Braun's response: "You made probably one of the most eloquent statements I've heard . . . about this country and the challenge we face as senators, and crossing the line. I mean, I know from firsthand experience being both a woman and an African-American, what it's like . . . to cross lines that have kept people out." She explicitly connects various forms of prejudice, referring to "racism and sexism and all the isms that divide us and pit us against one another" (*Nominations* 1993, 31).

In the same vein, Senator Dianne Feinstein implicitly compares discrimination on the basis of sexual orientation with racial discrimination when she alludes to "bleak periods of prejudice and bigotry" in U.S. history. She pleads, "Let us not today create another ugly chapter in this country's history" (S6201). In the discourse of the confirmation process, the gains of gays and lesbians precipitated by the nomination are framed as parallel to those of other, "similar" minority groups. Senator Joseph Lieberman announces that "this is . . . an historic nomination because of Roberta Achtenberg's sexual orientation" (*Nominations* 1993, 21). He compares strides made to eliminate racial and gender inequalities with the issue "in our time" of discrimination based on sexual orientation (S6212).

Feinstein suggests that with Achtenberg's confirmation, "the doors of opportunity will open once again." She urges, "Let us swing those doors open today, once and for all" (S6097). In the double inflection that characterizes much of the language of the confirmation process, the "doors of opportunity" are perceived as opening both for Achtenberg as a lesbian in government and for those minority families whom she would serve as assistant secretary of HUD. However, Lieberman, who supports Achtenberg's nomination despite his stated disapproval of homosexuality, notes, "This question of discrimination based on sexual orientation is in some ways like the earlier questions of discrimination based on race or gender, but in some ways they are quite different" (S6213).

While such a comment attempts to dissociate gays and lesbians from other, more "legitimate" or established minority groups, most of Achtenberg's Senate supporters emphasize her capacity for empathy with her constituents, drawing a strong parallel between her situation and theirs: "She knew what it meant to be discriminated against, to be told that you weren't wanted, that you were not the right type of tenant" (*Nominations* 1993, 20) Here the comparison between Achtenberg and other minorities draws its strength from a common experience of victimization. In several of her supporters' statements, the problems of housing discrimination and discrimination against Achtenberg are merged, so that their words appear to address both issues at once. Senator Barbara Boxer argues, for instance, that "when we confirm Roberta Achtenberg . . . we will be taking a real step forward because we will be saying that discrimination is unacceptable, and we will be saying that the promise of equal opportunity is alive and well" (*Nominations* 1993, 20). Likewise, Lieberman asserts that Achtenberg "is superbly qualified to serve . . . as Assistant Secretary of Fair Housing and Equal Opportunity, and . . . that of course I think is the larger message of equal opportunity that speaks out from this nomination" (*Nominations* 1993, 21). Both statements leave unclear whether the "promise" and "message" of equal opportunity apply to Achtenberg or to the people she will serve, and this ambiguity strengthens the identification between them.

Like other categories of identity already protected by law, homosexuality is located by Achtenberg's supporters in the realm of the private, which they discuss as entirely distinct and separable from the public realm: "Sexual orientation . . . is essentially a matter of privacy" (S6213). Boxer reinforces this distinction by reassuring her colleagues that "Roberta Achtenberg is supported by the mainstream. This is not someone who had dedicated her life to the fringes of our society . . . in her public life . . . she is mainstream" (S6208). Senator David Durenberger, likewise, asks rhetorically, "When the Senate considers a Presidential nominee, are we undertaking the task of moral policemen—endorsing or condemning the *private conduct* of nominees? . . . It is not up to me to judge her *private behavior*" (S6216, emphasis mine). The senators argue that sexuality should be treated as a matter of personal preference, devoid of political significance. Boxer urges, "We are all God's children. We are. And let us not judge each other based on our differences. Let us all put aside differences that do not matter" (S6118). Senator Patty Murray remarks bluntly, if less eloquently, that Achtenberg's "private life is about as important to me as her hair color or her style of shoes" (S6353).

In this liberal discourse, homosexuality is defined as an individual preference, an "eccentricity" with no implications beyond the bedroom. The doctrine of privacy "excuses" Achtenberg for her private tendencies, as long as her politics and her commitment to public life remain unquestionably mainstream. However appealing this discourse might appear—and there are indisputably seductive elements of an ideology like that articulated by Boxer —it is important to recognize its limitations. The goal of setting aside differences is a worthy one, if the attribution of "difference" is evenly distributed; that is, if there is no standard or norm against which difference is measured. Too often, however, difference is ascribed only to the minority, the "Other," while the dominant group remains unmarked. That which is male, white, and heterosexual maintains its privilege as the unspoken norm. It is possible to maintain this inequity despite an apparent commitment to Boxer's principle because the power to judge, and to support that judgment with material rewards and sanctions, remains unequally distributed among "different" groups.

This recourse to private identity, moreover, is not without its risks. In defining lesbianism as properly located within the private realm, supporters inadvertently encourage criticism of any public actions Achtenberg undertakes that are influenced by her "private" sexual orientation. Her opponents, unsurprisingly, make the most of this opportunity. With the exception of Jesse Helms, who is unreserved in his absolute condemnation of homosexuals, Achtenberg's opponents claim that it is her public actions, not her homosexuality per se, that ground their opposition. Nevertheless, all the activities for which they condemn her are explicitly connected to her sexual orientation. They are able to uphold these seemingly contradictory claims by calling on the deliberate separation of public actions from private identity maintained by her supporters.

For example, having referred to Achtenberg as "neither qualified nor temperamentally fit for this position" and as possessing a record "of intolerance, discrimination, and vendetta against those who do not share her values and beliefs," Senator Trent Lott says, "I want to reemphasize that the issue before us today is not one of sexual preference or orientation" (S6093). Yet his criticism is based on a conflict in which Achtenberg voted to revoke United Way funding for the Boy Scouts unless they changed their discriminatory policy against homosexuals (discussed below). Later Lott concedes, "My problem is not *just* with her lifestyle" (S6180; emphasis mine). Opponents insist that it is not her sexual identity but her public actions that raise doubt about her ability to do the job. Lott addresses the issue of "temperament" by asking rhetorically, "Is she tolerant of the views of others? Can she administer her duties fairly and without bias? Or will she be a militant extremist promoting a narrow special interest agenda?" (S6093).

The distinction drawn here between private identity and public actions is premised on the condemnation of a supposed gay and lesbian lifestyle that is characterized by immorality and depravity. Attacks on lesbian and gay individuals as such may be difficult for lawmakers to defend, given Americans' general mistrust of government interference in "private" lives. However, *advocacy* of such an ostensibly corrupt lifestyle is another matter entirely, suggesting an influence on the government, and on society more broadly, that many people are unwilling to grant to gays and lesbians. Senator Strom Thurmond states, "I would like to note that my opposition to Ms. Achtenberg's nomination lies not with her personal lifestyle but with her radical activism in pursuing her own political agenda" (S6218). An article in the *Washington Times* on May 24, subsequently entered into the *Congressional Record*, quotes Martin Mawyer, president of the conservative Christian Action Network, taking the dichotomy lesbian/homosexual, or public/private, one step further. Mawyer's statement divides the terms into two meanings with still greater specificity: "We're not opposed to gays and lesbians holding federal office, but her performance in that [San Francisco Gay and Lesbian Pride] parade is evidence *she's a lesbian activist, not just a lesbian*" (S6333; emphasis mine). In addressing the issue of activism, we reach a key point in the controversy over Achtenberg's nomination: her political activities become the site of displacement for her opponents' negative responses. Activism becomes the reservoir for their suppressed attitudes toward her unacceptable (sexual) behaviors that are at all times implied but always unstated.

Notably, the characteristics that make Achtenberg's "lifestyle" objectionable are never explicitly laid out; nor is the particular narrow "agenda" she is expected to pursue clearly defined. The ambiguity of these concepts is not a result of oversight but the consequence of a rhetorical strategy that enables the artificial separation of identity from behavior. The flimsiness of this distinction is evident in the comment of Senator Pete Domenici, who, while voting to confirm Achtenberg, nevertheless asserts, "I cannot accept, as I believe the majority of the American public cannot accept, the promotion of alternative lifestyles as appropriate surrogates for what we refer to as 'the traditional' American family. And, I want to add that this has nothing to do with the issue of gender or sexual preferences" (S6354). The bandying about of terminology such as "alternative lifestyles" offers evidence that "gay lifestyle," which has been described as "the most respectable of current homophobic slogans," is "a phrase promulgated by the antigay right to alarm heterosexual Americans by associating gay civil rights claims with extreme sexual practices" (Nava & Dawidoff 1994, 127). *Lifestyle* carries a connotation of particular behaviors, presumably sexual, that are too offensive to mention by name. By leaving the definition unspecified, the implication (but not the outright accusation) of objectionable and extreme sexual practices is raised, while the discussion of Achtenberg's behavior ostensibly remains focused on her political activism. In this way, sexuality and activism are subtly but effectively linked.

This connection is even more powerfully reinforced by the discussion and the accompanying video of Achtenberg's participation in the San Francisco Gay and Lesbian Pride parade. In the parade, Achtenberg hugs and kisses her partner, Judge Mary Morgan, while riding on a float with their seven-year-old son, Benjie. In the portion of the video shown to the senators by Jesse Helms, the image of the women's embrace is juxtaposed with the image of another float, elsewhere in the parade, that portrays God sodomizing Uncle Sam while a Boy Scout looks on. In the not-so-subtle parallel implied here, Benjie is equated with the Boy Scout, the icon of young, "uncorrupted," heterosexual masculinity, watching a (presumably offensive or perverted) expression of love between women, an expression that is equated with the sexual act depicted by the other float. The importance of this link and the power of these images were not lost on Helms, who sent a copy of the parade video to every senator's office and threatened to send copies to the hometown newspapers of any senator who voted in favor of Achtenberg (Franken 1993). These images provided visual rein-forcement for the claim that it was Achtenberg's actions—her "lifestyle," her activism, and, implicitly, her sexual acts—and not her identity that made her an inappropriate candidate for the job. In this way, the split between "homosexuality" and "lesbianism," between private and public, marks a di-vision between what is, at least arguably, a constitutionally protected "iden-tity" and unprotected "actions." Such actions provide something of a dump-ing ground for the unexpressed and inexpressible condemnation generated by identity.

By invoking the separation of public and private spheres, the undesirable qualities associated with homosexuality can be displaced from a realm that is relatively protected onto one that is not. Achtenberg's *behavior* is referred to again and again as indicting her, and it is discussed as though it were a matter entirely separate from her identity. Senator Bob Dole states that "we must show respect and tolerance for those among us who happen to be gay. But showing tolerance and respect should not force us to embrace an ideo-logical agenda that most Americans do not accept" (S6348). Senator Frank Murkowski agrees: "Ordinarily . . . questions of personal life or lifestyle would not be at issue. However the nominee goes beyond the point of just choosing a lifestyle, but, in fact, advocates her lifestyle forcefully, as an ac-tivist. What disturbs me is that she promotes that lifestyle and suggests it rep-resents family values" (S6169). He insists bluntly that "her activism is inap-propriate . . . and therefore I feel it is necessary that I vote against the nom inee" (S6170).

The discourse of nonconformity or outright perversion often used to condemn homosexuality but inaccessible to the senators in the (semi)pro-tected realm of identity is shifted instead onto the category of lesbian be-haviors that remain available for critique. For example, in a discussion on the first day of the debate, Lott quotes a purported editorial in the *San Francisco Chronicle* that refers to Achtenberg as having a "twisted mind" and "tearing down what is good and wholesome in others" (S6093).[13] Achtenberg is characterized later by Senator Robert Smith as having a "twisted value sys-tem," as illustrated by her refusal to support the closing of San Francisco's gay bathhouses after the outbreak of AIDS (S6215). Here again, the accusa-tion links the overt description of "twisted" values and public actions with the implication of sexual perversity and disease.

Most of the senators carefully avoid using the word *lesbian* at all, their discomfort with the term sometimes resulting in obscure or convoluted speech. In a striking example of one such verbal contortion, committee chair Riegle says to Achtenberg, "I think it's important that we separate what's important from what isn't, in terms of you here as a nominee, and the fact that you may be the first person to come and to sit in a nomination seat in a situation, such as you do" (*Nominations* 1993, 30–31). Senator William Cohen also seems disinclined to use the term and attempts what is no doubt intended to be a more neutral approach: "She has a sexual orientation that is not followed by a majority of people in this country" (S6212). Helms is one senator who is willing to use the word, and with no one actively contesting his usage, the term assumes the negative connotations with which he endows it, ultimately sounding like a curse itself: "damn lesbian," "militantly activist lesbian" (S6352).[14] While others talk around the word, and around the issue entirely, Helms uses the term repeatedly and effectively. A reporter for the *San Jose Mercury News* observed, "On the Senate floor, Feinstein and Boxer spoke eloquently on [Achtenberg's] behalf, as did other senators. But Helms shouting the 'L' word was what grabbed national attention" (Shepard 1994, A2). Whereas *homosexual* becomes a depoliticized term in this discussion, just the opposite effect occurs for *lesbian*, which becomes a threatening category imbued with strong political overtones. If it is true that "it is the goal of the gay and lesbian movement to make 'gay' and 'lesbian' words one expects to hear, registers, and considers without reluctance," it is nevertheless also the case that, "at this point, the religious right still controls these words" (Nava and Dawidoff 1994, 105).

Among Achtenberg's opponents, only Helms refuses outright to maintain the public/private split, condemning equally "homosexuality" and "lesbianism." Helms appropriates a variant of the metaphor of "crossing the line" in articulating his concerns: "Any Senator who assumes that this is not a national issue should be advised that it is. Not because it is just a nomination, but because we are crossing the threshold into the first time in the history of America that a homosexual, a lesbian, has been nominated . . . for a top job in the U.S. Government. That is what the issue is" (S6099). While this quotation indicates that Achtenberg's identity itself is "the issue," he later identifies "the issue" as her behavior, suggesting that he draws no distinction between identity and actions: "That is what this issue is . . . how she has acted in public" (S6207). While taking a less provocative stance, Domenici also cautions against an overly rigid delineation between public and private spheres. He argues that "nominees do not come neatly sliced—they come as a whole loaf. Their personal value systems and their professional capabilities cannot be compartmentalized" (S6354). Domenici continues, "The debate on this candidate portrays clearly that professional expertise and private values are not easily separated or seen in isolation of one another. They are, instead, intricately intertwined" (S6355).

Despite the attempts of both supporters and opponents to deny the relevance of Achtenberg's private life to their evaluation of her competence, the centrality of sexual orientation to the tenor of the debate did not go unremarked, either by those in the Senate chamber or by those outside. The *San Francisco Chronicle* of May 20 observed, "Much of the Senate hearing into her nomination has not involved her qualifications to serve, but her sexual orientation" (S6177). Lieberman likewise notes on the second day of the debate that "the question of discrimination based on sexual orientation . . . is not explicitly on the line in this nomination but it is, in my opinion, implicitly on the line" (S6212–13). In her closing statement on the second day, Boxer concurs: "We know what this is all about. . . . It is not about qualifications. It is not about tolerance. It is not about demeanor. It is not about those things. It is about a private lifestyle that some feel disqualifies this woman" (S6223).

When the Senate returns to the issue three days later, Riegle reiterates this view, noting, "I think the only real challenge against this nominee boils down to her sexual orientation. . . . I believe all the other arguments that have been raised here are a smokescreen" (S6350). Boxer echoes his comment, remarking, "This kind of name calling is a smokescreen for disapproval of her private life" (S6350). Feinstein, too, supports the view that "the focus has not been on her qualifications. . . . Instead, critics have tried to use Roberta's sexual orientation to deny confirmation" (S6351). Through the representation of Achtenberg as a lesbian activist, the association of activism with bizarre sexual acts, and the added characterization of her "twisted" mind and values, opponents condemn Achtenberg for an implied and occasionally stated perversity that undermines her fitness to serve in high political office, even as they continue to insist that her sexual orientation is irrelevant to their condemnation.

The focus on identity raises another problem for supporters, one that arises from the very analogies with race and gender that they employ to fortify their position. Despite the progress of white women as well as people of color, it is still widely assumed that these groups constitute "special interests," and that the political vision of their representatives is largely bounded by these interests. Put differently, women are often seen primarily, if not solely, as spokespeople for other women. Their ability to represent or speak for a broader constituency is often questioned. This is equally true for racial and other minorities, who are often required to prove themselves able to address issues beyond those of particular interest to their group. This expectation is striking because white, middle-class, heterosexual males are never asked to do the same. They are not seen as representing (or even belonging to) a particular constituency based on their race, class, sexuality, or gender, nor are the concerns of this group characterized as "special interests."

Achtenberg's supporters equate her with other qualified minority candidates, comparing her appointment to the appointment of women, of blacks, and, finally, of a black woman. However, the difference between Achtenberg and Carol Moseley-Braun is that Moseley-Braun represents a constituency whose right to a political voice is at least given lip service by mainstream political representatives. For minority candidates, it is widely assumed that one's marginalized characteristic influences one's political interest and vision, and that one therefore speaks at least in part, if not primarily, for a particular constituency. The question then becomes whether or not this constituency has been granted the right, or at least a token right, to such political representation and public voice.

In the cases of gender and race, most politicians today would assert publicly (whatever their private views) that women and racial minorities have a right to such representation. Members of minority groups who speak out on behalf of racial and gender equality are increasingly admired for furthering their civil rights causes. However, this is not the case for gays and lesbians, who constitute one of the last groups against whom public condemnation remains acceptable. Certainly, there is no consensus among even mainstream politicians that gays and lesbians deserve political representation or voice. In fact, even Achtenberg's Senate supporters are unwilling to make such a claim. To address this difficulty, they need to assert that, *unlike* women or African American politicians, Achtenberg's marginalized characteristic is irrelevant to her politics. They must show that her political views are not affected by her sexual orientation, and that she therefore will not become a spokesperson for a gay and lesbian constituency or an advocate for the purported "gay agenda."

Achtenberg's supporters are caught in a dilemma: they need at once to claim that sexual orientation is an identity like other marginalized categories, such as gender and race, and to assert that it is different. They need to reject one particular implication of the identity claim without dismantling the framework of identity that enables them to compare gays and lesbians to other oppressed minorities. The strategy is, needless to say, a risky one. While moderate senators might be persuaded to cease discrimination based on the claim that sexual orientation is an irrelevant characteristic of identity, they will not then grant that "irrelevant" characteristic a political voice. In granting this degree of visibility to a lesbian politician, they claim the right to withhold voice, a strategy that permits lesbians and gays to be seen but not heard. Achtenberg may be confirmed as an out lesbian, but she may not speak as a lesbian or on behalf of lesbians.

This tacit compromise effectively forecloses any public conversation that could arise from Achtenberg's confirmation. It therefore leaves the compulsory nature of heterosexuality and the dominant definitions and institutions that privilege heterosexuality intact. It frees the senators from having to concede that homosexuality is an acceptable or equal alternative to heterosexuality. Many of the senators seem to find it incumbent upon them to condemn homosexuality even if they support Achtenberg's nomination. Lieberman, who votes in favor of Achtenberg and even identifies himself as her friend (*Nominations* 1993, 20), distances himself and his colleagues from any tacit approval of homosexuality: "This is not a vote on whether a Senator accepts homosexuality, approves of it, accepts it as the equal of a heterosexual lifestyle. I do not" (S6213). Some senators might be convinced that Achtenberg, and lesbians and gays generally, should not be disqualified from holding office on the basis of sexual orientation (as is the case with race). However, they are largely unwilling to suggest that lesbians and gays as such be given a voice in national politics—a concession all but the most profoundly right-wing politicians generally grant to racial minorities, at least in public discourse.

Thus Achtenberg's Senate supporters, while willing to grant her *visibility* as a lesbian through their self-congratulatory discourse about social progress, are uniformly reluctant to grant her *voice* as a lesbian. She must promise not to advocate for gay and lesbian rights, and her supporters must explain away and defend her past activism on behalf of such rights. The ostensible social progress achieved through Achtenberg's confirmation is thereby held in check by the understanding that one attains such high status only by sacrificing one's right to speak as a lesbian. On the one hand, as Torie Osborn, former director of the National Gay and Lesbian Task Force, asserts, "A young lesbian coming up, secretive at college, can come out and have more hope for her life because there's a Roberta Achtenberg at HUD" (in Shepard 1994, A4). Stoddard likewise writes that Achtenberg's achievement "set new levels of aspiration for young lesbians and gay men who yearn for success without sacrificing their identities" (1993, 45). Yet, on the other hand, if

Achtenberg becomes a role model for gay and lesbian youth through her success, she does so at the cost of her activist politics, and those who wish to model themselves after her learn a harsh lesson about the sacrifices such an achievement entails.

The danger here for the lesbian and gay rights movement is not only that the language of this debate denies Achtenberg the right to speak on behalf of lesbians and gays. Through her supporters' own rhetoric, her identification with a broader gay and lesbian community is itself eroded. The result is that her legitimacy as a nominee for this position is premised on the contrast between her and the members of such a community. Achtenberg's supporters go to some lengths to differentiate and isolate her from other gays and lesbians. In addition to their characterization of sexual orientation as "private conduct" (S6216) and their assertion that "her personal life should have nothing to do with this nomination," they build an argument for her integrity as a politician precisely upon her *distinction* from other gays and lesbians. Boxer, responding to the characterization of lesbian and gay rights as a "special agenda," does not deny this description but instead argues that Achtenberg does not share this agenda, thereby disengaging the nominee from the struggle for gay and lesbian rights. Boxer notes that "it is an issue of great importance to all of us that we do not confirm people for the position of Assistant Secretary, or as Cabinet members, if they have a special agenda and they are going to push that agenda." In Achtenberg's testimony, Boxer reminds the senators, the candidate asserted her understanding that if confirmed, her job will be "to enforce fair housing laws, not to push any envelopes" (S6212).

Boxer goes so far as to quote from a letter written by Art Agnos, the former mayor of San Francisco, relating an incident in which Achtenberg was criticized by other gays and lesbians. Agnos writes that "the sharpest opposition to her work [as a city supervisor] came from a small sector of the lesbian and gay community" who criticized her for "failing to subscribe to a single-issue approach that advanced their own narrow agenda and which would have ignored the needs of other families. It is consistent with the integrity that characterized Roberta Achtenberg that she withstood such criticism" (S6222). In citing this example, Boxer dissociates Achtenberg from the pursuit of "special" rights, at the same time highlighting the selfish appeals of other lesbians and gays. This rhetorical strategy effectively divides "good" lesbians and gays—those who do not work to advance their own rights—from "bad" ones—those concerned only with their own special interest agenda. This particular discourse of "support" simply repeats a historical pattern of oppression, familiar to numerous minority groups, that advances one individual at the expense of the group rather than enhancing the group's status through her success.

## DISPLACING THE CLOSET

Notably, in the discourse of both Achtenberg supporters and opponents, the figure of the closet is displaced by the metaphor of "crossing a line" to describe the liberal invitation, extended to various minority groups at various points in history, to assimilate and therefore attain heightened political status. Only one reference is made to the figure of the closet, midway through the three-day debate, and even in that instance, the allusion is quite vague. Senator Tom Harkin, speaking in support of Achtenberg's nomination, states, "This is one Senator who believes there is more to housing than just closets." He continues, "I have always believed that people should be judged on the basis of their abilities, not upon the basis of fear or prejudice, unfounded accusations or centuries-held beliefs that we now find should not be held any longer" (S6200). In contrast to the closet metaphor, Riegle introduces the notion of crossing a line in his opening statement during the committee's nomination hearing. Addressing Achtenberg, Riegle states, "In a sense you are crossing one of those invisible lines that we have in our society in terms of this issue that is there raised by some with respect to sexual orientation" (*Nominations* 1993, 30). He repeats his opening statement at the beginning of the Senate confirmation proceedings, establishing at the outset the framework within which Achtenberg's "difference" and her accomplishment are to be viewed.

Rather than suggesting the act of coming *out*, the metaphor of a line represents an act of coming *over* or coming *in*, emphasizing an entrance rather than an exodus. More specifically, while "coming out" leaves ambiguous the nature of the new location, "coming over" is quite explicit in identifying the site at which the act concludes. Coming over clearly indicates the assimilation of that which was "Other," distant and distinct, to that which is self, nearby and similar. The figure of a line solidifies, in a different manner than does the closet, the opposition between heterosexuality and homosexuality. In the closet metaphor, the relationship between inside and outside allows for some complexity. This metaphor implies that gays and lesbians are "locked away" by those who condemn us, but it also suggests that we achieve a degree of safety by locking those same people out. The closet may suffocate us yet it may protect us; it may be externally imposed or strategically chosen. This understanding continually undermines a unified or stable meaning, making the determination of perspective always ambiguous and undecidable.

Although the metaphor of the closet has its own limitations as a means of representing the complexities of lesbian and gay oppression, it does communicate the feeling of being wholly surrounded. It thereby hints at the numerous and interconnected forms of oppression that impose invisibility and silence. The figure of the closet conveys a sense of how heterosexual institutions envelop lesbian and gay individuals and communities. It suggests how our hiddenness places us in a particular "outsider within" status that is not entirely comparable with the experience of other, more easily identifiable minority groups. Such a status may seem particularly threatening because gays and lesbians are already within our society's most intimate spaces: families, schools, workplaces, synagogues, and churches. For this reason, we cannot be excluded by the same means and with the same certainty as are members of other minority groups; our exclusion must be accomplished through alternate means. To be in a closet, in this context, is to be sequestered within, rather than exiled without. It is at once treacherous for those "inside" and threatening to those "outside," because it is banishment to a place very close to the oppressor. The "closet" is *inside the oppressor's own home*, and so it represents a very particular and highly contradictory position of marginality. The closet metaphor acknowledges that those whom the mainstream attempts to exclude are always within, making the dividing lines between "us" and "them" extremely precarious. The maintenance of these lines demands constant vigilance from those who desire to keep such boundaries intact.

The notion of crossing a line, in contrast to the closet metaphor, rhetorically situates the oppressed group at a more distanced position. Lines are used, literally and figuratively, to divide "us" from "them" (Nava and Dawidoff 1994, 70). This implicit division is borne out blatantly in a comment made by Senator Alan Simpson. Despite his stated belief that "sexual preference . . . should not be a disqualifying factor," Simpson makes the startling assertion that "Ms. Achtenberg will not be simply presiding over and making judgments that effect [*sic*] people who are solely citizens of her country. It is our country, and our Government" (S6355). Simpson offers no further explanation of what he means by this reference to "her country." However, his comment offers vivid evidence that "in this (hetero)sexist social ontology, there are two distinct groups: 'Americans' and 'gays and lesbians'" (Phelan 1995, 196).

Because it creates false oppositions and simplifies complex relationships, the metaphor of crossing a line misleads in a variety of ways. The image presumes not only an infallible definition of homosexuality but also a clear biological differentiation between heterosexuals and homosexuals. It thereby fortifies the bounds of heterosexuality, such that "we" and "they" are distributed on respective "sides." There is no possibility of confusion, no need for potentially uncomfortable questioning of the self. This view precludes any suggestion that apparently biological categories are *themselves* constructed, that "what we believe to be a physical and direct perception is only a sophisticated and mythic construction, an 'imaginary formation'" (Wittig 1993, 104). Nor can there be any possibility of perceiving the categories of biology not as bipolar but as dispersed and differentiated across a spectrum of possibilities. The presumably "natural" binary opposition of heterosexuality/homosexuality is never called into question.

This linguistic division recurs throughout the Achtenberg debate. The clear distinction represented by the figure of a line is particularly necessary to establish in this case because, as the metaphor of the closet suggests, gays and lesbians are not identifiably outsiders but are hidden instead within society's most sacred institutions. The metaphor of a line erases the ambiguity that surrounds the definition and classification of homosexuals and substitutes a distinctive "Otherness." Through this alternate metaphor, visible and/or vocal gays and lesbians can be perceived as exiled without, observably different, and clearly distinguishable through what are perceived as their "reprehensible" actions and the flaunting of their infamous "lifestyle." The images and locales that Achtenberg's opponents reference—most notably those of the gay bathhouses and the gay and lesbian pride parade—are used to represent gays and lesbians as visibly different (not like us) and as outsiders (not among us). This rhetorical exile is a crucial strategy for opponents, a means of establishing and maintaining clear boundaries despite the existence of gays and lesbians within all institutions, despite the resounding accuracy of the lesbian and gay rights slogan "We Are Everywhere."

The metaphor of crossing a line, however, oversimplifies not only through the deceptive clarity of its insider/outsider dichotomy. It also misleads by forwarding an understanding of oppression not as a systematic network of obstacles but rather as a single barrier to be overcome. Once a group has crossed the line, the barrier is instantly removed. As an expression of any oppressed group's experience, such a model is misrepresentative and reductive. "The experience of oppressed people is that the living of one's life is confined and shaped by forces and barriers which . . . are systematically related to each other in such a way as to catch one between and among them and restrict or penalize motion in any direction. It is the experience of being caged in" (Frye 1983, 4).[15] This description illuminates the complex and *systemic* character of oppression and suggests the unyielding quality of oppression that may persist after one or more of the barriers are removed.

The metaphor of crossing the line replaces the ambivalence surrounding the relative gains and losses involved in coming out of the closet with a clear-cut notion of movement from a worse to a better place, an image of achievement that suggests the unequivocal and irrevocable success of crossing a finish line. It suggests as well the linearity of a group's progress, in which hard work and good behavior are rewarded with permission to cross over into a position of greater privilege and, implicitly, of greater moral uprightness. This is suggested by Lott's remark that his job is to consider the appropriateness of the candidate based on "their ethical conflict, if they have any, and whether or not they have any legal problems" (S6092). Similarly, Simpson, opposing confirmation, complains that "we are all entitled to public servants who at least listen and try to be objective" (S6355). Such statements imply that gay and lesbian political candidates, like other minority candidates historically, are morally suspect by virtue of their difference, their presumed allegiance to a special interest group, and their consequent ulterior motives. If they can overcome the inherent moral inferiority conveyed by their difference and free themselves of these purported biases, then they may be judged capable of serving as political representatives.

Although the expression "crossing a line" often signifies a transgressive act, this sense of the phrase is virtually absent from the discourse of Achtenberg's supporters, who use the phrase only to convey a sanctioned traversal. The line represents a degree of expected conformity, as Murkowski's comments illustrate: "I think that we all have an obligation to some degree for conformity within bounds.... If we are too out of conformity ... somebody is going to say hey, you are a little out of line." Such lines, then, mark off "certain bounds within which we should be expected to conform" (S6169).[16] In this sense, the very possibility of coming out as an act of self-determination chosen by gays and lesbians is steadfastly suppressed. It is replaced, instead, by a benign crossing in response to the beckoning of the powers-that-be, where the initiative and impetus are clearly on the side of the senators.

While Achtenberg's supporters avoid the transgressive connotations of "crossing the line," her opponents deploy the metaphor in a quite different manner. The notion of transgression is both implicitly and explicitly pre-

sent in opponents' discourse, portraying the crossing of established boundaries as an unacceptable incursion into sacred territory. Helms turns Riegle's
words around when he characterizes the Banking Committee's nomination
hearing as a "love-in" for Achtenberg. Helms tells his Senate colleagues, "I
wish you could read the statement that the chairman made just like it was a
time for celebration that the President of the United States has *crossed a line*
and has nominated a lesbian for high Government office" (S6207; emphasis
mine). Senator Slade Gorton also emphasizes what he sees as inappropriate
public behavior on Achtenberg's part, arguing that "there is a crucial distinction between legitimate advocacy of an agenda and a hostile and irre-
sponsible intolerance of those who do not share that agenda, between spir-
ited advocacy and punitive harassment. Ms. Achtenberg *crossed this line*"
(S6349; emphasis mine).[17]

Significantly, both supporters and opponents suggest that the line being
crossed with this nomination is one of inclusion rather than visibility. That
is, Achtenberg's nomination is seen as significant in that it ostensibly marks
the "first time" a lesbian or gay man has been nominated for a cabinet post
(S6099), crossing from outsider to insider status. This contention is most
likely incorrect. What makes Achtenberg's nomination a first is that she is
*openly* lesbian, and that this fact is therefore a subject of open discussion
among the senators. It is highly unlikely that in the history of American
government there have been no nominees to high office who would fit the
most common definition of homosexual—one whose sexual and affectional
preferences are for members of one's own sex. In this way, the metaphor of
the line misleads us into accepting the narrowest possible definition of homosexuality by suggesting that only "announced" or "out" gays and lesbians
*are* gay or lesbian. This interpretation permits supporters and opponents to
agree confidently that Achtenberg's nomination is unprecedented, thus
avoiding the disquieting possibility that closeted gays and lesbians have held
important political appointments historically and that they do so currently.

Because the metaphor of crossing a line equates the politics of gays and
lesbians with those of other minority groups, it highlights intergroup similarities while suppressing distinctive features. Such a discourse obscures
those elements that are specific to gay and lesbian identities, such as "closetedness" and a particular insider/outsider status. In this way, it neutralizes the
intrinsic challenge that homosexuality presents to heterosexist institutions.
Homosexuality is already hidden within heterosexuality and its institutions.
The nature of its challenge to dominant culture thus differs in important
ways from the challenges presented by differences of gender or race. The

metaphor also disguises the way in which heterosexuality itself is a default category that can be perceived only in relation to its opposite, homosexuality. The category of "heterosexuals" relies for its definition and clarity upon the existence of a group of "homosexuals" who constitute a distinct and observable category of outsiders. Only through their exclusion can heterosexuality define its borders. Upholding the category of "homosexuality" is thus crucial for shoring up these inherently unstable boundaries (Halley 1991).

By presenting homosexuals as a single entity, the line metaphor borrows from the closet metaphor a tendency to subsume lesbians' and gay men's experiences under the broader category of "homosexuality," thus denying each its particularity and difference. "Heterosexuality is the paradigm, and all deviations from it constitute a single category." Within such a framework, "that lesbians, gay men, and bisexual women and men might have legally distinct concerns is unimagined" (Robson 1992, 85). The result is most often a privileging of white, professional gay male experience, while attention is diverted away from lesbian specificity. This is an especially disturbing omission if we accept Rita Mae Brown's assessment that "lesbians are as different from gay men as straight women are from straight men" (in Kasindorf 1993, 35).

In the identification of Achtenberg as a representative of lesbians *and* gay men, lesbianism is concealed within the male-identified category of homosexuality. This is evident in Helms's use of the male image in the gay pride float to sabotage the female image of Achtenberg's family. Equating lesbian sexuality with gay male sexuality obscures important differences in how the two are perceived and publicly discussed. Lesbian sexuality and relationships are often portrayed quite differently than, and evoke responses quite different from, gay male sexuality and relationships. At the same time, this equation ignores or denies the connections between lesbianism and feminism and between lesbians and heterosexual women.[18]

Such a rhetorical strategy conceals the fact that not sexuality alone but gender itself is at stake in this debate. Attacks on homosexuality are undergirded by a condemnation of those who are perceived as refusing or failing to fulfill their assigned gender role. Achtenberg is condemned by opponents for her inadequacy *as a woman*, as evidenced by both her "poor judgment" and her failure to conform to political propriety. If lesbianism is linked to rebellious behavior and poor judgment, it is additionally and unsurprisingly associated with insufficient femininity. Achtenberg is repeatedly criticized for actions that are viewed as falling outside the range of acceptable feminine behavior. Yet in a classic example of oppression's double bind (Frye 1983), Achtenberg is also criticized for failings associated with a feminine gender role. She is represented at various places in the discussion either as exhibiting insufficiently feminine behavior or, conversely, as embodying too many of the negative stereotypes of women.

As a woman, Achtenberg is depicted by opponents as irrational, enslaved by her emotions, and possessing inferior powers of judgment. Such characteristics have long been associated with stereotypes of women. Senator Christopher Bond comments, "Ms. Achtenberg has a tendency to let her passions and ideological inclinations overshadow her judgment" (S6176). Rather than being admired for her convictions and commitment, Achtenberg is censured for standing up for her beliefs. Senator Don Nickles states, "She has been so adamant in her belief and her activism that her judgment and impartiality are clouded" (S6210). Moreover, some opponents employ language that explicitly belittles her. In one example, Simpson states, "I am not personally convinced that Ms. Achtenberg has demonstrated that level of maturity, objectivity, and fairness as to warrant my support of her confirmation to this important position" (S6355). On another occasion, Helms refers to her demeaningly as a "lady" who, he implies, threw the equivalent of a temper tantrum when "her little resolution" was vetoed (S6101).

In critiquing her *un*feminine demeanor, Helms characterizes Achtenberg as "pushy, demeaning, demanding; she is a mean person, mean-spirited" (S6100). Such terms describe the antithesis of the feminine ideal in Western culture. Achtenberg herself viewed this comment as an attack on her not only as a woman but, in particular, as a Jewish woman. In an interview with the *Jewish Bulletin of Northern California* after her confirmation, she commented on the implied anti-Semitism of this characterization: "There was no question it was anti-Semitic, and there was misogyny as well. . . . Every chance they got, they called me pushy. I don't think I'm the only Jewish person who has thought it [is anti-Semitic] when someone says 'pushy.' Jewish people know what that means" (Wolkoff 1993, 1). Achtenberg's rabbi, Yoel Kahn, who was present at the Banking Committee's nomination hearing, agreed that *pushy* is one of the "code words for Jews as well as for women who are in leadership positions" (Wolkoff 1993, 41).

The Republicans' theme of "meanness" continues with Lott's criticism that Achtenberg "has not been just a *passive* lawyer. . . . She has been an *aggressive* activist in representing a lot of extremist positions" (S6179; emphasis mine). This familiar passive/active opposition provides a clear parallel to the dichotomy of femininity/masculinity, condemning Achtenberg for failing to be feminine in her predominantly male profession. One wonders who would applaud a "passive lawyer" or nominate her for an influential government job. Nevertheless, Lott uses this assessment to assure the senators that "this is not some nice middle-of-the-road, pleasant[,] well-educated, well-trained, well-qualified person that has never shown any indication of intolerance or extremism." Instead, he warns, "there is too much of a record of aggressive advocacy that involves punishment, retribution, intimidation and . . . intolerance of different views" (S6180). Achtenberg is also accused by Senator Malcolm Wallop of carrying out "coercion" and "threats" (S6104), by Senator Charles Grassley of "persecution" (S6354), and by Senator Phil Gramm of having "a long history of engaging in vendettas against people with whom [she] disagreed" (S6222).

Achtenberg's supporters respond to such attacks by emphasizing those positive traits she possesses that are stereotypically feminine. They focus in particular on her nurturance and her skill at gaining cooperation from various people. Feinstein remarks that those who know Achtenberg best "know her as a sensitive individual, a caring individual. We also know her as a rather quiet individual" (S6200). Boxer notes, "Roberta Achtenberg is a healing person. She brings people together." She highlights Achtenberg's "abilities to bring people together, to solve problems, to build coalitions, to listen to all sides" (S6092). She explicitly rejects Helms's characterization of Achtenberg, arguing, "She is a good person . . . she is not pushy and she is not demeaning and she is not demanding and she is not mean" (S6115). She quotes from a letter to defend Achtenberg against a negative female stereotype: "Roberta is neither shrill nor uncompromising" (S6116). It is difficult to imagine any man needing to respond to accusations that he is shrill. Finally, Boxer characterizes the Senate debate, in brief, as an act of "tearing down a good woman" (S6208). While these claims are not harmful or demeaning in themselves, they illustrate the constraints that are placed on her supporters. They feel they must portray Achtenberg as conforming to an appropriate gender role yet not falling victim to the stereotypical weaknesses of that role.

Achtenberg's actions as a politician, as well as her association with what is viewed as a hostile and threatening community of gays and lesbians, discredit her in the eyes of opponents as an acceptable woman. The argument of Achtenberg's opponents that lesbians and gay men promote their lifestyle by enforcing their own political agenda invokes a conspiracy theory, fashionable in some right-wing political circles, that gays and lesbians are attempting to impose a secret agenda on unsuspecting Americans, particularly on susceptible American youth. While the accusation of a conspiracy is never explicitly expressed in this debate, it is insinuated by her opponents, with Achtenberg seen as a leader of these subversive forces. There is more than a hint of "unladylike" aggression and even violence in the discussion of the gay and lesbian community's alleged efforts to impose a particular lifestyle on the American public. This aggression is attributed directly to Achtenberg, as well as to the gay and lesbian community with whom she is associated. Grassley, for example, accuses Achtenberg and gays generally of "forcing homosexuality upon those who oppose this lifestyle and all it entails" (S6354). Helms insists more forcefully, "The homosexual community is trying to ram their way of life down someone else's throat" (S6207). This "way of life" and its representatives are viewed as insidious, thoroughly immoral, and utterly destructive. The gay and lesbian community and its representatives are thereby portrayed as the oppressors rather than the oppressed. This reversal is accomplished through a "devious process of inversion," by which "gays and lesbians are cast as not . . . vulnerable to discrimination, violence and indignity, but as aggressors against a vulnerable society, able to 'force our agenda down unwilling throats'" (Cerullo 1990, 13–14). In the service of this reversal, Smith characterizes Achtenberg as "one who, if she had her way, would shut down all the Boy Scout troops in America and replace them with sex clubs festering with disease" (S6216).

Achtenberg's conflict with the Boy Scouts is the example her opponents use repeatedly to illustrate the threat she poses to American values. Achtenberg served on the board of directors of the United Way of the Bay Area, which had a policy requiring all organizations it funded to practice nondiscrimination based on "race, national origin, gender, age, status of having been involved in military service, marital status, sexual orientation, disability and the like" (*Nominations* 1993, 36). It came to the board's attention that the Boy Scouts, a recipient of United Way funds, refused to provide services for gay or bisexual boys and prohibited openly gay men from becoming scout leaders. The United Way then directed a task force (of which Achtenberg was not a member) to investigate the matter. The task force reported to the board that the charges of discrimination were true. The board, including Achtenberg, then voted unanimously to cease funding the Boy Scouts organization unless and until it changed its rules to provide services for all boys on a nondiscriminatory basis (*Nominations* 1993, 36). In addition, Achtenberg introduced a resolution to transfer $6 million of city money out of the Bank of America, which continued to fund the Boy Scouts despite their discriminatory policies. At her nomination hearing, Achtenberg is also accused of urging the San Francisco School Board to bar the Boy Scouts from using public school facilities, although this charge is not borne out by the evidence presented (*Nominations* 1993, 36–37).

Achtenberg's opponents argue repeatedly that her "efforts to destroy the Boy Scout troops in the San Francisco Bay Area" (S6215) represent a "vendetta" (*Nominations* 1993, 79; S6093; S6222). They cite this incident to confirm their accusations of both her perversity and her poor judgment. She is reproached for being "more than a critic. She has been the ringleader of an ideological crusade to remake the Boy Scouts in her own image" (S6348). One quotation from Achtenberg, taken from an Associated Press article published in August 1991, is repeated seven different times in the transcript of the debate.[19] The quotation reads: "Do we want children learning the values of an organization that provides character building exclusively for straight, God-fearing male children?" Her attitude toward the Boy Scout organization is characterized by Smith as that of a "Scoutophobe . . . hacking away at the values held by Boy Scouts" (S6216).

This discussion portrays the Boy Scouts as the embodiment of all that is admirable about heterosexual masculinity and, by extension, heterosexuality in general. Achtenberg's politics presumably attack all this: "The Scouts teach young men to value important things, such as honor, integrity, honesty, duty, God, country, and family" (S6215). Thus Achtenberg's statement is interpreted as a rejection of that which is good and right about patriarchal America. Helms argues, "The Scout oath says 'On my honor as a Scout, I will do my best to do my duty to God and my country and to obey the Scout law; to help other people at all times; to keep myself physically strong, mentally awake, and morally straight.' . . . These are the values that were—and still are—under assault" (S6206). Finally, Lott complains, "This lady is not attacking some extremist group, for heaven's sake. She is going after the Boy Scouts. She might as well be going after motherhood" (S6180).[20]

In contrast to the equation of heterosexual masculinity and duty to God with the clean-cut image of the Boy Scouts, homosexuality is represented by the sex clubs or bathhouses that Achtenberg fought to keep open at the beginning of the AIDS crisis, and by the values presumably associated with them: "Sex clubs encourage anonymous sex, promiscuity, unsafe sex and the spread of AIDS" (S6352). Achtenberg's one-time support of these clubs is presented as further evidence of her perversion and of the kind of America she would impose, given the chance. She is described as "a radical liberal who is hostile to the values held by the Boy Scouts yet would fiercely defend promiscuous, dangerous sex" (S6216). Despite the fact that lesbians did not participate in the bathhouse culture, Achtenberg is seen as doubly implicated. She is found guilty based on both her presumed membership in the subculture that perpetuated the "immoral" lifestyle of the bathhouses and her decision as a politician to try to keep them open. Smith claims Achtenberg is "the only" American who could believe that "the Boy Scouts are an insidious group bent on undermining society while sex clubs are a valuable institution that provides important cultural stability" (S6216). Helms refers to her as a "militantly activist lesbian" in the same sentence that he discusses her refusal "to shut down the so-called public bathhouses in San Francisco, where hoards [*sic*] of homosexuals were engaging in their perverted activities" (S6352). In a similar vein, he condemns "the *pornographic* and *blasphemous* activities during last year's San Francisco Gay Pride parade led by Roberta Achtenberg and her partner—and their son" (S6332; emphasis mine).

As the Boy Scouts become the repository for a sacred heterosexual masculinity and Achtenberg's own femininity is attacked, the discussion inevitably turns to Achtenberg's son. Opponents question her capability and even her legitimacy as a parent. In fact, Achtenberg's own unconventional family structure and the questioning of her parental judgment in bringing her son to a gay and lesbian pride parade coincide neatly with Lott's suggestion that Achtenberg, through her actions related to the Boy Scouts, has as good as attacked motherhood. The issues of Achtenberg's views regarding families and her relationship with her own partner and son take on considerable importance for a cabinet position largely concerned with helping families, particularly families with children.

This issue marks yet another site at which the public/private distinction begins to rupture. The continuity between private values and public commitments is highlighted by the long-standing debate over American "family values." The debate over families and family values permeates the confirmation hearing, although it surfaces only intermittently. Attention is focused on Achtenberg's own family, including her partner, Judge Mary Morgan, and their son, who was born after Morgan was artificially inseminated. Achtenberg's opponents condemn the parenting behavior of Achtenberg and Morgan. They particularly criticize the women's decision to ride with their son in the San Francisco Gay and Lesbian Pride march on a float carrying a banner that read: "Celebrating Our Family Values." During the parade, Achtenberg and Morgan "hugged each other and at one point, they embraced and kissed each other fervently" (S6100) in the presence of their son. Nickles asks, "What kind of environment is that to be showing a 7-year-old?" (S6210). Helms adds his condemnation by presenting a newspaper article in which the family relationship itself is challenged, through a reference to Achtenberg and Morgan's "claim to be his 'parents'" (S6333). Even biological kinship is thrown into question, as though a lesbian who bears a child is not legitimately the child's mother. At the same time, the claim of a gay or lesbian partner to a family relationship with the child is ridiculed outright.[21]

Achtenberg's relationship to this nontraditional family is the inevitable lead-in to the question of family values, the catchwords of George Bush's presidential campaign and of the religious right in opposing homosexuality. Both sides draw on issues of family to support their positions. Achtenberg's supporters are careful to specify her involvement in the Parent-Teacher Association (PTA) at her son's school when referring to her involvement in "numerous organizations" (S6091). They also emphasize her loyalty to her family of origin, particularly her brother: "Because of Ms. Achtenberg's familial experience with a brother who was disabled, she has been sensitive to disability issues" (S6109). Her opponents' contrasting view is stated bluntly by Helms, quoting a Boy Scout spokesman: "We don't believe homosexuals provide a role model consistent with . . . family values" (S6099). Achtenberg's "attack" on the Boy Scouts translates into a rejection of all things American, from masculinity to motherhood. It serves as the representative case of her undermining of family values, which organizations like the Boy Scouts are seen to uphold.

Yet the first mention of family values during the nomination hearing is made not by an opponent but by Boxer, an Achtenberg supporter, most likely in an attempt to forestall the inevitable family values debate. At the beginning of the discussion she asserts, "Roberta Achtenberg already has been a champion for families with children" (S6092). Boxer reads a letter she wrote with seven other Achtenberg supporters, in which they emphasize that Achtenberg has been "a strong advocate for the rights of families and children" (S6098). Boxer asks Achtenberg to tell the committee "about your very important fight that made history in San Francisco, which was to pass a local ordinance which stopped discrimination against families with children. Because when I think of family values, I very much think about it . . . I think that shows where your priorities are" (*Nominations* 1993, 39). Boxer, like other supporters, counters the right-wing discourse of family values by presenting evidence of Achtenberg's positive work in helping disadvantaged families gain equal access to fair housing.

As the discourse of femininity ultimately comes to rest in the issue of motherhood, so the discourse of family values gains much of its legitimacy from its religious foundation. In this way, religion inevitably makes its way into the debate as well. Here again lies hotly contested territory, particularly in light of the standard Christian anti-gay argument that homosexuality is prohibited by the Bible, that it defies the will of God and so is inherently sinful. It is hardly surprising, then, that both opponents and supporters attempt to stake a claim to this influential territory, despite the constitutional separation of church and state that should render the issue irrelevant. Supporters deny what they perceive as "implications that Roberta Achtenberg does not love God" (S6116). They portray Achtenberg as "a Jewish woman... [who] freely professes her own belief in God" (S6179) and who is actively involved in her synagogue (S6091; S6116). They emphasize, "Roberta is deeply respected by the Jewish community in San Francisco and is greatly admired as an advocate for civil rights and for Jewish concerns" (S6114). In contrast, opponents quote her favorable comments about the group ACT-UP as evidence of her endorsement of "harassment and terrorism of Catholics and other religious groups." They cite her participation in the gay and lesbian pride parade as evidence of her intolerance toward those who hold religious views (S6094). Lott argues that "Roberta Achtenberg has participated in events and parades where those with religious views were ridiculed and parodied." To illustrate his point, he cites the "San Francisco parade where she was an honored guest and participant, [where] there were graphic depictions of God sodomizing Uncle Sam while a Boy Scout looks on" (S6094). In highlighting this illustration, Lott summarizes the views that Achtenberg's opponents express implicitly and explicitly throughout the debate. They strategically portray Achtenberg and the entire gay and lesbian community she represents as subversive to America, menacing to the traditional values embodied by the Boy Scout organization, and hostile to God and believers in God.

In the Senate debate, supporters and opponents remain locked inside traditional gender roles and dominant social institutions. They struggle to represent Achtenberg as either in sympathy with or a menace to so-called American values. By arguing with opponents over Achtenberg's femininity, supporters more firmly validate and entrench ideals of femininity in American culture, rather than challenging these ideals as anachronisms. Even in their efforts to defend Achtenberg as a good mother and a religious woman, supporters are put on the defensive, forced to uphold traditional gender stereotypes. It remains clear that opponents control much of the discourse and determine the ways in which the issues in this debate are framed. This constraint is inherent in civil rights arguments that strive for equality for marginalized groups *within* existing institutions, rather than challenging the authority of the structures themselves. As a result of this strategy, the terms of the argument and the classifications assigned to minority groups remain those imposed by the dominant ideology. In the final section of this chapter, I investigate some of the drawbacks that attend these civil rights approaches to lesbian and gay liberation.

## CIVIL RIGHTS: LIMITS AND CONTRADICTIONS

The clash that takes place in the Achtenberg nomination is over the separation of that which Achtenberg's supporters claim is private—lesbian identity—from that which is public—lesbian activism. The rhetorical moves of Achtenberg's supporters reflect the strategies that dominate gay and lesbian civil rights discourse more broadly. The Achtenberg case thereby provides an opportunity for us to examine how such strategies function and what their effects might be, in practice rather than in theory. As in lesbian and gay civil rights discourse generally, Achtenberg's supporters create and uphold the category of "homosexuals" as a discrete and protected class and simultaneously dismiss or erase the potential challenge this class presents to dominant ideology and institutions.

The mismatching of political strategies captured here occurs at numerous levels. First, Achtenberg's own politics have consistently been, as her opponents correctly observe, activist. Her appearance on a float at the San Francisco Gay and Lesbian Pride parade, her kissing and embracing of her partner during that parade, her seven-year-old son Benjie's presence on the float, and the banner that proclaimed "Celebrating Our Family Values" are, in fact, public behaviors. As Helms points out, despite her supporters' insistence that sexual orientation is a private matter, her actions during the parade neither were private actions nor were carried out in a private space (S6351).

In interviews, moreover, Achtenberg praises the actions of such groups as ACT-UP, an organization that utilizes direct action, such as demonstrations and other forms of street activism, to increase AIDS funding. She acknowledges her belief in the limitations of working within the system to bring about social change, and she notes that politicians are inherently limited in their ability to bring about such change. In an interview with the *Advocate* she states, "I am very cautious about the role of electoral politics in our own liberation movement. . . . I remain extremely concerned that people are inclined to turn over our movement to elected officials. People who have been elected to office are extraordinarily incapable of being leaders of indigenous movements" (Stoddard 1993, 49). Her desire for the position at HUD, she explains, is based on her commitment to implementing the existing fair housing policy—a policy that currently excludes any reference to sexual orientation. A civil rights lawyer by trade, her own politics nevertheless strongly support extragovernmental action. Thus, while the Achtenberg nomination is employed as a means of arguing for the irrelevance of sexual orientation to the political process and Achtenberg's behavior is defended under the mantle of "privacy," her own statements and actions suggest a stance not entirely sympathetic with this position. "Achtenberg is someone whose life and work have balanced on the edge between inside and outside, between professional politics and grassroots activism, between confrontation and coalition" (Miles 1995, 70).

But the juxtaposition of Achtenberg's own politics with the politics of her nomination represents only part of the often self-defeating paradox of her supporters' arguments. As her opponents observe, Achtenberg's nomination by Bill Clinton came, in part, as a payoff to gays and lesbians who had contributed both money and support, in the form of a strong voting bloc, to help him get elected. Achtenberg herself was the first elected official in California to support Clinton and was instrumental in advancing his campaign in that state (Brown 1993). Moreover, at the time of her nomination, Clinton was embroiled in the battle over the ban on gays and lesbians in the military, a ban he had made a campaign promise to lift. Unable or unwilling to fulfill this commitment to an important constituency, his credibility with gays and lesbians had faltered badly. By appointing Achtenberg, Clinton could fulfill at least one campaign promise, which was to appoint more gay and lesbian officials to high government posts. Thus, although Achtenberg was clearly an excellent and well-qualified candidate for this position, it also seems likely that Clinton's choice of a lesbian for this position was more than coincidence—that he particularly needed this timely nomination.

By supporting a presidential candidate with time and money, by creating organizations such as the Gay and Lesbian Victory Fund to help elect openly lesbian or gay political candidates, and by employing lobbyists on Capitol Hill to represent their interests, gays and lesbians have worked to attain political power and to establish an influential political identity. In organizing around a shared sexual orientation to support particular political candidates and causes, lesbians and gay men are proclaiming and, indeed, creating identity as an outgrowth of political concerns. This identity, then, cannot be defended as private or irrelevant to politics. Achtenberg's achievement, her ability to stand before the Senate Banking Committee as a candidate for a highly placed political office, came about precisely because of the *political* nature of claiming a gay or lesbian identity. Her opportunity resulted from gays' and lesbians' insistence on being recognized as an influential constituency, from efforts to bring gays and lesbians together as a political force to be reckoned with. From this perspective, the claim that sexual orientation is private and irrelevant is not only unconvincing but in direct contradiction to gay and lesbian political initiatives.

Achtenberg herself opened the Banking Committee hearing by introducing Mary Morgan to the committee as her "beloved partner" in the same way that other nominees introduce their spouses. In doing so, she asserted openly and publicly her love for and commitment to another woman. In an interview with the *San Francisco Examiner* after her confirmation, Helms described Achtenberg's introduction of Morgan as "rubbing her ways into the noses of heterosexuals and other people who don't approve of that lifestyle" (in Satter 1993). Women's strength and assertiveness have long been held in check through the threat of being labeled a "lesbian." Lesbianism has been portrayed as a source of shame and thus expected to be kept hidden. Heterosexuality, in contrast, has been made compulsory by a multitude of interlocking institutions and expectations. In this context, to speak with pride of one's lesbian partner or of oneself as a lesbian is itself an act of rebellion and challenge. Where only silence is acceptable, speaking openly as a lesbian or gay man is automatically interpreted as advocacy or activism, as "flaunting it"; or worse, as imposing or forcing one's sexual orientation on others. Where identity is relegated to the private realm, public acts that lend visibility and voice to lesbians *as* lesbians are inevitably seen as "ramming it down people's throats." Such public actions are viewed by opponents as unacceptable, unnatural, and "out of line." Thus, in this single act of proudly claiming voice and visibility for the relationship between herself and her "beloved partner," Achtenberg took a rhetorical initiative long forbidden to gays and lesbians. In doing so, she illuminated the artifice of a public/private division that is not imposed on other candidates. Despite her supporters' intentions to isolate and insulate her "private" life from public discussion, Achtenberg's introduction rejected such confinement.

Within the framework of a civil rights discourse that relegates identity to the private realm, such public actions are left open for attack, undefended and indefensible. This framework enables the criticism that Achtenberg is "a lesbian activist, not just a lesbian." Perhaps more to the point, as long as supporters fail to challenge the equation of homosexuality with private sexual acts, publicly expressing or affirming homosexuality is akin to being publicly sexual, or at least publicly explicit about sex. Achtenberg's supporters never challenge the equation of lesbian identity with lesbian sex, as though sexual acts between women exhaust the meanings of the word *lesbian*. With this equation intact, public lesbianism (whether marching in a gay and lesbian pride parade, hugging in front of one's son, or introducing one's partner) equals public sex. As in the gay and lesbian pride parade video, this scenario equates the hugging and kissing of committed lesbian partners with illicit sex. This connection is reinforced by the discussion that associates Achtenberg with the gay bathhouses of San Francisco. The bathhouses, and often gay men in general, are linked in the public imagination with promiscuous and dangerous sex; here, lesbians are drawn into the picture as well. With lesbianism undefined and activism, or even visibility, undefended, all that is public is subject to condemnation and censure.

Civil rights arguments leave intact these negative associations and fail to challenge the misleading notion of a single, homogeneous gay and lesbian "lifestyle." They preclude exploration of the wide range of differences between and among gays and lesbians, prohibiting the formulation of broader definitions and better understandings of the gay and lesbian movement. They foreclose any interrogation of heterosexuality, refusing to challenge its compulsory nature or privilege. The framework provided by civil rights lacks the means to examine critically the hierarchical opposition between hetero- and homosexuality. It fails to question the illusory clarity of these categories or to reveal how slippery the distinctions might be.

A civil rights discourse, moreover, forestalls any investigation of how and why a class of persons distinguished by particular sexual practices came to be created. "Since homosexual *practices* are widespread but socially threatening, a special, stigmatized category of *individuals* is created so as to keep the rest of society pure" (Epstein 1987, 16). Rather than revealing the arbitrariness of this system of classification and undermining its apparent stability, a civil rights approach reinforces existing boundaries and categories by solidifying the distinctions and validating the labels the dominant group imposes. In this way, such a strategy may actually enhance the power and status of the dominant group, further entrenching the subordinate status of the oppressed.

But the civil rights argument as it is presented here not only neglects the need for social change; its splitting of identity from action actually condemns or prohibits the very means through which such change can be accomplished. This is where such an approach becomes most limiting, and perhaps even counterproductive, for the cause of gay and lesbian rights. "Homosexuality has been recast as a civil rights issue. But this is accompanied by a new distinction between conduct and orientation, between *being* homosexual and *acting* homosexual" (Fejes and Petrich 1993, 405). As identity is split from action, acceptable or "good" gays and lesbians are differentiated from those whose activities render them disruptive and, consequently, "bad" or unacceptable. Just as "'good' blacks in the 1960s civil rights movement were not supposed to be angry or militant" (Fejes and Petrich 1993, 405), in the civil rights movement of the 1990s, "good" gays and lesbians are not supposed to be angry, militant, or sexual.

It is precisely the public/private distinction, so earnestly set forth by Achtenberg's supporters, that her opponents seize upon in their attacks on her. They attack her for her voice and her visibility as a lesbian, emphasizing public behavior that they judge inappropriate. In this way, opponents turn the identity argument around and use it against Achtenberg. They insist that they do not object to her identity; in doing so, they clear the way to attack her for her actions. They thus displace their disapproval onto her activism, which they recast as "terrorism," "vendetta," or simply "meanness."

It is her activism, finally, that enables an open season to attack Achtenberg. Her opponents use it to justify their critiques of her conflict with the Boy Scouts, her efforts to keep the bathhouses open, her appearance in the gay and lesbian pride parade, her alleged irresponsibility as a mother, and her inadequacy as a woman. It is here that sexuality is smuggled back into the discussion through the accusations of "twistedness" and "perversion." Opponents attack not her lesbianism per se but her activism on behalf of lesbian and gay issues. Activism is thereby equated with perversion in an indirect but reliable way. While sexual perversion is not explicitly mentioned, it always waits just offstage in this debate, and activism becomes its camouflaged code word. Activism is set on the side of perversity, in opposition to the "morally straight" values of the Boy Scouts: "In the twisted value system of Roberta Achtenberg, the Boy Scout tradition is a menace to society that needs to be quashed, and the sex club tradition is one which is beneficial and deserving of our protection and encouragement" (S6215). Activism is aligned with plague, as opposed to health—a particularly potent opposition in the AIDS era. Activism is linked with aggression and meanness, as opposed to passive heterosexual femininity. Finally, *activism* becomes a synonym for *heretical activity*, as opposed to religious belief. Through this series of associations and oppositions, "lesbianism," as it can be tolerated within the framework of civil rights, is limited to its most narrow sense. Its existence is momentarily affirmed, only to subject it to vicious condemnation before returning it decisively to its former status of invisibility and silence.

## CONCLUSION

During the Achtenberg debate, contests over the meanings of "homosexuality" and especially "lesbianism" illustrate vividly how politics and power help create the categories and provide the frameworks within which we define experience and organize knowledge. Such contests serve as startling reminders of the degree to which "our" identities, and the identities of "Others," are constructed by dominant institutions. Interlocking social, political, legal, and historical discourses interact with the accidents of our personal histories to produce in each of us a sense of who we are and how we do or do not "fit" in the larger world.

In the case of Roberta Achtenberg, the significance of this single event lies both in its positioning as a "historic nomination" and in the perception of Achtenberg as representative of gays and lesbians as a group. While on one level the debate can be said to conclude with Achtenberg's confirmation, in fact this debate produces a multiplicity of results. The participants and audience in this debate are American lawmakers and the American body politic, collectively. The debate's consequences therefore are wide-reaching, ranging far beyond this particular historical site or moment. The outcomes of this debate must be judged on more than the single issue of Achtenberg's personal success. Ultimately, the discourse of this historic moment creates at once a broadening and a narrowing of possibilities for a burgeoning lesbian and gay rights movement.

Ironically, Achtenberg's supporters and opponents do not produce respectively these two contrary outcomes. Rather, the discourse of *each* group yields *both* consequences. Both supporters and opponents invoke the metaphor of crossing a line. This creates the boundaries of a group's identity by defining them through difference yet simultaneously invites their participation, if not full inclusion, in sameness. In this framework, crossing the line implies tolerance, perhaps even equality. Where the arguments of the two sides diverge, those who support Achtenberg's nomination "mainstream" her as much as possible, downplaying and depoliticizing her lesbianism. Achtenberg's supporters are caught in a double bind. Their means of creating a liberating discourse, understood here as one that will win confirmation for a publicly identified lesbian, relies on their ability to uphold the category of "homosexuality" while restricting it to its most confining and least threatening definition. Their position calls for a resolute underscoring of sameness and the attendant denial of difference. Achtenberg's opponents take the opposite approach, presenting "lesbianism" as politically radical and extraordinarily subversive.

The Achtenberg debate encompasses a broad array of issues surrounding gay and lesbian rights, offering a sometimes startling insight into the continuing acceptability of homophobic expression in the political realm. Achtenberg is the target of tremendous hostility in these hearings, as gay and lesbian lives are depicted as antithetical to family values and anathema to righteous Americans. Such portrayals cause incalculable harm to the images of gays and lesbians that heterosexuals hold and dispirit the hearts and minds of countless gays and lesbians. They constrict the horizons within which any of us can see gay and lesbian individuals and hear gay and lesbian voices. In doing so, these representations effect a narrowing, rather than a broadening, of human potential and self-understanding.

Although this debate ostensibly addresses one candidate's qualifications, it ultimately raises questions about the interwovenness of gender roles, sexual identity, and political subjectivity. On the positive side, the nomination forced a staid Senate to confront the complex relationship between minority identity and political commitments. By confirming Achtenberg, the senators stopped short of demanding the absolute suppression of activism for unpopular causes among would-be political candidates. On the negative side, however, the senators' efforts at grappling with these issues maintained Achtenberg, and gays and lesbians as a group, as "Others." Throughout the debate, sexual orientation is a characteristic associated only with gays and lesbians. At no point in the discussion does anyone acknowledge that *everyone* present, not only Achtenberg, has a sexual orientation. Nor do the senators recognize how their own arguments and opinions are influenced by their own sexual orientation. Finally, none of the senators demonstrate any awareness of the ways in which other privileged elements of their identities might directly or indirectly influence their political views and decisions.

Inevitably, the social changes that can be identified with "lesbian and gay liberation" will be as contradictory as the phrase itself. Every effort to be free of the confines of categorization only creates a new set of "regulatory imperatives." The invocation of identity in an effort to free oneself of its limitations is an act with both the clear promise of success and the inevitability of failure. To free oneself is always to subject oneself again, though to a more acceptable or desirable level of subjection—a repositioning rather than a release. Like the closet metaphor, "liberation" is always elusive; locking oneself in begins to look more and more like being locked out.

For Roberta Achtenberg, and for those who aspire to her honesty and achievement, it is crucial to remain constantly watchful of the forces that construct our meanings. These meanings provide the range of possibility for defining who we are and who we can become.

## ⟆ 3 ⟅

# AND THE BAN PLAYED ON
## Politics and Prejudice in the Cammermeyer Case

Military Justice is to Justice, what Military Music is to Music.
—Georges Clemenceau (in Lehring 1996, 269)

## PROLOGUE

On July 14, 1991, exactly thirty years to the day after her initiation into the United States military, Colonel Margarethe (Grethe) Cammermeyer went before a military board on charges of being a homosexual.[1] In the hearing that followed, Cammermeyer's military and civilian counsel presented a case that highlighted her great value to the military. They cited her nearly twenty-seven years of service,[2] her tour of duty in Vietnam, and her numerous honors and awards. These included the Bronze Star for service in Vietnam, recognition as an outstanding Vietnam veteran, and the Veterans Administration (VA) Nurse of the Year Award. They also included membership in a national nursing honor society, Who's Who of American Women, Who's Who in the West, and Who's Who in Science and Engineering. Cammermeyer's attorneys praised her thirty-three published articles and book chapters, her completion of a doctorate, and her subsequent faculty appointments at the University of California–San Francisco and the University of Washington. They spoke of her current position as chief nurse of the Washington State National Guard and her candidacy for chief nurse of the entire National Guard.

Cammermeyer's legal counsel presented testimony from her supervisor, who requested a special exception to policy so that Cammermeyer might

83

be retained by the military for her superior service despite the charges brought against her. They provided evidence from two psychological experts, who testified that homosexuality does not interfere with mental health, hinder the performance of military duties, or increase the likelihood that a soldier will engage in prohibited sexual behavior. They put on the stand Cammermeyer's superiors, subordinates, and peers, who praised her nursing skills and leadership abilities and asserted unanimously that her presence had never disrupted the cohesion of her military unit, either before or after she disclosed her sexual orientation.[3]

The lawyers even put on the stand Cammermeyer's oldest son, Matthew Hawken, and his wife, Lynette, both devout Mormons. Matthew and Lynette assured the board that every member of Cammermeyer's family, including her aging father, knew of her sexual orientation. They explained that not only did her entire family support her but her three unmarried sons, as well as her father, had all chosen to live with her *after* her disclosure. Because her sexual orientation was already known to her entire family, Cammermeyer's lawyers argued that she could never be subject to blackmail based on the threat of disclosure of her sexual orientation (a common argument supporting the military policy). Matthew and Lynette, along with the other witnesses called in the case, spoke of their pride in Cammermeyer and their belief that she should retain her position in military service.

During Cammermeyer's military board hearing, the government offered only a single piece of evidence, calling to the stand no witnesses. In lieu of testimony or argument, it presented a statement made and signed by Colonel Cammermeyer. The statement was made to an officer of the Defense Investigative Service (DIS) in the course of a security clearance interview, set up at Cammermeyer's request, for the purpose of upgrading her clearance to "top secret." This status was a prerequisite to enrollment in the War College, and such enrollment was necessary to qualify Cammermeyer for her next career goal: the position of chief nurse of the National Guard. The DIS officer who conducted the interview, Agent Brent Troutman, had forwarded Cammermeyer's answer to one of his routine questions to the Defense Department, which subsequently initiated military discharge or "separation" proceedings against her. As Cammermeyer later confessed, despite her many years of military service, at the time of her meeting with Agent Troutman she was woefully naive about the military's policy on gays and lesbians. She was therefore unaware of the consequences of answering truthfully what she later referred to as "the question [that] would change my life" (1994, 3).

In the decision of the military board hearing of Colonel Margarethe Cammermeyer, rendered July 15, 1991, Colonel Patsy Thompson, who headed the hearing, addressed Cammermeyer with this pronouncement: "I truly believe that you are one of the great Americans" (Department of the Army 1991, 131). Nevertheless, she read the following decision of the board:

> Col. Cammermeyer has proven to be a great asset to both the active and re-serve component, the medical profession as a whole. She has consistently pro-vided superb leadership and has many outstanding accomplishments to her credit, both military and civilian. Notwithstanding, the board finds that Col. Cammermeyer is a homosexual as defined in AR 135-175 and as evidenced by her statement to DIS Agent Brent B. Troutman on 28 April '89, her ad-mission under oath to this board that she is a lesbian, and statements made under oath to this board by five character witnesses. We recommend that Col. Cammermeyer's federal recognition be withdrawn. (Department of the Army 1991, 132–33)

In the absence of other evidence, witnesses, or testimony, the board's de-cision rested on a single piece of evidence: a four-word statement affirmed by Cammermeyer to be her words and to be true. After nearly twenty-seven years of unblemished service to the United States military, the highly dec-orated Colonel Cammermeyer was summarily dismissed, with an honorable discharge, from her military office and from further military service. She was consequently denied her rank and a portion of her retirement benefits. At the same time, she lost the opportunity to become chief nurse of the Na-tional Guard, to achieve her goal of attaining the rank of general, and to re-tire with full military honors. These ambitions were thwarted as a result of her own brief statement—a statement she steadfastly refused to retract, de-spite a number of opportunities to do so. She refused to deny her statement, although to have done so would likely have allowed her to remain on the path to fulfilling her lifelong dream.

Grethe Cammermeyer's four-word statement read: "I am a lesbian."[4]

## INTRODUCTION

The events that led to Grethe Cammermeyer's honorable discharge, like the events that led to Roberta Achtenberg's political appointment, were part of a larger political context that marked a shift in status for gays and lesbians. That the Senate hearings on lesbians and gays in the military and the Sen-ate debate over Achtenberg's confirmation took place almost simultaneously is neither coincidental nor insignificant. The events of 1993 followed on the heels of a year that was characterized by a "dramatic shift in visibility and credibility" of the gay and lesbian movement (Vaid 1995, 151). The events surrounding both Cammermeyer and Achtenberg were precipitated, although in different ways and with differing results, by the nomination and election of the first Democratic president who made lesbian and gay rights a plank in his official campaign platform. Bill Clinton's presidency, with its promise of broader opportunities and acceptance for gays and lesbians, both reflected and reinforced the heightened visibility and newly amplified political voice belonging to gays and lesbians.

Candidate Clinton drew strong support from gay and lesbian communities, both in the form of political endorsements—Achtenberg, for example, was the first elected official in California to endorse him—and through generous campaign contributions from lesbians and gay men. In return, Clinton vowed not to forget his gay and lesbian constituents if he won the election. More specifically, Clinton promised gays and lesbians greater recognition and increased political access. He pledged to appoint gays and lesbians to important posts in his administration, and he promised, in what seemed no uncertain terms, to lift the ban on gays and lesbians in the military. When Clinton was elected and announced his intention to fulfill these commitments, in particular the lifting of the ban, the intense debate that ensued with Congress gave rise to equally intensive media coverage, sparking the interest of national constituencies on both sides of the military issue. It was in this context that both Achtenberg and Cammermeyer rose to the status of national figures, as the attainment of their personal goals became linked to the raging national debate over lesbian and gay rights, whose flames were fed by Clinton's bold promise.

Whereas Achtenberg was an active player in the political game and a longtime lesbian activist who chose to stake her fortunes on Bill Clinton's political acumen, Cammermeyer's role was much less deliberate. She was pulled almost unknowingly, at least initially, into the political fray. A nurse by training and profession, a soldier by lifelong commitment, Cammermeyer had dedicated much of her life to serving her country and caring for its ailing soldiers, both on the battlefield and in the VA hospitals where she later worked. Like many other gay and lesbian service personnel, Cammermeyer had no intention of committing a rebellious act or of taking a political stand when she stated that she was a lesbian. She simply responded with the honesty she believed the situation, and the army, demanded. Her case illustrates former *New Republic* editor Andrew Sullivan's claim that the military debate "took place not because radicals besieged the Pentagon, but because of the ordinary and once-anonymous Americans within the military who simply refused to acquiesce in their own humiliation any longer. Their courage was illustrated not in taking to the streets in rage but in facing their families and colleagues with integrity" (1993, 33). It was precisely this integrity that would implicate Cammermeyer, almost by chance, as a central figure in a complex debate. Before it was over, this debate would encompass the nature of military service, heterosexual masculinity, and sexual expression and identity. It would examine the nature of language itself and the links between self-expression, personal conduct, and human freedom.

Despite the clear differences between the Achtenberg and Cammermeyer cases, the similarities between the rhetorical strategies they employ are striking. In both debates, supporters focus attention on the qualities of the individual, downplaying each woman's connection with a larger constituency and attempting to isolate her from membership in the group "lesbians" or "homosexuals." Opponents in both cases take the opposite approach, strengthening the identification between each woman and the larger group by emphasizing her representative status. No one in either case is willing to defend gays and lesbians as a group or to challenge negative stereotypes of them. Thus the defense of both women rests in their *differences* from the despised group, especially in their ability to prevent the stigmatized quality of homosexuality from interfering with their work.

In both cases, this argument is made through the legal concept of the "right to privacy," through which each woman's identity or "status" as a lesbian is distinguished from the presumed behavioral manifestations of that status. Through the careful separation of public behavior from private identity, the women are defended on the basis of their ability to be "mainstream." In other words, there is no protection here for difference unless it can be successfully recuperated as sameness: a difference that makes no difference. What is never questioned in either of these discussions is the presumption that homosexual *conduct*, the military's equivalent of the popular but ambiguous term *lifestyle*, is abnormal, undesirable, and immoral.

Whereas Achtenberg's opponents denied that sexual orientation was at issue, ostensibly objecting not to her lesbianism but to her activism, Cammermeyer's opponents emphatically argue that sexual orientation is the *only* issue. This distinction parallels the difference between the "new" and "old" military policies. It reflects the changes in acceptable government anti-gay arguments between 1991, when Cammermeyer's hearing was convened, and 1993, when Achtenberg was confirmed. Under the guidelines of the new policy, status and conduct are considered at least conceptually distinct, while under the old policy challenged by Cammermeyer, they were indistinguishable. In 1991, simply being a lesbian or gay man in the military, even without engaging in speech or conduct that communicated that status to others, provided necessary and sufficient grounds for discharge.

In Cammermeyer's military board hearing, the debate officially pitted the government's stated regulation against an individual's petition for an exception to that policy. In seeking an exception, Cammermeyer's lawyers presented extensive evidence of her individual contributions and consequent value to the military, keeping the focus on Cammermeyer herself. Yet the government's disinterest in refuting or even questioning such evidence reveals that this case was not about a person but a policy. As a result, Cammermeyer's subsequent civil court suit against the military was designed not only to enable her to continue her own military career but to challenge the rationale under which she and others were excluded from service.

From most vantage points, it appears that the military had everything to lose and nothing to gain by discharging one of its most qualified nurses and a highly decorated colonel in whom it had invested countless hours and innumerable dollars for education and training. In all ways but one, her discharge marked a severe loss for the military: a loss of irreplaceable talent and skill, given the professional standing she had attained. Yet the military board, with stated regret but without hesitation, took the action that would uphold policy even in the face of such loss. It discharged Colonel Cammermeyer with the same surety of purpose it would have shown in dismissing an unsuitable new recruit. Despite the loss represented by Cammermeyer's separation, the military emerged from this battle "victorious" because it reaffirmed that, even at the highest levels, it could and would apply its ban absolutely.[5]

Because of the priority of the policy over the individual in legal challenges to the military, making sense of the Cammermeyer case requires examining the broad context of the military debate. Cammermeyer's story is but one piece of a much larger puzzle of interlocking legal, moral, and cultural concerns. What makes her case especially noteworthy is that she was the highest ranking officer ever to be discharged because of homosexual status (*Cammermeyer v. Aspin* 1994, 7n. 6). In addition, hers is one of the few dismissals, especially of lesbians, that attracted national attention. Her case generated widespread media coverage and her autobiography, *Serving in Silence*, became a network television movie produced by Barbra Streisand and starring Glenn Close.

Cammermeyer's case is also of particular interest because her discharge preceded the adoption of the "Don't Ask, Don't Tell" policy. The revelation of her sexual orientation occurred because she was asked a direct question, a question she refused to answer dishonestly. Under the new policy, Cammermeyer would presumably not have been asked such a question and so would not have been classified as a homosexual by the military. Consequently, her military career would never have been placed in jeopardy. This shift in military policy illustrates that homosexuality, and the definition of who is homosexual, is not an unchanging universal but instead a social construction, in this case a creation of the military. Through the Cammermeyer case and the larger debate over gays and lesbians in the military, the social construction of homosexuality is carried out at a level of visibility rarely available, affording an unusual glimpse of this work in process.

More specifically, Cammermeyer would not be *identified* as a lesbian under the new policy, presuming that she continued to act as she always had, keeping her sexual orientation a secret. Therefore she would, for all practical purposes, not *be* a lesbian under military policy. Thus she could have remained in the service and likely received the security clearance and the promotion she sought. Perhaps equally revealing is the fact that if Cammermeyer had been willing to retract her statement, as she was requested to do several times during the course of the proceedings against her, she would probably have been allowed to remain in the military until her retirement, despite the "knowledge" the military had already obtained about her sexuality.

Technically, the civil case Cammermeyer brought against the Department of Defense challenged only the old policy under which she was separated from military service. However, by the time Cammermeyer's case reached the Ninth Circuit Court, where it was to be heard, this policy was no longer in effect. "Don't Ask, Don't Tell" was announced by Clinton in July 1993 and went into effect on February 28, 1994. The ruling on Cammermeyer's case was issued on June 1, 1994. Yet, as her case and the broader debate about gays and lesbians in the military reveal, the differences between the old and new policies are negligible, and the two policies ultimately stand or fall as one (Bull 1994).

In the first section of this chapter, I examine the background and significance of the military's policies on homosexuality, exploring the nature of the ban itself. By investigating the relationship between homophobia, racism, and sexism in military ideology, I show how the exclusion of gays and lesbians from the military arises from the gendered nature of the organization and its preoccupation with upholding an image of heterosexual masculinity. Through a reading of Defense Department arguments presented at the 1993 hearings on the Policy Concerning Homosexuality in the Armed Forces (hereafter referred to in references as *Policy Hearings*), as well as the Defense Department's arguments in the Cammermeyer case, I analyze the controversial way in which the new military policy equates speech with sex through the linking term of *conduct*.

In the second part of the chapter, I turn to the legal arguments that support both sides of the debate. As in the case of Achtenberg, I examine how the discourse of supporters as well as opponents broadens *and* narrows gay and lesbian freedoms, expanding and constraining the range of possibilities for envisioning gay and lesbian lives. I focus in particular on arguments about the immutability of sexual orientation, the right-to-privacy principle, and the distinction between status and conduct. I highlight the ways in which arguments for lifting the ban may inadvertently undermine broader goals of gay and lesbian self-determination and liberation. In this way, advances in one area of rights may exact a significant cost in other areas from individual gay and lesbian service members, as well as civilians. I also explore how the discourse of the military debate, like the discourse of other lesbian and gay rights initiatives, consistently misinterprets the meaning of sodomy statutes through its insistent but illegitimate equation of sodomy with homosexuality. Finally, I examine the impossibility of complying with the "Don't Tell" directive, given the connotations of secrecy in American culture.

I conclude this chapter with an assessment of the role that heterosexual prejudice has played and continues to play in the formulation and maintenance of military policy on lesbians and gays. Such prejudice is an unconstitutional basis for exclusion, as the judge's finding in Cammermeyer's civil court case affirms. For this reason, elucidating the role of such prejudice and redirecting attention from the "gay problem" to the "homophobia problem" in the military and elsewhere offer a promising direction for future gay and lesbian rights initiatives.

## A BATTLE OF NECESSITY

The military is a somewhat surprising and unlikely site to become a focus of lesbian and gay rights efforts, and it was not an issue many activists would have chosen. For those with liberationist politics, arguing for the right to participate openly in what is often perceived as the most fundamentally repressive institution of our time is hardly an inspiring prospect (Robb 1993; Smith 1993). Some writers express misgivings about allocating movement resources toward this goal, cautioning that this effort, "while solving one egregious case of heterosexist oppression . . . may very well contribute to the reinforcement of a wider regime of repression against gay and nongay people around the world" (Adam 1994, 116). The concerns of many lesbian and gay rights activists run more to such causes as environmentalism or the peace movement, which are largely at odds with the activities of the U.S. military.[6] "For most gay people, the military ban was not the issue of choice. . . . But it was the issue of opportunity. For as far as gays have come, they cannot yet determine the order of their own social agenda" (Kopkind 1993, 9). Not yet in a position to choose their battles, movement leaders knew that when the discussion of gay and lesbian rights came to national attention by way of the military debate, their strong presence and vocal participation were essential.[7]

The military battle is a symbolic as well as a practical issue, and its consequences are ultimately much more far-reaching than gaining the right to serve one's country.[8] As the largest employer in the nation and one of the most influential institutions in the socialization of young adults, the military's acceptance or exclusion of a group becomes a prototype for a group's status in civilian life. "Participation in the military stakes claim to political and civil equality generally" (Rolison and Nakayama 1994, 128–29). Consequently, "if lesbians and gay men are judged unfit to serve their country, their second-class status is reemphasized. If, on the other hand, they are deemed acceptable, the rationale for stigmatizing them is greatly weakened" (Cruikshank 1994, 11). The ban creates a climate of hostility that has psychological as well as material consequences for the quality of life of millions of gay men and lesbians, both in and out of the armed forces:

> The military's policies have had a sinister effect on the entire nation: Such policies make it known to everyone serving in the military that lesbians and gay men are dangerous to the well-being of other Americans; that they are undeserving of even the most basic civil rights. Such policies also create an ambiance in which discrimination, harassment, and even violence against lesbians and gays is tolerated and to some degree encouraged. (Shilts 1993, 4)

In the past, the military at times has led the way for social change. The integration of African Americans into the armed forces preceded their widespread integration into society, and evidence that integration was successful in the military set a precedent that encouraged integration in other institutions. Equality in the military thus supports and promotes broader equality, whereas military discrimination legitimizes widespread prejudice. In this way, while military policy may have no *direct* influence on the practices of civilian life, as an institution that commands great national respect, along with a substantial share of national resources, the policies the military adopts have effects that circulate far beyond the uniformed rank and file. This influence becomes even more pronounced at a historical moment in which the military debate is receiving such rapt attention from all forms of national media. To understand the nature of the messages the military conveys to the larger community, we must look more closely at the content of the military ban, its theoretical grounding, and its practical consequences.

## MILITARY POLICY AND THE INCOMPATIBILITY OF HOMOSEXUALS

The ban on gays in the military has not always existed, nor has such a ban been universal among nations past or present (Korb 1994). Classical scholars are fond of pointing out that, historically, same-sex eroticism has a "long and hallowed relationship to democracy and military valor" (Boswell 1993, 15). In ancient Rome, for example, the love of warriors for one another was considered advantageous in building an effective fighting force, and erotic bonds between soldiers were regarded as increasing both morale and military readiness (Boswell 1993; D. Cohen 1993). More recently, although the exclusion of gays and lesbians from military service began during World War II, it was also during this war that thousands of gay men and lesbians served their country and created an active gay and lesbian subculture within military life (Bérubé 1990).

The military ban was implemented in the 1940s "on the advice of military psychiatrists" and was based on the belief, widely held by the psychiatric establishment at the time, that homosexuality was a mental illness and therefore incompatible with military service (Scott and Stanley 1994, xi). The American Psychiatric Association removed homosexuality from its list of mental disorders in the 1974 edition of the *Diagnostic and Statistical Manual of Mental Disorders (DSM)*, but the ban on military service continued. On January 16, 1981, just five days before his administration was due to leave office, President Jimmy Carter issued a revised and more restrictive version of the policy. The most cited paragraph of this policy, called the "Directive on Enlisted Administrative Separations," announced the military's infamous view that "homosexuality is incompatible with military service." The statement continues:

> The presence in the military environment of persons who engage in homosexual conduct or who, by their statements, demonstrate a propensity to en-

gage in homosexual conduct, seriously impairs the accomplishment of the military mission. The presence of such members adversely affects the ability of the Military Services to maintain discipline, good order, and morale; to foster mutual trust and confidence among servicemembers; to ensure the integrity of the system of rank and command; to facilitate assignment and worldwide deployment of servicemembers who frequently must live and work under close conditions affording minimal privacy; to recruit and retain members of the Military Services; to maintain the public acceptability of military service; and to prevent breaches of security. (in Burrelli 1994, 19)

It was this version of the ban, now referred to as the "blanket ban" or simply the "old" policy, that remained in effect until its suspension pending the Senate Armed Services Committee's hearings during the summer of 1993.

The old policy's assertion that "homosexuality is incompatible with military service" exploited concerns about national security to justify the military's use of any and all means to prevent gays and lesbians from enlisting and to discharge them from military service if they were discovered to be already in uniform. New enlistees were routinely asked Question 27 on the standard military processing forms: "Are you a homosexual or a bisexual?" While this inquiry was designed to screen out homosexuals initially, thus obviating the need for military concern over gays and lesbians in its ranks, the approach failed for several reasons. Some individuals familiar with the policy may simply have lied when responding to the question. But more often, young people enlisting in the military, many only eighteen or nineteen years old and away from home for the first time, might never before have considered the question and might not yet have come out even to themselves. Alternatively, some young men and women who felt unsure or unhappy about being gay or lesbian might have hoped that responding in the negative would make that answer true.

The most infamous rationale supporting the old policy was that because homosexuality was often kept a secret, gays and lesbians were particularly vulnerable to blackmail and thus were poor security risks. The fact that "there is not one documented case of a homosexual person disclosing national secrets based on blackmail about their homosexuality" (Department of the Army 1991, 62) did not deter those who supported the ban; nor did the reasonable argument that if homosexuality were not banned in the first place, there would be less need for secrecy and less of a basis for blackmail. Another expressed rationale for both the old and new policies was a belief that the presence of lesbians or gay men disrupts unit cohesiveness, an element essential to military readiness and effectiveness. This reasoning suggests that homosexuals would make heterosexual service members uncomfortable in the already intimate confines of bunks and showers, because heterosexuals would not want to be looked at by or share sleeping quarters with individuals presumed to be physically attracted to them, and who would presumably be unable to control the sexual desires and impulses generated by this attraction.[9] Military commanders also expressed concern about fraternization among gay or lesbian service members, that is, the possibility of two members of the same unit, or a commander and a subordinate, becoming involved in a sexual relationship.

What is notable about these justifications is that they are all problems that can be and have been caused by heterosexuals, and each potentially troublesome behavior is already addressed and proscribed by the military's governing code of laws, called the Uniform Code of Military Justice (UCMJ). There is nothing specific to gays or lesbians that suggests they are any more likely to commit these crimes than are heterosexuals. No evidence indicates that identifying oneself as gay or lesbian is inherently incompatible with honorably serving in the military. In other words, while these concerns have been used to justify the necessity of excluding gays and lesbians solely on the basis of sexual orientation, there is a difficulty in constructing the necessary links that would prove these criteria sufficient for the blanket exclusion of gays and lesbians.

This difficulty provides the basis for numerous challenges to military policy that have made their way through the U.S. court system. Under the guidelines of the Constitution, and based on the precedents established by legal challenges to exclusionary policies in civilian life, an institution that excludes a particular group or "class" of people must provide a reasonable basis for doing so. That reasonable basis must be related to the accomplishment of the institution's mission and must not be based on prejudice. The legal procedure for judging exclusionary processes is as follows: "Initially, the court must determine whether the challenged classification serves a legitimate governmental purpose. If the court answers this question in the affirmative, the court must then determine whether the discriminatory classification is rationally related to the achievement of that legitimate purpose" (*Cammermeyer v. Aspin* 1994, 12). This is known as the "rational basis review" requirement, and it calls for a lesser degree of scrutiny than is demanded by the criterion of suspect class status (Halley 1993).

It is in response to this rational basis requirement that the issue of unit cohesion has become so prominent in anti-gay military discourse. The military defines unit cohesion as "the bonds of trust among individual service members that make the combat effectiveness of a military unit greater than the sum of the combat effectiveness of the individual unit members" (*Cammermeyer v. Aspin* 1994, 36n. 19). Military leaders claim that the presence of gays and lesbians decreases effectiveness by disrupting these bonds. However, this claim is difficult to substantiate. Because the military has been loath to admit the presence of gays and lesbians in the armed forces, it has conducted no studies and compiled no statistical evidence on whether their presence detracts from military effectiveness (Department of the Army 1991; *Policy Hearings* 1993). At the same time, the recent disclosures of many gay and lesbian service members who have served, and served with distinction, before and after making their sexual orientation known to others provides abundant anecdotal evidence to the contrary.

One of the most dramatic contradictions in the claim that gays and lesbians impair the military mission is the military's policy of "stop-loss," which was put into force most recently during the Persian Gulf War (Department of the Army 1991, 89). The stop-loss policy prevents any individual from leaving military service in the event of an emergency that requires military mobilization. Under this policy, during the Gulf War and other national crises, military personnel who had been identified as gay or lesbian but had not yet been discharged were retained in military service and sent to the Persian Gulf, even if they were expected to be discharged when they returned home. Nor did such service exempt them from discharge upon their return. What is most telling about this policy is that despite the claim that gay and lesbian soldiers are disruptive and unfit for military service, the military will send these soldiers into a situation where military cohesion and readiness are of the utmost importance. The circumstances of war provide precisely the conditions that are called on to justify the ban: facilities are at their least private and living quarters at their most crowded, unit cohesion is a matter of life and death, and the effectiveness of the military is put to the ultimate test. Yet this is also the situation in which military leaders choose to suspend their exclusion of gays and lesbians from the armed forces.

When newly elected President Clinton announced his intention to lift the ban, those who opposed this move were urgently pressed to offer a rationale for excluding homosexuals that was strong enough to justify the ban's continuation. By this time, as even Secretary of Defense Dick Cheney had conceded, the argument that gays and lesbians posed a security risk was "a bit of an old chestnut" (Lehring 1996, 273), and this theme was quietly dropped.[10] Moreover, as many who supported lifting the ban argued, existing UCMJ laws could be enforced to prevent or punish inappropriate sexual conduct among gay and lesbian service members. The codes regulating sexual impropriety could and should be applied to everyone equally, supporters asserted, to address and assuage the fears of heterosexual service members.

During the summer of 1993, after Clinton's announcement, the Senate Armed Services Committee, chaired by Senator Sam Nunn, held hearings to determine what, if any, changes should be made to the military ban. Despite Clinton's commitment to lift the ban, Congress promised to overrule the president if he issued an executive order to do so and threatened to pass into law an even harsher discriminatory policy (Cammermeyer 1994, 297). As Lawrence Korb, former assistant secretary of defense under Ronald Reagan and current supporter of lifting the ban, asserted, "In many ways, Clinton was the worst person to try to end the ban," because of his lack of military experience and the controversy over his evasion of the Vietnam draft (1994, 227). Faced with the possibility of a standoff with Congress, Clinton agreed instead to a six-month moratorium on discharges while the Armed Services Committee held hearings on the policy and the military established a working group to study the issue.

For nine days during the spring and summer of 1993, Nunn's committee heard testimony from military experts, legal counsel, a number of heterosexual service members, and a significantly smaller number of lesbian and gay current and former service members. Although there was some pretense of providing a balanced representation of views, the presentation of witnesses and testimony was noticeably skewed. Cammermeyer relates the tone and substance of the hearings:

> They were designed only to justify the military's policy of discrimination. I watched in amazement the testimony of so-called experts who had no personal experience regarding gay people in the military. I listened to the top brass repeat fears and biases without being challenged. Prejudice was justified on the basis of "that's how we've always done it." . . . A parade of witnesses went before the committee, handpicked to support the existing ban and justify the prejudice. (Cammermeyer 1994, 298–99)

Later she recalls, "I wasn't surprised to hear that some of the soldiers who had been interviewed by the committee revealed that though they wanted the ban overturned, their superiors had told them not to disagree with the existing policy."

The testimony of other military personnel supports this claim. In a deposition submitted on Cammermeyer's behalf, General Vance Coleman asserts that anti-gay sentiments constitute what he refers to as the military "company line," which "discourages any vocal disagreement with current policy." He charges that "the leadership of the military is responsible for the vocal opposition to lifting the ban," and that the military personnel who are chosen to state their views are "hand-picked by leadership to voice their [negative] opinions" (Plaintiff's Reply Memo 1994, 27–28). Similarly, during the Senate hearings, Sergeant Justin Elzie, a gay marine, explains:

> If you stick a microphone or a camera in a Marine or young sailor's face and ask them, how do you feel about this subject, chances are that no matter what their personal beliefs they will stick to the party line and support the ban. That is what the chain of command promotes, and they are afraid of being labeled as gay themselves. (*Policy Hearings* 1993, 667; see also 880–81)

Unsurprisingly, then, the heterosexual military personnel who spoke at the hearings unanimously agreed that they would be uncomfortable serving with gays and lesbians, that the presence of open gays and lesbians would undermine unit cohesion, and that having to serve with openly gay or lesbian service members would cause them to rethink a decision to reenlist. On the other side of the issue, Cammermeyer was the only lesbian to testify at the hearings. When two gay ex-service members were brought in, their testimony was sandwiched between that of two larger panels of heterosexual service personnel who opposed lifting the ban. Tellingly, the Senate heard no testimony from heterosexual service members who advocated lifting the ban (*Policy Hearings* 1993, 572). General John Otjen, a member of the Military Working Group who supplied the Senate with military representatives, acknowledged that no effort was made to solicit the participation of heterosexual service members who supported lifting the ban (Otjen 1994, 257–60).

When the hearings concluded, President Clinton and the Senate Armed Services Committee announced that they had reached a "compromise" between ban supporters and opponents. Dubbed "Don't Ask, Don't Tell, Don't Pursue" by Secretary of Defense Les Aspin (*Policy Hearings* 1993, 727), the compromise replaced the former blanket ban on gays and lesbians with a policy that was grounded in the separation of homosexual "status" from homosexual "conduct." In drawing this distinction, the new policy ostensibly accommodated Clinton's view, shared by a number of senators on the committee, that "the issue ought to be conduct" (in Miller 1994, 88). The policy claimed to limit "the issue" to conduct by allowing gays and lesbians to serve as long as their homosexual status was not manifested by homosexual behavior, which remained "conduct unbecoming."

A key problem with this ostensible compromise lay in the ambiguity of the terms *status* and *conduct* and the fluidity of the boundaries between them. Even as this distinction was drawn, it was undermined by the wide expanse of territory covered by the category "conduct" and the extreme narrowing of the meaning of "status." The new policy retains the grounds for discharge outlined under the old policy: the commission of homosexual "acts, statements, or marriages" (*Policy Hearings* 1993, 770). More specifically, under the new policy as under the old, an officer will be separated from military service under any of the following conditions, barring subsequent findings to the contrary:

1. The officer has engaged in, has attempted to engage in, or has solicited another to engage in a homosexual act or acts
2. The officer has stated that he or she is a homosexual or bisexual
3. The officer has married or attempted to marry a person known to be of the same sex

Most notable and contested in this definition is the interpretation of condition (2), the prohibition on speech. The manipulation of speech in the changeover from old to new military policy is revealing. In the old policy, the statement "I am a homosexual" or variants thereof would be cause for separation from the military because of their reference to status. In *Pruitt v. Cheney*, Dusty Pruitt, an officer in the U.S. Army Reserve, was discharged from the army after stating in an interview with the *Los Angeles Times* that she was a lesbian. While Pruitt's lawyers argued that her statement comprised protected speech under the First Amendment, the army won its case by arguing that the First Amendment was not at issue (*Policy Hearings* 1993, 83). The army claimed that her speech itself was not the reason for her discharge. Instead, it was the status to which the statement referred that justified her dismissal, for this status was not protected. The army further contended that its knowledge of her status, however obtained, necessitated her separation.

Under the new policy, in which only conduct provides grounds for dismissal, speech itself is reclassified. No longer associated with status, statements such as "I am a homosexual" now constitute prohibited conduct. Under the old policy, "the admission of being a homosexual is not treated, ipso facto, as a propensity to engage in homosexual behavior. Rather it is considered a reasonable cause for conducting an investigation" that could then lead to a discharge (Burrelli 1994, 19). In contrast, the new policy considers the admission itself to be conduct punishable by dismissal. It declares that "a person's sexual orientation is considered a personal and private matter and is not a bar to service unless manifested by homosexual conduct." However, the category of conduct encompasses all acts of self-identification as a homosexual; it therefore includes "acts" that are simply speech. "Current regulations are based on conduct, including statements" (Burrelli 1994, 28).

In the new policy, then, speech and conduct are indistinguishable. The statement that one is a homosexual is taken not only as an indicator of status but also, and more important, as an instance of conduct. Nunn explains the chain of associations that equate self-identification with conduct: "When someone stands up and announces they are gay or lesbian, does that not indicate something about their sexual conduct? . . . Is that not also stating that there is a basic tendency, at least, for the sodomy statute to be breached? . . . How do you then distinguish that from conduct?" (Policy Hearings 1993, 482). The effect of this line of reasoning is to sabotage the very division the new policy is intended to uphold: the possibility that "you can have the orientation without the propensity," that is, the status without the conduct (Policy Hearings 1993, 800). The new regulation extends "the domain of 'homosexual conduct' to circumscribe even further the public construction of a homosexual identity. The identity/conduct distinction that advocates for gay, lesbian and bisexual rights have been so eager to assert is collapsed, in this instance through the mediating category of speech." As a result, "speech, conduct and identity remain inextricably bound up together" (Currah 1995, 66).

Whereas voice is generally associated with the mind and the body linked to behavior, then, these connections are ruptured within the framework of a policy that equates speech with conduct. Voice and body are equated through the characterization of verbal statements as certain, even infallible predictors of the body's sexual behaviors.[11] "Conduct unbecoming" includes all manner of "statements unbecoming," so that any behavior or statement that is interpreted as expressing a same-sex orientation is equally prohibited and actionable. Both acts and statements are read as improper, public sexual acts. Jamie Gorelick, general counsel for the Defense Department, clarifies the policy change: "We used to say, in the old policy, 'If you say you are a homosexual, we will presumptively conclude that you are.' . . . We say now, 'If you say you are a homosexual, we presumptively conclude that you engage in acts or have a propensity or intent to do so" (Policy Hearings 1993, 805). Navy lieutenant Tracy Thorne, who was discharged after announcing on ABC's *Nightline* that he is gay, notes wryly the practical consequence of this policy "change": "The policy used to be that if the military found out that you were gay, they would kick you out. And now, if they find out that you're gay, they're going to kick you out" (Koppel 1994).

Ultimately, "the Clinton administration's 'Don't Ask, Don't Tell' policy worsened the status-conduct distinction by treating speech itself as conduct" (Vaid 1995, 135).[12] One danger of treating speech as conduct is that this equation provides a strategic opening for those hostile to gays and lesbians. Opponents connect the regulation of speech—a questionable proposition at best, given the broad protections of the First Amendment—with the regulation of a prohibited form of conduct: the act of sodomy. Sodomy has a long history of censorship and its condemnation has much broader appeal in the popular mind than does speech. By subtly yet strategically linking speech with sodomy, the "new" policy decisively reasserts its condemnation of gays and lesbians, renewing its insistence on their silence and invisibility.

The issue of sodomy provides a stronghold for opponents of lifting the ban. In the wake of *Bowers v. Hardwick*, an already widespread association of homosexuality with the sexual practice of sodomy was solidified in the minds of American lawmakers and the public. The military's UCMJ contains a law specifically prohibiting sodomy. Article 125, section a, of the UCMJ reads: "Any person subject to this chapter who engages in unnatural carnal copulation with another person of the same or opposite sex or with an animal is guilty of sodomy. Penetration, however slight, is sufficient to complete the offense." Because the UCMJ functions as a legal code for the military, sodomy is not only prohibited but illegal behavior for military personnel; that is, it constitutes a criminal act that is punishable by court-martial and jail time, and it may result in a general or a dishonorable discharge. In contrast, homosexual status without evidence of conduct is against military policy but not against the law, resulting most often in an honorable discharge and no criminal charges.[13]

The regulation itself, like the majority of state sodomy laws, does not single out homosexuals.[14] Its language prohibits "unnatural carnal copulation"—a highly ambiguous reference that has been interpreted to mean anal or oral sex—without regard to the gender or sexual orientation of the participants.[15] Nevertheless, in *Padula v. Webster*, an influential court decision that followed in the wake of *Hardwick*, the court deliberately ignored the gender-neutral language of most sodomy laws to conclude that sodomy is "the behavior that defines the class" of homosexuals. It is precisely this view that has been adopted, implicitly and explicitly, by military leaders as the key to sustaining the ban. Linking homosexuality with sodomy sets it in opposition to the military, which presumably stands for "normal" heterosexual sex—which is represented, not incidentally, by those acts in which men penetrate the territory of the female body. The opposition between gay sex and military sex is further reinforced by a number of references to AIDS during the military hearings that associate the disease with homosexuality. By characterizing homosexual sex as perverted and diseased and heterosexual sex as normal and wholesome, the military debate forwards the same potent contrast of plague and health, moral bankruptcy and moral purity, that the Boy Scout discussion put forth in the Achtenberg debate. Importantly, this argument is advanced even in the face of evidence that the particular sexual acts being performed by heterosexuals and homosexuals do not differ significantly, if at all (see "Sodomy and Sexuality," below).

## HOMOPHOBIA, RACISM, AND SEXISM

The parallel between the segregation of African Americans and the exclusion of gays from military service has been heavily drawn upon by those who support lifting the ban and vehemently rejected by those who wish to maintain it. Operation Desert Storm commander General Colin Powell, one of the most famous and most frequently quoted opponents of lifting the ban, is unequivocal in his rejection of any similarity between these groups. Powell insists, "Skin color is a benign, nonbehavioral characteristic. Sexual orientation is perhaps the most profound of human behavioral characteristics. Comparison of the two is a convenient but invalid argument" (in Burrelli 1994, 63).

Nevertheless, some of these denials themselves provide the best evidence for recognizing the validity of the comparison. For example, Lieutenant John Burnham, a military leader who testified at the Senate hearings, denies that anti-gay sentiment is an example of prejudice, explaining:

> Prejudice against somebody because of their skin color or the fact that they are a woman or because of their nationality is the result of an attitude that you have because of what you have experienced, what you have been taught by your parents or your community or any kind of an outside influence. That can be educated away, and that is why the[y] call it prejudice. (*Policy Hearings* 1993, 547)

It is difficult to read such a definition without thinking of the subtle but pervasive ways in which heterosexism and homophobia are instilled in each of us by dominant institutions.

Burnham further weakens his point when he argues that this issue is unlike the question of allowing women to serve. He insists that although "some people may have reservations about different issues involving women serving," permitting men and women to work together "does not go against the grain" in the same way that integrating homosexuals and heterosexuals does (*Policy Hearings* 1993, 547). History, of course, proves him wrong; until very recently, the thought of women serving on active duty with men went entirely "against the grain." As the ongoing debate over women in combat illustrates, for many people it remains so.

Whether or not these groups themselves can be seen as comparable, their situations in relation to the military share an undeniable resemblance, as do the military rationales that have been used to exclude them. Supporters of lifting the ban have identified a number of striking similarities between the rhetoric historically used to keep African Americans segregated within the military and the justifications that currently uphold the ban on gays and lesbians (Adam 1994; Cammermeyer 1994; Department of the Army 1991; Horner and Anderson 1994; Korb 1994; Robson 1992; Rolison and Nakayama 1994). Cammermeyer's lawyers argue in a legal brief that "virtually every justification used for the military's ban on gays was used to justify the military's discrimination against African-Americans in World War II" (Memo in Support 1994, 43). These justifications include the rationales, frequently cited in both cases, that white or heterosexual service members will object to sharing intimate space with members of the black or gay/lesbian minority; that they will refuse to take commands from or respect the authority of members of the minority group; that the presence of these outsiders will disrupt the cohesion of the unit and thereby decrease military effectiveness; that the military will experience difficulties sending integrated forces to foreign countries because of the negative attitudes of those countries toward the minority group; and, finally, that integrating the forces will ultimately cause good soldiers to refuse to serve in the armed forces (Horner and Anderson, 1994).[16]

While there is much to learn from analogies with groups such as African Americans and women, it is equally important to keep in focus the ways in which this issue is distinct. Most notably, African Americans and women were historically placed in separate, segregated units in the military, forbidden from serving in the same units as white male service members. These groups therefore sought desegregation of the military, whereas gays and lesbians already serve in every military branch and unit. They therefore seek recognition for the service they already provide, arguing "not from the premise of suppliance, but of success, of proven ability of prowess in battle, of exemplary conduct and ability" (Sullivan 1993, 36). Gays and lesbians have served in the military throughout its history, as writers such as historian Allan Bérubé (1990) and journalist Randy Shilts (1993) have painstakingly documented. Even General Norman Schwarzkopf, who adamantly opposes lifting the ban, admits, "I have finally come down to the fact that yes, homosexuals have served in the military and can serve in the future if they are not openly admitting so" (*Policy Hearings* 1993, 613).

However, although even most military leaders now concede that gays and lesbians already serve in the armed forces, not everyone with influence does. Senator Lauch Faircloth, for example, comments on the eighth day of the Senate hearings that "in all of the hearings I have been to, not one person has said that the service would be improved by bringing homosexuals into it" (*Policy Hearings* 1993, 795). In light of the evidence presented in the hearings, however, the issue is not whether to add a new group of people to the existing military. Instead, it is whether to recognize the members of this group who are already in uniform, to acknowledge their historical and contemporary contribution to all branches of military service, and to accept their right to serve, openly and without fear, as gay and lesbian service members.

Resistance to lifting the ban relates directly to the military's symbolic force in society, and the intensity of the resistance suggests how deeply such a change would challenge the existing military ethos. This challenge lies at the heart of both the military's frequent denial, in the face of copious evidence, of the presence of lesbians and gays and its unwillingness to permit open gays and lesbians to enlist. The military perceives itself as the stronghold of heterosexual masculinity and the soldier as the epitome of what it is to be an American, which is to say an American male. The U.S. military is the quintessential instance of a gendered organization, and its gender is unquestionably male, as is that of the nation it serves (Adam 1994).[17] Moreover, war itself, like the role of the soldier, constitutes a traditionally male rite of passage. "For generations . . . the military has been an institution that has promised to do one thing, if nothing else, and that is to take a boy and make him a man" (Shilts 1993, 5).

Just as the military tasks of protecting the nation and defeating aggressors are gendered masculine, those entrusted with these responsibilities are perceived and often perceive themselves, in terms of their heterosexual manhood. A comment from a former Marine Corps commandant in 1982 illustrates just how integral this self-image has been: "War is man's work. . . . When you get right down to it, you have to protect the manliness of war" (in Benecke and Dodge 1996, 81). Gay men, however, are seen as failing or refusing to conform to the rules and image of heterosexual masculinity. The presence of gay soldiers performing their duties with skill is thus particularly galling to military officials who want to maintain the military's masculine image, and who fear that gay men will undermine ideals of masculinity (Shilts 1993). Whoever or whatever threatens the military ethos is perceived as undermining the military mission as well. "The crux of the issue in the United States is the culturally embedded view that homosexuality represents a feminization of men and that this feminization entails a world of implications debilitating to military effectiveness, namely, all of the traditional traits assigned to the feminine . . . all of which detract from military readiness" (Adam 1994, 104).

The perception of gay men as effeminate is linked to the idea that any man who willingly submits himself sexually to another man places himself in the passive, "feminine" role, the role of the woman who is penetrated rather than the role of the aggressor (Mohr 1994, 116). "Many non-gay people believe that gay men and lesbians exhibit 'cross-gender' behavior: behavior stereotypically associated with the other gender. In this view, gay men behave like 'normal' women and lesbians like 'normal' men" (Fajer 1992, 515). The belief that homosexuality is characterized by "inverted" or opposite-gender traits leads to a stereotype of gay men as effeminate: weak, "swishy," overemotional, and generally frail of mind and body. These qualities are seen as antithetical to military service and destructive to the military's image and effectiveness. "The construction of a 'homosexual threat to the military' is a story about the perceived potential emasculation of American masculinity" (Adam 1994, 104).

The fear of a loss of masculinity is a fear of men losing control over women as well. The ban strengthens such control by authorizing sexual harassment and reinforcing male dominance and female submission, sexually and otherwise. Under its terms, "the way women can prove themselves to be nonlesbians is to have sex with men. Thus antigay regulations have encouraged sexual harassment of women. Those who will not acquiesce to a colleague's advances are routinely accused of being lesbian and are subject to discharge" (Shilts 1993, 5). Cammermeyer herself reports, "As women have attained more rights and opportunities in the military, the accusation of being a lesbian has become a weapon of sexual harassment. Continuing the ban is a perfect mechanism to perpetuate sexism either by keeping women out of the military or by controlling and abusing women who do serve" (1994, 294).

These observations are supported by the comments of other female service members, as related by Congressman Gerry Studds: "We've heard a lot of women say, especially aboard a big ship, if they're not willing to put out for sailors, they're accused of being a lesbian, whether they are or not" (in Gallagher 1992, 21). Representative Patricia Schroeder likewise reports, "If you're a woman in the military, you can't make sexual-harassment charges, because you're going to face the countercharge that you're a lesbian" ("Lesbians" 1993, A23). By enabling and abetting sexual harassment, the ban encourages not only homophobia but also sexism. It thus serves as an effective means of keeping *all* women, regardless of their sexual orientation, "in line" and submissive, as well as sexually available, to men (Benecke and Dodge 1996).

Despite the advances of women in the military, the institution and many of its members remain at best ambivalent about having women as military colleagues, as evidenced by revelations of sexual harassment and rape in such military settings as Tailhook and the Aberdeen Proving Ground. Historically, heterosexual women, like gay men, have been perceived as suffering a failure of masculinity, which serves as the basis for their exclusion. However, heterosexual women are somewhat redeemed through their conformity to traditional sexual roles. While, in the eyes of some male soldiers, women remain inferior to men, particularly in the fulfillment of military duties, their presence is acceptable only because—and as long as—they participate within their assigned gender role. It is instructive to note that the remaining conflicts over women's role in the military fall into two main categories: the question of implementing a female draft during wartime and the issue of allowing women to perform combat roles. The former issue hints at what the latter makes explicit: the violation of the gender taboo that forbids women to become military aggressors, "penetrating" the territory of foreign lands.

The vigilance of the military in safeguarding gender roles directly conflicts with its need to recruit women who will be skilled in military service. It is exactly those qualities that make a good soldier—independence, strength, skill, resourcefulness—that, when displayed by a woman, suggest the transgression of an appropriate female gender role. The resulting irony is that "women who show independence, resistance to sexual harassment, or the 'masculine' qualities so valued by the military are particularly vulnerable to the charge of lesbianism" (Adam 1994, 112). Lesbians are frequently stereotyped as "masculine" women, or women who display character traits stereotypically associated with heterosexual masculinity. Yet these are precisely the characteristics one must possess to be an effective soldier.

In a military that bans lesbians, this situation places all women in a double bind. A woman's success in the military and her ability to convince others that she can be a good soldier require her to exhibit those qualities that could also get her summarily dismissed as a lesbian—regardless of the sexual practices she engages in and with whom. The consequences of this catch-22 are aptly illustrated by a memo written by Vice Admiral Joseph S. Donnel. Although Donnel characterized lesbians as generally "hardworking, career-oriented, willing to put in long hours on the job, and among the command's top performers," he offered this description not as praise for their work but as a means of helping senior officers identify possible lesbians for investigation and discharge (Lehring 1996, 274). The better a soldier she is, the more a female service member risks being targeted as a lesbian.

The congruence between the qualities that make a good soldier and the characteristics associated with female gender-role transgression thus encourage the identification of female soldiers as lesbians (Halley 1991). This phenomenon undoubtedly accounts in part for the disproportionate number of women who are discharged for homosexuality in all branches of the military (Benecke and Dodge 1996; Robson 1992). One report indicates that in the decade from 1980 to 1990, women accounted for 10 percent of all military personnel but made up 23 percent of all discharges for homosexuality (Stiehm 1994, 158). In 1996, under "Don't Ask, Don't Tell," women accounted for 13.1 percent of the armed forces but made up 29 percent of those discharged from all branches (Moss 1997); in the army they accounted for 41 percent ("Could It Be a Witch-Hunt?" 1997, 15).

The statistics on female dismissals are particularly notable in light of service member polls that show significantly less resistance to lifting the ban among female than among male service personnel (Robb 1993, 12). According to the RAND Report, an independent study commissioned by the Clinton administration in 1993, 37 percent of male and 72 percent of female military personnel would not object to lifting the ban (Plaintiff's Reply Memo 1994, 28n. 14). One possible explanation for this disparity is that "some servicewomen feel this debate has advanced their own concerns about sexual harassment and women in combat roles" and thus welcome the lifting of the ban or at least profit from the national discussion this issue has engendered (Miller 1994, 69). In addition, polls indicate that even among civilians, "a significant majority of men in America are opposed to lifting the ban, and a significant majority of women are in favor" (*Policy Hearings* 1993, 620). Thus, although the argument against gays in the military is largely premised on the anticipated negative reactions of other service members, the largest percentage of separations is taking place precisely where service member opposition is at its lowest—among the ranks of women.

For women of color in the military, racial discrimination magnifies the intensity of the discrimination and oppression they experience. Kendall Thomas, a professor of law at Columbia University, observes that "the discriminatory policies of the military strike disproportionately women—especially women of color" (in Deitcher 1995, 180). Given the existence of pervasive racism as well as a disproportionate number of women of color in the military, there is little cause to question such a claim. Although there are no statistics on homosexual discharges broken down by race, some activists have compiled interviews and other anecdotal evidence to illustrate the difficulties women of color confront in the military (Benecke and Dodge 1996).

Thomas's assertion is further supported by evidence from the earliest investigations of lesbianism, instigated shortly after women were first integrated into active duty. In a 1980 incident aboard the USS *Norton Sound*, twenty-four of the sixty women on board were investigated for lesbian activity (Deitcher 1995). Two of these women, both of whom were African American, were discharged. Eight of the nine black women serving on the ship were targeted in the initial charges. Susan McGrievy, American Civil Liberties Union (ACLU) counsel in the case, observed, "It just smelled of racism. . . . They were convicted because people believe that African-Americans are oversexed" (in Deitcher 1995, 169).

These statistics and observations on women's separations suggest that gender and race, as well as sexual orientation, operate in applications of the ban. Significantly, "the branches of the service most resistant to allowing women in their ranks—the Navy and Marines—are the branches that drum out the most women for being gay. The Navy releases twice as many women as men on grounds of homosexuality. In the Marine Corps, the figure is seven times higher for women than for men." These figures demonstrate that,

> especially for lesbians, the issues are far more complex than simple homophobia, because they also involve significant features of sex-based discrimination. There are many men who never wanted women in *their* Army or *their* Navy in the first place, and the military regulations regarding homosexuality have been the way to keep them out for the last decade.

As a result, "until proven otherwise, women in the military are often suspected of being lesbian" (Shilts 1993, 4–5).

The inordinate number of women discharged may seem to discredit the hypothesis that *masculinity* is at stake here. (One might argue that gay men should pose the greater threat and evoke the more intense purging.) In fact, this inequality supports the hypothesis. The very entry of women into a traditionally male preserve constitutes a transgression, and thus the presence of women who refuse sexual or other submission to men is particularly subversive of male authority and superiority. The inclusion of women who are perceived to "act like men," sexually or otherwise, introduces the threat that such women will demand access to male privilege and power.

While this threat alone may justify the ban in the minds of many military leaders, it is insufficient as a rationale to satisfy the courts. In recent years, the success of legal challenges presented by Cammermeyer and others has necessitated a more explicit rationale for continuing the ban. In light of Clinton's promise to lift the ban, military leaders were forced either to justify the existing blanket ban or to articulate a new policy that would hold up in the civil courts.[18] No longer would the simple assertion that "homosexuality is incompatible with military service" suffice. At this historical moment, the military was called on to establish a compelling concern that necessitated unequal treatment but was not based on identity or "status," a category that had repeatedly been extended legal protection for other minority groups. Instead, the military had to justify its apparent discrimination based on a realm in which the U.S. courts had always given it a great deal of leeway: the arena of conduct (Burrelli 1994, 28). However, in Cammermeyer's case and a number of others, no evidence of "conduct" per se exists. To uphold dismissals like hers, the new policy would have to outlaw declarations of identity by defining such statements as a category other than status. Indeed, this is precisely what the military did. In its effort to maintain its ban, it presented the issue with a new twist, defining statements of gay, lesbian, or bisexual self-identity not as references to an individual's status but as conduct in and of themselves.

## Speech and Sexuality: Constructing the Homosexual

The issue that Cammermeyer's case brings to the fore is one that has for centuries engaged scholars of communication, law, philosophy, psychology, and linguistics: What does speech *do*? What is it that silence contains and speech releases? This question also lies at the heart of legal challenges to the new military policy, contests that focus largely on reclaiming speech as an artifact of protected status rather than as an instance of prohibited and actionable conduct. In the distinction the new military policy draws between status and conduct, status is characterized first and foremost by silence and inactivity. The "compromise" the new policy announces is the tolerance of this silent status, which Attorney General Janet Reno refers to in a memo as "unmanifested orientation" (*Policy Hearings* 1993, 706). Under the old policy, officers and recruiters were required to root out status by asking questions and conducting aggressive investigations. Under the new policy, at least in theory, military personnel are no longer asked direct questions or subjected to "witch-hunts" regarding their sexuality, as long as their status does not manifest itself through word or deed.

According to the new policy's supporters, the restriction on speech relates to military leaders' concern that gay and lesbian soldiers will be gay first, soldiers second, and that the primacy of their gay or lesbian identity will disrupt military readiness and unit cohesion. Strom Thurmond, in his opening statement at the hearings before the Committee on Armed Services, offers his perspective on the importance of silence, at the same time accounting for the apparent hypocrisy of the "Don't Ask, Don't Tell" compromise:

> This is not an issue of being for or against homosexuals as a group or homosexuality as a lifestyle. This is not an issue of whether individuals who are gay can serve on active duty. The record is replete with instances of dedicated and heroic service by many gays in the ranks of our armed services. The difference is that they served then and serve now as soldiers, sailors, airmen and marines and not as gays in the military. This should be a question of military readiness and determining the best course of action to enable our military, from general to private, to provide the security and stability necessary for America to continue to be a world leader and ensure the American way of life. (*Policy Hearings* 1993, 5)[19]

The words of Lieutenant Burnham reinforce the prevalence of this concern. While acknowledging that "homosexuals have served with distinction," Burnham offers this qualification: "But one of the primary reasons that they have served for full careers is that they served with discretion. And again, that was one of the aspects of their lifestyle that they subordinated to the overall good of [the] unit—was the fact that they were homosexual and it was not open" (*Policy Hearings* 1993, 556).

Later in the hearings, Senator Joseph Lieberman counters the claim that if soldiers are permitted to be openly gay or lesbian, "the homosexual orientation will become a more dominant part of that person's service." Referring to the testimony of the chief psychiatrist at Walter Reed Hospital, he argues that as long as gays in the military identify *primarily* as soldiers, and secondarily as gay or lesbian, their presence ought not disrupt unit cohesion (*Policy Hearings* 1993, 465). However, he concedes, in the reverse case, the existence of individuals with a "confrontational sexual orientation" would indeed disrupt the bonding and overall readiness of the unit. From this perspective, self-identification amounts to advocacy; advocacy is confrontational; and confrontation is, by definition, disruptive. Such a framework permits no conceptual space for statements of identity that are not interpreted immediately as having that identity "rammed down my throat," in the phraseology of one Department of Defense representative (Otjen 1994, 270). Senator John Warner's comments illustrate this leap from self-identification to activism and even recruitment when he states, "Homosexuals have served in many instances in a commendable way. . . . But the transition from the quiet manner in which they perform their duties to an open advocacy of their sexual preferences is the difficulty that this Senator, and I think many others, have" (*Policy Hearings* 1993, 468).

When speech is defined as indistinguishable from sexual conduct, declaring one's sexual orientation constitutes improper public behavior. "The new policy's ideology would have us believe that saying one is gay is itself an act of sex" (Mohr 1994, 64). This link between speech and sex is particularly striking when viewed through the lens of public address history—in particular, the traditional prohibition against women's speech. Feminist rhetorical scholars such as Karlyn Kohrs Campbell (1989) have established the role of sexism in mandating women's silence, as public discourse has historically been considered the exclusive domain of middle-class, heterosexual white men. The construct of the orator is traditionally gendered masculine, and public address has consequently been viewed as a singularly unfeminine activity. Historically, a woman who spoke publicly, especially to a "promiscuous" audience, where the clear separation of the sexes was not maintained, was looked upon as immoral and sexually impure (Zaeske 1995). This longstanding association links women's public speech with the specter of uncontrolled female sexuality. Thus the connection between speech and sexuality, particularly abnormal, unnatural, or hypersexuality, is well supported by historical precedent.

Just as Roberta Achtenberg's opponents saw lesbian activism as antithetical to a politician's role and threatening to a male-dominated government,

the military ban's supporters view the expression of homosexuality as antithetical to the soldier's role and subversive to the patriarchal military. In both
cases, the claim to identity is read, probably accurately, as marking an absence
of shame and the assertion of self-esteem and pride. In a context that deems
homosexuality a cause for secrecy and silence, to speak without shame of
being lesbian or gay is to challenge, if not reject, political and military ideologies. "To break silences that are systematically and ubiquitously enforced
in public life, is profoundly political," so that affirming a lesbian or gay identity can be construed only as advocacy or "flaunting it" (Gamson 1996,
79–80). Such an assertion of pride, moreover, is correctly viewed as a threat
to the dominant belief system that insists on the inferiority and marginality
of gays and lesbians.

What gives the military's anti-gay discourse and its appeal to shame such
a profound resonance is the sometimes implicit, sometimes explicit connection of homosexual orientation with the practice of sodomy. The very term
*conduct* has come to be a military code word for sodomy, as has its popular
equivalent, *lifestyle*. The courts have identified sodomy as "the behavior that
defines the class" of homosexuals, and from this perspective, the declaration
of a lesbian or gay sexual orientation is read as a statement that one has committed or intends to commit sodomy or has at least a propensity or desire to
do so. In *Padula v. Webster*, as discussed above, the Washington, D.C., circuit
court judge denied legal protections to lesbians and gays, arguing that "practicing homosexuals" could not constitute a suspect classification. The judge
concluded that "if criminal or criminalizable sodomy is the inevitable consequence or the essential characteristic of homosexual identity, then the class
of homosexuals is coterminous with a class of criminals or at least of persons whose shared behavior is criminalizable" (Halley 1989, 919–20).

The *Padula* decision, however, is based on a misapplication of the precedent set by *Bowers v. Hardwick* (Halley 1991). Although the authors of the
*Hardwick* decision explicitly asserted that they were *not* setting a precedent
for equal protection rulings, their decision was applied as a precedent for
such rulings through the linking term of *sodomy*. The *Padula* judge reasoned
that if there is no right to commit sodomy (the finding of the Court in
*Hardwick*), and if sodomy is the behavior that defines the class of homosexuals, then there can be no legal protection for homosexual status. According
to *Padula*, the *Hardwick* case "forecloses [any] effort to gain suspect class status . . . for practicing homosexuals" (Halley 1991, 354). However, there is no
support for this definition of homosexuals even in the sodomy statutes
themselves, the majority of which do not equate sodomy with a particular

sexual orientation. Indeed, "the peculiar slippages that attend this definition of the class of 'homosexuals' all seem to require some sort of willful blindness to the actual scope of most sodomy prohibitions" (Halley 1991, 355).

The equation of homosexuality with sodomy has widespread significance for withholding gay and lesbian rights. Nan Hunter, former director of the ACLU's Lesbian and Gay Rights Project, explains that "sodomy laws have functioned as the linchpin for denial of employment, housing, and custody or visitation rights; even when we have proved that there was no nexus between homosexuality and job skills or parenting ability, we have had the courts throw the 'habitual criminal' label at us as a reason to deny relief" (in Deitcher 1995, 146). Thus, despite its misinterpretation of *Hardwick*, the *Padula* ruling has had devastating effects. Through its precedent, speech and sodomy are inextricably linked, so that the act of identifying oneself as a lesbian or a gay man is akin to, and as incriminating as, committing sodomy. The category of "conduct" provides the bridge joining the otherwise disparate concepts of "speech" and "sodomy." Moreover, the military has taken this equation one step further. Whereas the court linked sodomy directly to homosexual status, the military—legally required to demonstrate a disruption to its mission—equates sodomy with all forms of "homosexual conduct," broadly defined.

What is perhaps most intriguing about this connection is that the trajectory from statements of self-identity to conclusions about conduct does not work as decisively in the other direction. Identifying oneself as lesbian or gay constitutes homosexual conduct sufficient for military discharge, whether or not one ever has or ever intends to commit sodomy or participate in other acts that are defined as homosexual conduct.[20] Nevertheless, the reverse is not true. Committing sodomy or other sexual acts with a partner of the same sex is *not* automatically considered sufficient evidence to classify one as a homosexual or to qualify one for dismissal. Almost unbelievably, in light of the vehement rhetoric that decries the effects of homosexual conduct on the military mission, even "the courts . . . found no problem with the Department of Defense directive that exempts heterosexuals who engage in homosexual conduct from dismissal" (Currah 1995, 67).

The reference here is to a provision in the military's policy on gays which states that a service member who is found to have committed same-sex sodomy will not be discharged under the policy if "such conduct is a departure from the member's usual and customary behavior" (*Policy Hearings* 1993, 70). This extenuating circumstance has been nicknamed the "Queen for a Day" rule (Otjen 1994, 339). It provides that a service member who has committed a sexual act or acts with a member of the same sex will not be dismissed from the military if he or she is found to be a heterosexual engaged in homosexual sex. In contrast, a service member whom the military identifies as gay or lesbian who is engaged in precisely the same act is subject to investigation and dismissal. Given the military's definitions, "an individual who identifies as heterosexual may engage in homosexual acts and experience homosexual attraction, while a homosexual person who engages in heterosexual conduct nonetheless *remains* a homosexual person" (Plaintiff's Memo 1994, 38).

The argument the military advances is that gays and lesbians are inherently more likely to violate the UCMJ's sodomy statute, *even if they have never engaged in an act of homosexual sodomy,* than are heterosexual soldiers who have admitted to or even been caught engaging in such an act. The explanation for what appears a blatant hypocrisy lies in the interpretation of sexual orientation as an essential and immutable element of character. This essential quality is inseparable from sexual conduct when such an association is convenient, that is, when arguing that homosexuals "by definition" commit sodomy. But such a quality is entirely distinct from sexual conduct when this dissociation is convenient, in the case of heterosexuals caught "slumming." From the perspective of military policy, clues to one's immutable inner self are provided more reliably by self-identification than by conduct—even sexual conduct.

The "Queen for a Day" rule illuminates and perpetuates the essentialist understanding of sexual orientation that underlies military policy. It suggests the existence of inflexible, a priori categories that allow the classification of individuals finally and certainly into two distinct and opposite categories of sexual orientation.[21] The internal incoherence of this policy reveals that it is not the acts themselves but the status to which they presumably refer that is subject to condemnation. "These actions are simply markers of sexual orientation status . . . rather than acts which are despised and censurable independently of reference to despised sexual orientation status. . . . These are homosexual acts only in that despised homosexuals perform them" (Mohr 1994, 64). This perspective is expressed vividly in the deposition given by Department of Defense representative General John Otjen in Cammermeyer's civil court case. When confronted with evidence that large numbers of heterosexuals violate the sodomy statute, Otjen defended the military ban by arguing that "there is a sense of core values that exist in the group that think that homosexuality, that sex *of any nature* between two people of the same sex, is inappropriate, [and] unnatural" (Otjen 1994, 216; emphasis

mine). Thus, despite the insistence of many lawmakers and of Clinton himself that "the issue ought to be conduct," this example exposes the persistent
reference to status that the censure of conduct conceals.

## IMMUTABILITY AND THE PRIVACY PRINCIPLE

The view of sexual orientation as an immutable characteristic of individuals has a certain legal utility for lesbian and gay rights initiatives. Legal arguments based on this principle "have been encouraged by the courts supporting gay rights that have justified their rulings by pointing to the supposed immutability of homosexuality, as well as by hostile courts that have
based their decisions to *deny* protection to homosexuals on the supposed
*mutability* of sexual preference" (Halley 1991, 360). Establishing immutability is the key to earning suspect class status for lesbians and gays, which
would compel courts to apply the strictest scrutiny to any distinctions made
on the basis of sexual orientation as they do for distinctions based on race,
religion, or physical disability. Although, thus far, all efforts to attain such status have failed, ironically, the military's view of sexual orientation as essential and immutable might actually fortify arguments for extending equal
protection laws to gays and lesbians. Whether or not an individual lesbian or
gay man personally shares the view that sexual orientation is immutable, this
perspective is undeniably attractive in its potential for gaining the sympathy
of the courts.

Despite their popularity, however, arguments based on immutability have
numerous drawbacks and even dangers when employed in the cause of gay
and lesbian rights, as evidenced by *Padula*. To begin with, despite claims to
the contrary, immutability is not a necessary prerequisite for classification as
a suspect class (Halley 1991). In fact, "recent Supreme Court opinions have
conceded that the trait in question need not be the result of nature but can
be the product of social or even legal constructions" (Currah 1995). This
provision is evident, for example, in the cases of religion and physical disability (Mohr 1994; Phelan 1994). Religion may be deeply rooted, but it can
also be chosen or changed, and religious conversion or "rebirth" (both examples of chosen status) does not exempt individuals from protection under
the law. Likewise, while one may be born with a disability, both physical and
mental disabilities may develop over time or may result from events such as
a careless accident, a self-inflicted wound, or drunk driving (Mohr 1994).
The law does not distinguish among various "causes" of one's religion or
disability in extending equal protection. The argument that if homosexual-

ity is "chosen" it is a matter of personal responsibility, and therefore need not or cannot be protected, fails to acknowledge elements of choice and responsibility in other protected classes.

Moreover, as discussed in the previous chapter, the very concept of an immutable or biological category is based on the paradigm of race, which is problematic in light of recent scholarship that deconstructs "biological" categories such as gender and race. To argue for immutability is to ignore an abundance of scholarship on sexuality, race, and other social categories that rejects essentialism and argues for the constructed nature of all social distinctions (Plaskow 1994). This includes the division of people into classes based on the gender of their sexual partners (Butler 1990; Foucault 1978). As illustrated by the "Queen for a Day" rule, challenging essentialist arguments may be a necessary step toward revealing the injustices built into the military policy. The concept of immutability may serve prejudice and discrimination to a greater degree than it can ever enhance minority interests. It may also play directly into the hands of those who would perpetuate and further entrench homophobia:

> It seems that arguments for lesbian and gay rights based on the presumed givenness of homosexuality are attractive precisely because they disrupt as little as possible the culture's deeper assumptions about sexuality. They allow us to see gays and lesbians as a "them" who are in some way different from the general population. They allow us to focus on the "causes" of homosexuality to the neglect of the "causes" of heterosexuality. They allow us to debate the religious and social acceptance of gays and lesbians, but to avoid the question of how heterosexuality comes to be constructed and accepted as normative. (Plaskow 1994, 31–32)

In this way, an essentialist view of sexuality, while advantageous in some respects, upholds the "Otherness" of gays and lesbians and reinforces the rigid categories established by and for a heterosexist, homophobic dominant ideology.

The risks of the immutability and associated right-to-privacy arguments are illustrated all too clearly by the majority opinion in *Hardwick*, which appropriates these claims and uses them against lesbians and gays. Despite its occasional legal successes, the immutability argument inherently constrains gay and lesbian freedoms because it rests on a premise that "'homosexuals' constitute a distinct class of persons existing in human nature and they must, by their very nature, commit sodomy." This view authorizes the homophobic construction of "a natural homosexual, a preexisting human class persistently marked and thus adequately defined by the act of sodomy" (Halley 1991, 358). The right-to-privacy argument attempts to protect a class of gays and lesbians while bracketing discussions of "conduct" (read "sodomy"). However, by attempting to sidestep the issue of conduct, the privacy argument leaves intact—and thus unintentionally reinforces—the belief that "gay identity emerges ineluctably from an irresistible propensity to commit sodomy" (Halley 1989, 921). Sodomy emerges as an uncontrollable, specifically homosexual desire, in need of privacy and legal protection. By reinforcing the equation of homosexuality with the illegal activity of sodomy, privacy arguments undermine efforts to obtain heightened scrutiny under equal protection laws.

Given the minefield laid down by the *Hardwick* decision that strikes down any legal argument for sodomy, "judges are far more likely to be sympathetic to arguments about status than to those regarding conduct" (Bull 1994, 30). Evan Wolfson, a senior staff attorney for a gay and lesbian legal organization, warns that "when we get to conduct, we will run smack into *Hardwick*" (in Bull 1994, 30). Consequently, arguments for equal protection generally distinguish status from conduct and challenge the presumption that conduct can be predicted by status. Such a legal strategy appears in a brief written by Cammermeyer's attorneys, who claim that "sexual orientation and sexual conduct are truly distinct" (Plaintiff's Memo 1994, 34). They support this assertion with the statement from Dr. Laura Brown, a well-known psychologist specializing in the study of sexual orientation, that "there is almost no relationship between an individual's orientation and his or her sexual conduct" (*Cammermeyer v. Aspin* 1994, 31).

According to Mary Newcombe, one of Cammermeyer's civilian lawyers, the intent of this argument was to challenge the presumption that particular, prohibited sexual acts—including sodomy, hypersexuality, promiscuity, unwanted sexual advances, and fraternization—follow from a given sexual orientation (1996). Just as one's self-identification as a heterosexual tells us nothing about that individual's sexual proclivities, the acknowledgment that one is gay or lesbian offers no clue as to the particulars of his or her sexual conduct. In fact, it does not even tell us what would seem to be the most obvious information—the sex of the individual's sexual partners. Again, just as those who identify as heterosexual may never have had sex or may occasionally or frequently engage in sexual activity with people of the same sex (a possibility made abundantly clear by the "Queen for a Day" rule), individuals who identify as gay or lesbian may never have had sex or may engage occasionally or frequently in sexual activity with members of the opposite sex. These observations support the claim that what we identify as sexual orientation is indeed distinguishable from sexual conduct.

This is not to say, as Cammermeyer's attorneys undoubtedly did not wish to argue, that gays and lesbians should be expected or required to refrain from engaging in expressions of same-sex affection, up to and including sexual intimacy. However, that is precisely how the separation of status from conduct has been interpreted by the military and the civil courts, including the court in the Cammermeyer case. Cammermeyer's lawyers sought to prove that homosexual status did not indicate a propensity to commit criminal acts, because a gay or lesbian sexual orientation can be expressed in many ways that are not outlawed by the military's definition of sodomy. But the courts, working with an implicit definition of sodomy as *any* expression of homosexuality, (mis)interpreted the splitting off of conduct from status to mean that being gay or lesbian need not result in the expression of same-sex desire through any behavior whatsoever. As a result, Judge Thomas S. Zilly's decision in Cammermeyer's favor is based, in part, on his conclusion that "there is no rational basis for the Government's underlying contention that homosexual orientation equals 'desire or propensity to engage' in homosexual conduct" (*Cammermeyer v. Aspin* 1994, 33). Cammermeyer's acknowledgment of her status, in the view of the court, "is not reliable evidence of her desire or propensity to engage in homosexual conduct."

Zilly's judgment that homosexual status does not indicate a propensity to engage in homosexual conduct, combined with Cammermeyer's insistence that hers is an "emotional orientation," both broadens and narrows the possibilities for understanding gay and lesbian lives.[22] The separation of gay or lesbian self-identity from particular sexual acts, or even (in the case of Cammermeyer's statement) the evasion or dismissal of sexuality altogether, diverts the obsessive focus on sex that grips the public's thinking about gays and lesbians. It forces us to look elsewhere for an understanding of what might more accurately be labeled, for some, "affectional orientation." Zilly's statement dissociates the insistent coupling of homosexuality with sexual practices and so invites us to reconsider this narrow definition. Such a definition excludes, for example, individuals who identify as gay or lesbian but choose celibacy or who do not engage in same-sex sexual behavior for any number of reasons: because they live with their parents or their children, are still heterosexually married, have not yet met a suitable partner, are nuns or priests, are HIV positive or fear contracting HIV. Moreover, Zilly's assertion raises the question of what it means to assign someone else or oneself a gay or lesbian identity if we can no longer rely on a simplistic equation of same-sex sexual contact and homosexuality. In the absence of a reliable sign that identifies a preexisting class of individuals who can be labeled "homosexuals," we might examine instead the way in which this class and its members are *constituted* as having a particular identity based on the fallible sign of sexual activity.

Zilly's statement adds an alternative to the original equation of homosexual status with prohibited sexual acts, specifically sodomy. Whereas the military claimed that acknowledging a gay or lesbian identity was tantamount to committing the forbidden and immoral act of sodomy, Zilly's decision establishes the possibility, even the likelihood, that acknowledging a gay or lesbian identity does *not* mean one is likely to engage in such an act. Embedded in this possibility, again, are potential gains and losses for gay and lesbian rights. What is gained is the distancing of gays and lesbians from a condemned behavior and the rescuing of the category of "homosexuality" from complete submergence in the potent discourse of sex. What is lost is the acceptance of gay and lesbian difference, and with it any possibility of gaining legal protections for and public recognition of same-sex relationships. If status and conduct are unrelated, as Zilly suggests, then gays and lesbians can legitimately be asked to refrain from engaging in any expression of affection, even as their identities are presumably protected.

This is precisely the situation implemented by the new military policy. The double bind for gays and lesbians is abundantly clear, as is their second-class status with respect to military and civil law: winning protection for identity means sacrificing one's right to express or share that identity. Again, homosexuality is presented as the difference that must make no difference as a condition of its tolerance. For lesbians and gays, as for no one else, the sacrifice of intimate relationships, love, and sexuality is demanded in return for the most fundamental of constitutional rights.

## SODOMY AND SEXUALITY

The equation of homosexuality with sodomy causes lesbians to vanish under the sign *gay* or *homosexual*. With both terms ambiguously gendered, they are read alternately as male or gender neutral. The result is that a stereotype of gay male sexual practices is translated without examination into an account of lesbian behavior.[23] In his testimony in the Cammermeyer case, Otjen, who was a member of the Military Working Group (MWG) that crafted the new policy, conveys the MWG's conviction that homosexuals are more likely than heterosexuals to commit sodomy. He concedes, however, that the group did not distinguish between lesbians and gay men in their study of the issue. In response to a question about whether lesbians are more or less likely than heterosexual men to violate the UCMJ sodomy law, Otjen circuitously replies, "I haven't frankly thought about that. . . . But my opinion is that when you tell me that you are a lesbian or you tell me that you're a homosexual is that you are [sic], in that you participate in those things which, those activities which identify that group. And if sodomy is part of that, then I believe my statement holds true" (Otjen 1994, 414–15).

In fact, substantial research suggests that sodomy is not a predominant activity in the lives of many lesbians. One study, for example, reports that 23 percent, or about one-quarter, of lesbians rarely or never engage in oral sex (Blumstein and Schwartz 1983, 236). A recent survey of a nationwide sample of lesbians found that 36 percent, or over one-third of respondents, had never performed fellatio (Lever 1995, 29). To suggest that sodomy "defines the class" of lesbians singles out an activity that might be relatively infrequent or unimportant to the subjective experience of self-identified lesbians, defining all members of this group in terms of a behavior that large numbers of lesbians may never even practice. Lest we think, however, that the stereotype paints an accurate picture of the sexual lives of gay men, this, too, may be misleading. In the age of AIDS, many gay men are forgoing sodomy as part of the practice of safe sex (Martin 1987).

The definition of homosexuals as those who commit sodomy is distorted not only because it excludes many self-identified gays and lesbians. It also vastly overincludes individuals who have never considered themselves gay or lesbian and who have never engaged in same-sex sexual behavior. If sodomy is the behavior that defines the class, then a huge number of heterosexual couples will suddenly find themselves classified as homosexuals. The numbers representing heterosexual acts of sodomy are striking, if not surprising. One survey found that 90 to 93 percent of heterosexuals have engaged in oral intercourse (Blumstein and Schwartz 1983, 236, 242). The respected *Hite Report on Male Sexuality* (1981) likewise reported that "approximately 96 percent of all [male] respondents had orally stimulated a female partner" (Editors of the *Harvard Law Review* 1990, 59). Similarly, *The Redbook Report on Female Sexuality* (1977) found "that 85 percent of women surveyed perform fellatio with their husbands 'often' or 'occasionally,' and 20.3 percent had engaged in anal intercourse with their husbands more than once" (Editors of the *Harvard Law Review* 1990, 59).

These statistics suggest that sodomy can legitimately be identified as the behavior that defines the class of *hetero*sexuals. As Michael Himes, one of

Cammermeyer's civilian attorneys, observes, in light of such findings, it is logical to assume that when people announce their heterosexuality, they are declaring that they have a propensity to engage in sodomy (Otjen 1994, 209–11). The statement that one is a heterosexual, and particularly a heterosexual male, provides good predictive evidence that one is at high risk of violating the UCMJ. Statistically speaking, it makes even more sense to say that sodomy defines the class of men, independent of sexual orientation. In this case, the identification of oneself as a male permits a strong presumption that one will engage in sodomy, whereas if one is a woman, one is statistically less likely to engage in this conduct. Given the rationale that dismisses gays and lesbians from the military because of a presumed propensity to commit sodomy, there is no defensible basis for not dismissing "avowed males" as likely criminals who are at a high risk of violating the UCMJ regulation.

The distinction between the homosexual "propensity" to commit sodomy and an equal, if not more pronounced, heterosexual propensity is upheld by the confusion surrounding the meaning of the term *sodomy*, and the peculiar and persistent slippage in the meaning of this term. The *Alyson Almanac*, a reference book on gay and lesbian subjects, defines sodomy as "sexual acts deemed unnatural by the person using the term. . . . *Sodomy* is variously used to mean any sex between two men; any sex between two men or two women; anal intercourse involving a man and a partner of either sex; or sexual acts involving a human and an animal" (Alyson 1993, 97–98). The ambiguity of the term permits and even encourages inconsistent legal interpretations. "Sodomy statutes maintain themselves in part by their equivocal reference to identities *and/or* acts. The duality of the sodomy statutes— sometimes an index of identity, sometimes an index of acts—is a rhetorical mechanism in the subordination of homosexual identity and the superordination of heterosexual identity" (Halley 1993, 1722). In light of this definitional instability, it is little wonder that Foucault referred to sodomy as "that utterly confused category" (in Halley 1993, 1740).

While the term *sodomy* is often used as if it encompasses any and all same-sex sexual behavior, "the criminality of sodomitical acts involving persons of different genders is simply assumed out of existence" (Halley 1991, 357). The equation of homosexuality with sodomy supplies the necessary diversion so that the question of heterosexual sodomy is willfully ignored or simply never raised. Through this mechanism, "designating homosexual identity as the personal manifestation of sodomy confirms its subordination," while "the ways in which homosexual identity is *not* sodomy are subject to an organized forgetting" (Halley 1993, 1722). The effectiveness of this strategic mental block is aptly illustrated by Thurmond's assertion that "heterosexuals do not practice sodomy" (*Policy Hearings* 1993, 493).[24]

Thus it is not surprising that in both formal and informal discussions of the military ban on gays, and even in the testimony presented before the Senate Armed Services Committee, the term *sodomy* was applied loosely, without reference to the legal definition upon which the argument was based, to mean *all* homosexual sex and *only* homosexual sex.[25] This identification is pervasive: "Sodomy in these formulations is such an intrinsic characteristic of homosexuals, and so exclusive to us, that it constitutes a rhetorical proxy for us. It is our metonym" (Halley 1993, 1737). The argument that bans gays and lesbians from the military because of an inherent tendency to commit sodomy is based on precisely this tautology, resting on the misunderstanding that sodomy refers to any sexual act that occurs between two members of the same sex; that is, that sodomy "is" gay or lesbian sex. Again, this definition is underinclusive of heterosexuals, overinclusive of gays and lesbians, and relentlessly circular. Its utility for maintaining the military status quo lies in the fact that, in the absence of statutes that specifically discriminate against homosexual (as opposed to heterosexual) sexual acts, this loose application of the term creates a dividing line that maintains the apparent distinction between "us" and "them"—a distinction that is then deployed to keep "them" out and "us" in.

This discussion returns us to one of the principal dynamics of gay and lesbian oppression: the fear or hatred of the "Others" who are always already among "us" and the need decisively to cast out, both symbolically and literally, those "Others." Precisely because of the almost desperate insistence on upholding these distinctions, we must view them with suspicion. The presentation of sexual categories as clear-cut and rigidly bounded is illusory, if not deliberately misleading. "Acts do not translate, one-for-one, into identities. Once that equation is gone, it becomes difficult to maintain the corollary assumptions that the world properly provides two and only two sexual-orientation identities, and that heterosexuality is pure of sodomitic practice and homoerotic impulse" (Halley 1993, 1738).

The need to maintain rigid boundaries around arenas of sexual activity in order to preserve difference and distance between heterosexuality and homosexuality is but a symptom of a deeper affliction. The category of "heterosexuality" is based on the most tenuous of foundations, constructed not from internally consistent characteristics but entirely through its status as "not homosexual" (Butler 1990; Foucault 1978; Halley 1991; Halley 1993).

The class of heterosexuals is "a default class, profoundly heterogeneous, unstable, and provisional" (Halley 1991, 372). Heterosexuality therefore remains entirely dependent on the existence of an abstract homosexual "Other" for its own definition. At the same time, it is threatened by the presence of the real men and women who engage in same-sex sexual practices—a threat based on the ambiguity of definition, on the pervasiveness of homoerotic desire and activity throughout a much broader population than that identified as "homosexual," and on the inability of anyone to distinguish reliably those who are gay or lesbian from those who are not. Homosexual "status" is thus a particularly untrustworthy foundation on which to erect an edifice of difference. In contrast, the military's definition of homosexual "conduct" as gay sex, and of gay sex as sodomy, provides clearly delineated and differentiated categories. This misleading categorization conveniently forestalls confusion, uncertainty, or (worse yet) overlap of sexual orientation, sexual identities, or sexual activity.

Redefining sodomy as homosexual sex and reinterpreting sodomy statutes to apply exclusively to gays and lesbians thus provide the means by which to maintain a binary system, comprised of two mutually exclusive categories of sexuality and two distinct modes of sexual practice. The slippage in the meaning of sodomy is not accidental, then, but deliberately upholds an apparent, if illusory, difference between same- and cross-gender sexual practice. It thereby suggests that, although not distinguished by the UCMJ rules of conduct, one form of sexual practice is nevertheless legally forbidden and morally abhorrent while the other is acceptable, appropriate, even natural (see Plaintiff's Memo 1994, 26).

Because it presumes an exclusive link between sodomy and homosexuality, this framing of the issue begs the real question raised by the outlawing of sodomy. The crux of the military's problem is how to reconcile its moral condemnation and institutional prohibition of sodomy with the widely held knowledge that this practice is prevalent among heterosexuals. The military's construction of the sodomy argument fails to acknowledge that sodomy is practiced by many groups, of which homosexuals are only one. It also fails to consider the possibility that this practice may be linked to a group defined by a characteristic other than sexual orientation. Such a logical fallacy is the equivalent of claiming that in the winter, many gays and lesbians get the flu. This may be an entirely true statement; however, when it is phrased this way, we are led to believe that lesbians and gays are *particularly* susceptible to catching the flu, based on their membership in the class of homosexuals. Of course, this is not the case. It would be equally true to say that in the winter, many heterosexuals catch the flu. The fallacy lies in linking an irrelevant characteristic with a particular outcome and inferring a causal relationship.

In the flu example, it is obvious that an illogical conclusion has been reached, but only because there is no stereotype linking sexual orientation to the flu in the public imagination. (For evidence of the power of stereotypes in shaping our acceptance of such associations, simply substitute "HIV" for "flu." Suddenly, the implications of the statement and the causality it implies will no longer seem questionable to many readers.) The question is not whether gays and lesbians will get the flu. The question is whether the flu will be prevalent this winter, for if so, we might expect it to be *equally* present across populations of varying sexual orientation. Having reached this conclusion, we can abandon the analogy but retain its message. Such reasoning narrows the scope of the argument to a false dichotomy gays and lesbians will, or gays and lesbians will not, commit sodomy. This erases the possibility of a third standpoint: that those who identify themselves as gays and lesbians are no more or less likely to commit sodomy than those who identify themselves as heterosexuals, and that sodomy, whether deemed acceptable or not, is not accurately viewed as a manifestation of a particular sexual orientation.

Moreover, nowhere in the two options delineated above is there space for imagining homosexual acts, sexual and nonsexual, that are *not* acts of sodomy, and that are therefore not prohibited by the UCMJ. This construction of the argument is, needless to say, both highly reductive and fundamentally misleading. The alternatives provided establish gays and lesbians as either hypersexual—their sexuality uncontrolled and uncontrollable, their identity and desires expressed exclusively through sodomitic acts—or as asexual, cursed victims of unnatural urges that they valiantly succeed in overcoming through sheer strength of will. Missing and desperately needed here are a multitude of other options that would account for other kinds of lesbian and gay identities, other expressions of lesbian and gay love, intimacy, and sexuality.

Simply stated, sexual orientation and sodomy "are two entirely separate phenomena: sexual orientation classifications are based on the direction of an individual's sexual and affectional attractions, while sodomy statutes proscribe particular sexual acts in which persons of any sexual orientation may participate" (Editors of the *Harvard Law Review* 1990, 58–59). Cammermeyer's own words illuminate this distinction, when she describes her love for women as an "emotional orientation" and "explicitly reject[s] the notion that her identification as a lesbian can be reduced to the mere presumption of sexual acts with women" (Plaintiff's Memo 1994, 33). The very concept of a *sexual* orientation may be revealed, under closer scrutiny, to be a patriarchal concept organized around the assumed centrality of sexual, specifically genital, interaction to the formation and maintenance of intimate relationships. For many lesbians, "a relationship with another woman can provide a far richer and more supportive intimacy than that possible with most men." Nevertheless, we find repeatedly that "this aspect of our lives is reduced, in culture and in law, to sexual preference, as though the only advantages of a same-sex relationship were genital" (Becker 1995, 149).

This is not to deny that sex is a focal point of intimate relationships for many people of diverse sexual orientations. Yet for many others, sex may be or become less important, even unimportant, compared to other facets of their relationship. It is surely the case that no single standard of sexual activity exists that ensures the success of all intimate relationships; nor are intimacy and sexuality identical. Thus even to designate one's emotional/affectional choice(s) as a "sexual" orientation denies the existence of a vast variety of primary, intimate relationships in which sexual/genital contact plays a relatively minor role.

To make such an argument is not to accede, reassuringly, to what Mary Newcombe has called a "sex-phobic" culture that sex and sexuality are, after all, insignificant or that they are best repressed (1991, 9). Nor is it to desexualize lesbians or gay men and thus to deny difference yet again. It is, however, to question the classification of individuals based on whom they engage in genital contact with and to challenge the hierarchy of traits that places sexual acts at the core of a person's being and identity, as the key to an essential or immutable self. The "sexual orientation" model derives from a focus on sexual activity, narrowly defined as genital contact (with its attendant and apparently necessary goal of orgasm), as the defining moment in intimate relationships and the defining characteristic of classes of people. However, this is but one of many possible criteria for categorizing intimate relationships. Alternatively, such partnerships could be classified according to whether they are monogamous or nonmonogamous, respectful or abusive, loving or indifferent, egalitarian or unequal, or according to whether they provide opportunities for individual growth or foster mutual stagnation—all without reference to sexual orientation. Each of these classifications may provide a more relevant and useful means of categorizing intimate relationships than does a system of classification based solely on the gender of the two participants.

In contrast to this narrow view, lesbians themselves have offered a broad variety of definitions of lesbianism. The notion of a lesbian continuum proposed by Adrienne Rich (1986), alongside widely varying perspectives on who "is" and who "isn't" a lesbian, suggests a more complex and less stable phenomenon than can be captured by reference to a particular sexual behavior or set of behaviors, let alone encompassed by a military regulation. As more than one lesbian writer has observed, the terms of the patriarchy and the concepts provided by patriarchal thought offer miserably inadequate means to express ways of living and loving that lie outside patriarchal institutions and beyond heterosexist understandings, imagination, and language (Lorde 1984; Newcombe 1991; Robson 1990; Robson 1992; Vaid 1995). By inviting us to contemplate the difficulties of simple classification and to investigate the intricacies of human emotional expression, Zilly's and Cammermeyer's statements uncoupling homosexuality and sodomy extend the horizons within which gay and lesbian lives can be seen and understood.

There is nevertheless an undeniably negative aspect to these well-intended assertions. In a society or a military that is phobic about gay and lesbian sexuality, Zilly's and Cammermeyer's words offer reassurance that gays and lesbians are not doing anything that undermines patriarchal power or heterosexual masculine dominance. They suggest that gays and lesbians are not, in fact, doing much of anything at all. This suggestion reinforces the dominant ideology in at least two ways. First, it maintains the priority of heterosexual, vaginal intercourse as the natural, original, and perhaps only kind of sex worthy of the name, while removing any potential disruption or threat that the presence and pervasiveness of alternate sexual forms pose. Second, it deliberately separates status from conduct and protects status at the cost of our right to engage in various forms of conduct. Such a sacrifice, however vigorously demanded and valiantly offered, is ultimately both impractical and inhumane.

## THE GREAT DIVIDE: DISTINGUISHING
## STATUS AND CONDUCT

Defending homosexual identity on the grounds that it is private and therefore off-limits to the long arm of military law accomplishes for Cammermeyer's supporters precisely what arguing for private, protected identity achieved for Achtenberg's Senate proponents: it leaves the public domain, broadly defined, open to attack. Achtenberg's opponents seized on the public/private distinction to hold her to a highly limited voice and visibility. In a military context, the public/private distinction translates easily into a delineation between conduct and status. This division produces a legal decision in Cammermeyer's favor that nevertheless subjects her, and the gay and lesbian constituency she represents, to similarly rigid constraints. These restrictions exact silence as the cost of individual rights and invisibility as the price of "affirmation." Difference may be protected only if it remains entirely hidden—a difference that makes no difference, that cannot even be acknowledged as such. The dissociation of identity from conduct enforces gay and lesbian invisibility and silence both within the military and beyond.

This protection of homosexual status but not conduct quickly becomes "a prescription for closetry" (Altman 1982, 135), a reminder that victories may be partial and produce potentially harmful outcomes. Zilly's ruling permitted Cammermeyer to remain in uniform after identifying herself as a lesbian, undermining the blanket ban under which she was discharged. However, this decision granted Cammermeyer and other soldiers permission to speak only with the most extreme limitations: they must not indicate their status in any other manner, and their statements must refer to status alone. Although handing the military a legal defeat, by upholding the separation of status from conduct Zilly paved the way for continuing discrimination against gay and lesbian service members. His decision carries the premise of civil rights to its logical extreme. He allows gays and lesbians to identify themselves as such only if no further evidence comes to light to support their claim; only if all the evidence, in fact, denies it. This legal ruling and others like it thus mandate a kind of closed, circular discourse in which the words *gay* and *lesbian* no longer signify anything concrete. The cost of being able to say the words is the sacrifice of their meaning. Gay and lesbian self-identification must refer not to observable behaviors in the external world but only to an inner world that is not otherwise expressed or shared.

The argument for protecting status alone exhibits the same fundamental flaw in the military case that it did in the political arena. By defending a distinct and severely limited private realm, this approach abandons the struggle to claim a public voice and virtually invites restrictions on public behavior. Moreover, the very concept of a private realm is foreign to the unique situation of military employees, who are considered to represent their government and the military at all times and who may have to live under conditions entirely lacking in privacy. In such situations, their conduct is inherently "public" and subject to censure. Thus the military context provides an extreme example of the dangers of separating private from public identity: the public arena constantly encroaches on an ever-narrowing private realm, threatening to overtake it entirely. Virtually any activity can be construed as "nonprivate" and thereby subject to censure.

The status/conduct distinction is appealing because it appears to refute the equation of homosexuality with sodomy and the consequent indictment of homosexuality on legal and moral (often biblical) grounds. It dissociates the individual from the act. The military's circular reasoning goes as follows: (1) homosexuals, by definition, have a propensity to engage in "homosexual conduct"; (2) homosexuals are defined by their sexual activity; (3) the conduct of homosexuals is therefore inherently sexual; (4) all sexual acts gays and lesbians engage in, and only these acts, constitute sodomy (i.e., sodomy and homosexual sex are coterminous); (5) homosexual conduct is therefore equivalent to committing sodomy (6) engaging in homosexual conduct (sodomy) prevents one from being a good soldier.

The status/conduct distinction does not challenge the overall illogic of the formula. It simply circumvents, without confronting, the troublesome equation of sodomy with gay or lesbian identity. By equating status with sexual or emotional desire and conduct with any visible manifestation of this desire, this distinction disputes only claim 1. It suggests that homosexuals do not have a propensity to engage in homosexual conduct, that is, that desire need not manifest itself through word or deed. The military uses this split to police sexual activity and enforce a separate homosexual standard. It legitimizes continuing discrimination against gays and lesbians with the presumption that if one's sexual orientation becomes known, through any means, then the individual must be culpable for an act of "homosexual conduct." In this circular definition, public knowledge provides evidence of improper conduct, regardless of the means by which this knowledge was actually obtained.

Zilly's decision echoes the praise offered by Achtenberg's Senate supporters: Cammermeyer is rewarded for being "mainstream," for refraining from homosexual conduct despite her lesbian status. Cammermeyer's appeal is successful because she is one of the "good lesbians" who was never identified as engaging in any form of homosexual conduct, and whose status came to light only as a result of a direct question. Zilly's decision thus advances acceptance for only those who, like Cammermeyer, are successful in concealing their status. By refusing to dispute the condemnation of gays and lesbians who do engage in homosexual conduct of any sort, Zilly's judgment reinforces the view that there is something condemnable about them.[26]

Of course, given the military prohibition, individuals who commit sodomy are subject to reprimand and dismissal.[27] At issue, however, is a failure to distinguish between the broad meanings encompassed by the phrase "homosexual conduct" and the specific practice of sodomy. The equation of these terms reinforces a "'sex-as-lifestyle' assumption," the idea that gay and lesbian sexuality "is all-encompassing, obsessive, and completely divorced from love, long-term relationships, and family structure" (Fajer 1992, 514). By dissociating status from conduct broadly defined, rather than from sodomy in particular, gay men and lesbians are dissociated from all the other behaviors involved in the everyday living of our lives: participation in families, communities, friendships, and intimate relationships; the pursuit of an education and a career; involvement in political and social organizations; fulfilling a religious or spiritual dimension of our lives; and simply loving other human beings.

By refusing to enumerate the ways in which conduct is not sex, and by failing to defend the right of gay men and lesbians to make visible all aspects of our multifaceted lives, the status/conduct distinction implicitly denies the need for voice and visibility. Upholding this distinction permits the condemnation of "avowed" gays and lesbians as aberrant, unnatural, and immoral beings even while professing tolerance toward homosexual status. It suggests that there is something at best unacceptable or abnormal, at worst shameful or reproachful, about gay and lesbian love and sexual expression. It requires us to jettison claims that nonheterosexual love and nontraditional families are legitimate and healthy alternatives to heterosexual nuclear families and must be recognized as such. It obligates us to abandon efforts to affirm a multitude of family structures, for gays and lesbians and for others, and to cease attempts to educate people about these alternatives. It prohibits expression of the joy and pride that emerge from being gay or lesbian. Such affirmation may be especially crucial to convey to gay and lesbian youth, as well as to many others who are tentatively beginning to claim a gay or lesbian identity. Lacking this affirmation during the critical coming-of-age years or during the process of coming out as an adult can make life seem dreary and hopeless and the future void of love.

Reducing gay or lesbian identity to sex thoroughly distorts understandings of gay and lesbian lives. Just as the meaning of heterosexual love is not exhausted by reference to the sexual acts in which men and women engage, neither is the love of gay or lesbian partners encapsulated by reference to their sexual practices. The love between two men or two women is no more reducible to sex (sodomitic or otherwise) than is the love between a woman and a man. Lesbian and gay relationships can be as stable or unstable, long- or short-term, monogamous or nonmonogamous as the full range of heterosexual relationships. Like any other intimate relationships, they can be highly or not at all sexual, involving any, all, or none of the range of possible sexual acts. For many gay men and lesbians, as for many heterosexual men and women, sex is only one part of a loving relationship that includes many other facets of intimacy and connection.

Equating homosexuality with sodomy distorts public understanding of gays and lesbians by reducing an enormous range of possibilities for emotional and sexual intimacy to a particular sexual behavior that many gays and lesbians never even practice. The status/conduct distinction perpetuates this distortion by adopting a legal classification and attempting to apply it to the understanding of individuals in a manner far too simplistic to encompass the complexity and variety of human sexual identity and behavior (Vaid 1995). The construction of a relationship between status and conduct as either directly causal or entirely unrelated offers a miserably inadequate conception of sexual desire. Moreover, it fails to provide anything close to an exhaustive classificatory scheme for sexual practice. The adoption of patriarchal categories of law—a law established by and for men, supporting what Ruthann Robson labels the "rule of men" (1992)—is an inadequate and possibly dangerous means of trying to encompass the feelings, behaviors, and self-understandings of individuals who do not fit neatly within the law's expectations. We must therefore be vigilant in identifying the limits of a system that is "premised on normative assumptions about who people are, what they need, and how they should live their lives—assumptions developed primarily to support and maintain the patriarchy" (Newcombe 1991, 7). We must employ the utmost caution when using this system to represent ourselves, to ourselves or to others.

The separation of status from conduct enables the armed forces to protect outwardly the constitutional rights of gays and lesbians while nevertheless placing an absolute limit on their self-expression. Such a policy eludes the confines of the First Amendment by defining speech itself as conduct. This equation is still under debate in numerous legal challenges to the policy; it will likely be resolved only by a Supreme Court decision.[28] In regulating speech, the military effects yet another division: the separation of status from self-identification. It attempts to prohibit the latter, including all acts of self-definition, self-naming, and self-expression. What is left "protected," though only in a relative sense, is the ambiguous category of "status." This comes to mean less and less, until it seems to encompass precisely nothing, except what lies in the recesses of the human mind, so deep and so hidden that it is not identifiable even by the person whose thoughts it inhabits.

## THE PERILS OF PRIVACY

The argument that supports protecting "private" status while relinquishing the right to "public" conduct leaves intact another problematic binary that underlies military policy: the false opposition between openness and secrecy. The "Don't Ask, Don't Tell" policy portrays "telling" as a willful act, with secrecy, or "not telling," as the effortless default category. It presumes that asking the military to "not ask" and a soldier to "not tell" are comparable directives, accomplished by refraining from certain undesirable behaviors. Yet this assumption is misleading, for the silence demanded of gay and lesbian personnel is excessive, and maintaining this silence requires constant deception and lies (*Policy Hearings* 1993, 569). The premise underlying "don't tell" suggests that gays and lesbians are the only ones who "come out" and make others aware of their sexual orientation, while heterosexual orientation lacks this public facet because heterosexuals rarely make such declarations. Senator John McCain, for example, describes the "Don't Ask, Don't Tell" policy as establishing a situation in which "one's sexual preference was not asked; in that way, we tolerate all sexual preferences" (*Policy Hearings* 1993, 692).

Such a claim is grossly misrepresentative, because the default is not silence but acknowledgment; it is silence that requires an act of will. A presumption of heterosexuality operates in this culture such that individuals are assumed to be heterosexual unless they specifically refute that assumption. Thus heterosexuals can be "out" without a word, while gay and lesbian visibility requires a more concerted effort. Just as important, however, heterosexual men and women announce or "flaunt" their sexuality in countless ways every day. Sometimes these statements are verbal: a reference to a lover or spouse by name or gender, the use of gender-specific pronouns when referring to a sexual attraction, or a statement of affection made to one's lover or spouse in a public setting. Heterosexual women and men may openly discuss with others the activities they engage in with a lover or spouse, such as having and raising a child, buying a house, taking a vacation, visiting relatives, celebrating a birthday or holiday, or simply going out for the evening. They may indicate their sexual orientation through numerous nonverbal messages as well: adopting their spouse's last name or hyphenating it with their own, displaying their lover's or spouse's picture on their desk, wearing an engagement or wedding ring, or publicly displaying affection through touching, hand-holding, hugging, or kissing. This sharing of one's supposedly private life occurs many times every day, without a second thought, in the lives of heterosexuals. The command to hide one's sexuality thus forbids not only explicit statements of identity but also hundreds, if not thousands, of everyday forms of verbal and nonverbal expression. "Don't tell" in this way demands an all-encompassing silence about one's own life, a silence that can be maintained only by unwavering vigilance and ceaseless self-censorship.

This situation is exacerbated by the living conditions of active-duty military personnel, whose work may require them to live together twenty-four hours a day in very close quarters. In such an environment, there is literally no distinction between supposedly private space and shared, public space. Yet this incursion of public into ostensibly private space is not unique to the military context. In fact, the public/private split, which has its roots as far back as the Greek *polis*, hearkens to a societal structure that no longer exists.[29] Given rapid technological expansion, the number and magnitude of the private spaces that a right to privacy ostensibly protects are quickly dwindling, and such spaces may soon be difficult to find at all. At a minimum, the advent of the Information Age and the encroachment of technology into many of our everyday activities mean that it is no longer possible to manage and restrict the dissemination of information about ourselves. Despite our best efforts, such information invariably reaches sources beyond our knowledge or control.

The line between public and private space is being challenged by sophisticated technological advances in ways it has never been before. Already there is dissension about whether and how such spaces should be regulated. Electronic mail, the Internet, the World Wide Web, and other developments have created a new kind of space: "cyberspace." This shared space may be inhabited by an enormous number of people from all over the globe simultaneously, a concept that is already challenging the ways in which we think about the division of public and private.[30] These changes and others ensure that whatever boundaries remain between public and private realms will be increasingly fluid and elastic.

Moreover, while the potential for securing a protected, private space may be appealing, privacy arguments are just as easily used to silence gays and lesbians as to liberate us. The pliant boundaries between public and private allow opponents to define any expression of same-sex orientation to any other human being as a public act, no matter how private the setting might appear. This definition narrows the realm of private life to encompass only that which goes on inside an individual's head, so that all words and behaviors fall outside the realm of protected private expression. The structure of daily life and interactions, both in and out of the military, is such that there is little space for such secrets to be kept, even with great effort. There is very little information about an individual that cannot be accessed by a determined pursuer, and the more one tries to hide information, the stronger will be the resolve of others to discover it. For these reasons, the private realm referenced by the privacy argument, with its impermeable, clearly delineated boundaries, no longer exists, and it would be nearly impossible for anyone to re-create or sustain.

By examining the connotations of secrecy in our culture, we can begin to understand the real costs of Nunn's advice to gays and lesbians to keep their "private behavior private" (*Policy Hearings* 1993, 501). In American society, we are expected to share good news, to speak of accomplishments of which we are proud, to celebrate publicly our achievements or good fortune. We are also helped through sorrowful times—divorce, heartache, illness, death—by our ability to share our grief with others. Our life cycles are built around public rituals and ceremonies, bringing people together to recognize and rejoice in happy occasions and to commemorate sadness or loss. Advocating legal protection on the basis of privacy discounts the amount of public discourse that swirls around our so-called private lives. It ignores the ambiguity of the dividing line between these realms and the personal cost of attempting to keep secret the nature of one's home and family life, including one's intimate relationships, in a context where such information is usually shared.

If we lived in a culture where discussions of personal life, family relationships, and social life were widely prohibited or rarely present in the workplace or other public settings, it might be possible and even reasonable to maintain this degree of secrecy. But in American culture, where these elements of so-called private life are frequently, even constantly, discussed, the idea that a particular group of people can maintain silence in such discussions, and that such a silence will not in itself be read as incriminating evidence, is entirely implausible. Abstention itself can be implicit admission. "No comment" is itself a highly charged comment, and there are moments of silence that communicate far more than speech. Imposing the silence of privacy on one particular group and not another is unjust and unequal, a prescription for second-class citizenry. It is also impractical, as a pointed silence can be nearly as incriminating as a forthright declaration. The testimony of gay navy lieutenant Richard Dirk Selland illustrates vividly this phenomenon. When asked by the senators how others in his unit knew he was gay, he responded that there was "no conduct, no action . . . one lieutenant told me afterwards just simply the fact that on Friday nights, not hanging out with him and a few others, and not discussing women at the wardroom table, discussing my dates and so forth" (*Policy Hearings* 1993, 575).

Within this culture, then, secrecy is never neutral. The need for inordinate secretiveness or deception about one's personal life conveys, both to the circumspect individual and to others who perceive this caution, a sense of something wrong, the sign of a troubled life. We associate secrecy about our personal lives with shameful problems: alcoholism, child abuse, domestic violence, drug abuse, mental illness. We hide that which we judge disgraceful: our weaknesses, embarrassments, failings, the "skeletons in our closets"— those things of which we are ashamed. Our culture maintains an implicit equation between shame and secrecy, such that those things that cause us shame lead us to keep secrets while those things that we are forced to keep secret take on, by virtue of their hiddenness and our deception, an aura of shamefulness. Those things that are not shameful we need not keep secret. Only that which is stigmatized needs to be hidden from public view. The more shocking the characteristic or deed, the more secretive we must be, and the fewer people we are able to tell. Our most shameful sins are those we can confess to no one, those we cannot and do not tell.

To the extent that it clears the way for a policy such as "Don't Ask, Don't Tell," the privacy argument implies that gay or lesbian identity is, by its nature, offensive and disgraceful and best kept well hidden. Here, then, lies the heart of the problem of the right-to-privacy arguments that abound in lesbian and gay civil rights discourse generally and in the rhetoric of the military debate particularly. The separation of status from conduct both is premised upon and invites a defense of privacy and the attendant sacrifice of the right to voice or visibility. Right-to-privacy arguments are antithetical to the achievement of the right to speak or be seen. They argue for legal protection that extends only to what one does out of earshot and out of sight, both in relation to the law and in relation to others who might be likely to report one to the law. Such an approach to gay and lesbian rights reinforces shame and undermines self-respect, precluding the achievement of individual or collective pride and empowerment. At the same time, it bolsters the efforts of anti-gay forces to portray homosexuality as a sordid lifestyle and gays and lesbians as engaging in reproachable and scandalous behavior.

By arguing for gay and lesbian rights based on the right to privacy, advocates dispense with several of the most powerful and effective tools of social change we have at our disposal. The means of empowerment available to us are the same strategies that have been utilized in the struggles of other oppressed minorities: the freedom to assemble and to protest the denial of our rights through marches and other actions; the ability to lobby for political change and to pursue legal redress through the courts; and, crucially, the freedom to tell the stories of our lives by coming out. The freedom to speak openly about our lives influences directly those in our immediate environments, and indirectly a much broader community. If gay and lesbian oppression is characterized by invisibility and silence, arguing for rights based on privacy not only fails to undermine that oppression but actually codifies it into policy. While some civil rights can be won for individual gays and lesbians on the basis of a right to privacy, significant social change has never been accomplished while the group striving to bring about and reap the benefits of that change has remained hidden. If "coming out made gay liberation possible" (Cruikshank 1994, 9), then a return to the closet threatens to forestall further gains.

Awarding rights based on privacy represents a stringently limited concession to an oppressed minority group, and any victory on these grounds must be considered a highly qualified success. Perhaps nowhere are the tremendous constraints on gays and lesbians clearer than in General Norman Schwarzkopf's explanation of what it would mean to accept gays in the military under the provisions of the "Don't Ask, Don't Tell" policy. He states:

> If a person chooses to come into the military and does not practice a homosexual lifestyle, practices celibacy, does not try and announce openly that they are homosexual, does not choose to marry someone of the same sex and does not engage in homosexual acts, then for all intents and purposes they are not acting like a homosexual. And if they are serving their country honorably, I see no reason why they should not continue to do so. (*Policy Hearings* 1993, 618)[31]

Yet even this extensive list of restrictions does not exhaust the possible constraints. Despite attorney Gorelick's assertion that "something like marching in a gay rights parade, having known homosexual friends, making a speech, or reading books are not, in and of themselves, evidence or credible information of homosexual conduct," she adds, "Now, that is not to say that they cannot be considered among other pieces of information by the commander in making his or her assessment" in an investigation of homosexuality (*Policy Hearings* 1993, 806). These statements jointly support the assertion that despite a "compromise" that ostensibly allows gays and lesbians to serve, ultimately it remains the policy of the U.S. military that "as a general rule . . . homosexuality is incompatible with military service" (*Policy Hearings* 1993, 790).

The "don't tell" directive employs the fluid boundaries of an ever-shrinking private realm and an ever-growing domain of public life to obscure the questions it raises. The concept of "not telling" at first glance seems simple: it is a directive that prohibits statements acknowledging homosexuality. Yet the difficulties embedded here are innumerable, including the clarification of what constitutes a statement, what constitutes homosexuality, and what constitutes acknowledgment. Despite the military's goal of a policy characterized by the utmost clarity, each of these questions is far more contentious, and the answers far more ambiguous, than the policy's catchy nickname implies.

Insofar as the "don't tell" directive rests on the underlying right-to-privacy argument, it raises the myriad difficulties enumerated above. An exchange between Senator William Cohen and Gorelick illustrates how much is conceded in the privacy argument. When Cohen asks Gorelick whether the new policy is designed as a measure that allows gays to "engage in a homosexual act or activities, provided it is not disclosed or discovered," she replies, "No. The policy prohibits homosexual conduct." She then confirms Cohen's understanding that the measure of privacy is intended to "prevent the military from prying into the private life . . . but not to allow any activity on the part of that individual" (*Policy Hearings* 1993, 786).

The consequence, if not the purpose, of privacy arguments is to maintain, first, a clear line between self and Other and, second, the appearance of uniform heterosexuality and the absence of lesbians and gays, regardless of the fact that everyone knows they are present. "The military is far less concerned with having no homosexuals in the service than with having people think there are no homosexuals in the service" (Shilts 1993, 6).[32] The privacy argument concentrates on accommodating fearful and prejudiced heterosexuals who, pressured to extend civil rights to gays and lesbians in the military, do so only under the condition that they need not see, hear, or in any way confront this issue or this group of people. Such accommodation perpetuates compulsory heterosexuality and its attendant privilege while ensuring the continued erasure of gay and lesbian existence. It neither challenges stereotypes nor encourages heterosexuals to change their attitudes or actions. On the contrary, it affirms the acceptability of their present behavior, resolutely reinscribing the military status quo.

## CONCLUSION: "OUTING" HOMOPHOBIA IN MILITARY POLICY

One of the most evident implications of the Cammermeyer case and the military ban generally is that the prejudices of heterosexuals, rather than the actual requirements of national security, govern military policy. This is a key point argued by Cammermeyer's lawyers, as well as by other opponents of the ban. In written testimony submitted to the Senate, a group of legal scholars argues that the ban is unconstitutional based on precedents in which "the U.S. Supreme Court has ruled that the government cannot discriminate against an unpopular group based solely on the hostility of others toward that group" (*Policy Hearings* 1993, 838). More specifically, they note, "Even if the government could show that the hatred of others might cause some disruption in military efficiency, it would still not be legitimate for the government to discriminate against lesbians, gay men and bisexuals to minimize the disruption" (*Policy Hearings* 1993, 857).

The words of military leaders themselves attest to the attitudes of some heterosexual soldiers (in addition to their own negative attitudes) that lie at the heart of the ban. In his testimony to the Senate committee, Captain James Pledger admits, "I do not think there is any physical or mental or any other difference in [homosexual] capabilities compared with the heterosexual. But . . . it is the attitudes of the majority of the heterosexuals and their reactions to this type of behavior or orientation which begets behavior. Once it becomes known, it creates the problem that we would face" (*Policy Hearings* 1993, 557). Both the "behavior" and the "problem" here refer not to the conduct of gays and lesbians but to the reactions of heterosexuals to the knowledge of gay and lesbian soldiers.

Despite the relatively open acknowledgment of homophobia as the basis for the military's exclusionary policy, military leaders design creative, if at times absurd, rationales that blame gay and lesbian service members for the reactions of their peers. In his testimony to the Senate committee, Commander Lin Hutton calls it "a real tragedy" when good soldiers come out. He states, "What those individuals have done is betrayed a trust, and they have betrayed that level of respect that their peers had for them by acknowledging their sexual orientation. . . . They have broken the bond with the rest of the group. And the rest of the group will just not trust them and they will not respect them" (*Policy Hearings* 1993, 557).

Similarly, Captain Gordon Holder identifies the prejudices of heterosexuals as responses that are intentionally evoked by gays and lesbians, a line of argument that bears a striking similarity to the "logic" that blames women who are battered or raped for "provoking" male attacks. Holder asserts, "In the case of a homosexual person who suddenly declares themself [*sic*] homosexual, I would ask what is the motive. . . . Is it possible that you are seeking a power move here to gain an advantage or to cause a divisiveness in the cohesion that we have worked very hard and that we need in order to effectively do our jobs?" (*Policy Hearings* 1993, 557). In light of the baldness of such statements in revealing the underpinnings of the military ban, Barry Adam asks rhetorically: "Can one avoid the conclusion then that the gays in the military question is not about gays in the military but about the dynamics and practices of the heterosexist mind?" (1994, 107).

The answer is readily supplied by the testimony of General Otjen. In his deposition for the Cammermeyer case, the general "candidly admitted" to have used terms of ridicule, such as *fag, fairy, queer,* and *dyke,* to refer to gays and lesbians. Even more to the point, as summarized in a legal brief submitted on behalf of Cammermeyer, the general "further candidly admitted that heterosexual servicemembers' fear of and prejudice against homosexuals forms the basis for heterosexuals' claimed unwillingness to serve with homosexuals, testifying that if there were no such prejudice there would be no basis for the military's concerns" (Plaintiff's Memo 1994, 15).

The recognition that heterosexual prejudice lies at the heart of the military ban is of great legal significance, because the motive of satisfying majority prejudice fails to fulfill the rational basis requirement. "A cardinal principle of equal protection law is that the federal government cannot discriminate against a class in order to give effect to the prejudice of others" (*Cammermeyer v. Aspin* 1994, 55). Despite the considerable latitude granted to the military by the civil courts in deference to its uniqueness as an institution (Robson 1992), the military is expressly forbidden to deny the constitutional rights of its members: "There is not and must never be a 'military exception' to the Constitution" (*Cammermeyer v. Aspin* 1994, 15). Thus, if the military's various rationales boil down to a sanctioning of heterosexual prejudice against an unpopular group, its ban cannot be legally upheld. "Mere negative attitudes, or fear, are constitutionally impermissible bases for discriminatory government policies" (*Cammermeyer v. Aspin* 1994, 52). There is no justification for the ban that can withstand such a challenge.

It is on this basis that legal scholar Janet Halley argues that "the key to winning such [gay rights] cases is shifting the debate away from same-sex intercourse to antigay discrimination" (in Bull 1994, 30). By continuing to focus on "gays in the military" as opposed to *prejudice against* lesbians and gays in the military, we locate the source of the problem in gay and lesbian service members rather than in the attitudes of homophobic military leaders and service members. As long as lesbians and gays are identified as the problem, they will likewise be the focus of the solution. The solutions implemented thus far have resulted in their removal or marginalization. Similarly, the military's emphasis on homosexual sodomy alerts us only to the prohibited behavior of this group and makes it appear that the behavior is specific to them. It diverts our attention from the practice of sodomy by other populations, even if this practice is more prevalent among these other groups.

As long as we fail to undermine the discourse that frames the situation in terms of a "gay problem," we leave unchallenged the underlying "homophobia problem" that truly needs resolution. Just as we ought not punish women for the pervasiveness of sexist behavior or blame people of color for the persistence of racism, we can find no acceptable rationale for eliminating gays and lesbians from military service, no matter what the sentiment against them. We need look no further than recent history to find examples of the magnitude of tragedy and injustice that ensue when an argument for "national security" is employed to give credence to national hatred and fear. Nazi concentration camps and World War II internment camps for Japanese Americans were "justified" under precisely such a rationale.

As this chapter illustrates, the assignment of group identity on the basis of a particular sexual behavior is not only controversial but inaccurate. The subsequent exclusion of members of that classification from the rights of citizenship is patently unconstitutional. Legal challenges to the ban will benefit from a mindfulness that "the equal protection clause requires courts to scrutinize not classes but acts of classification—not preexisting, given biological groupings of human persons but governmental determinations that certain persons shall belong and others shall not belong to a special favored or disfavored group" (Halley 1991, 356). More generally, a broad range of lesbian and gay rights initiatives would benefit from this same mindful focus. Arguments for gay and lesbian rights would be well served by expending less energy on establishing claims about the immutability of sexual orientation and directing greater effort toward challenging heterosexist biases and homophobic fears. In doing so, we open up the categories through which others see us and broaden the horizons within which we are able to view ourselves.

# ⊮ 4 ⊰

## CONCLUSION

### Envisioning Our Future

You can't live in a post-revolutionary fashion in pre-revolutionary
times.                              —Rita Mae Brown (in Ponse 1978, 188)

A button marketed recently at gay and lesbian events declares, "If we give
gays and lesbians civil rights, everyone will want them." In fact, it is difficult
to identify any other group of American citizens who are currently less protected under the U.S. Constitution than are gays and lesbians. "There is
nothing in current constitutional doctrine that prevents those otherwise
bound by the Constitution (public or state entities) from discriminating on
the basis of lesbianism" (Robson 1990, 39). Despite the substantial progress
achieved by lesbians and gays over the past thirty years, there remains no
legal protection for homosexuals as a group. Instead of moving toward eliminating discrimination, the pendulum sometimes seems to be swinging in
the opposite direction.

The backlash against gay and lesbian rights forces the movement, along
with individual gays and lesbians, to reassess our goals, strategies, and vision
for the future. Lesbian and gay rights advances have prompted a forceful re-
action from a well-organized and well-funded radical right, whose resources
increase in direct proportion to its constituents' fears. As anti-gay forces
grow increasingly hostile, the gay and lesbian movement's response will lie
somewhere on a continuum that runs from affirmations of difference to as-
surances of sameness. At one end of this spectrum, the assertion of difference correlates with an insistence on greater political voice and cultural vis-

139

ibility for the group and all its members. It demands not only rights, though certainly rights are central, but also liberation. At the other end lies the effort to assimilate, a kind of political and cultural "laying low." This approach takes a road less contested, in the hope of gaining legal protections even at the sacrifice of more fundamental social change.

In recent years, influential segments of the gay and lesbian movement have committed themselves to the latter end of the spectrum, concentrating on legal challenges and political access. Activist and writer Urvashi Vaid distinguishes between a politics focused on rights, which she terms a strategy of "legitimation," and one whose goal is liberation:

> Gay and lesbian legitimation seeks straight tolerance and acceptance of gay people; gay and lesbian liberation seeks nothing less than affirmation, represented in the acknowledgment that queer sexuality is morally equivalent to straight sexuality. Legitimation seeks to change hearts and minds by educating the general public to understand that gay and lesbian people are human beings. Liberation seeks that same shift in consciousness, but it also looks for a transformation in social institutions—in government, family, religion, and the economy. (1995, 37)

Despite the limitations of legal action in effecting social change, "rights-focused strategies continue to be adopted by groups seeking reform. . . . Legal guarantees are secured as symbolic victories and as the initial step for powerless groups seeking improved social status" (Bumiller 1988, 51).

For many of us who have suffered oppression or discrimination in any form, it is easy to understand the attraction of rights-based approaches. Civil rights initiatives have an immediate, concrete appeal. They promise to secure the basic constitutional rights that lesbians and gay men have previously lived without: freedom from discrimination in areas such as housing, employment, child custody, military service, legal marriage, and spousal benefits. For individuals who live in a country that ostensibly provides these protections to all of its citizens, yet in practice denies them to particular groups, the simple granting of such rights often seems like the ultimate luxury: all we can hope for and, at the same time, too much to hope for. We continue to fight for the privileges others take for granted. These include, but are not limited to, medical and other insurance coverage for our partners and families, rights of hospital visitation, the ability to adopt children as a couple, and the recognition of a family relationship in issues of guardianship and inheritance. For gay and lesbian couples, the possibility of having our relationships legally recognized and afforded all the benefits granted to heterosexual couples is, as yet, only a dream.

Because even these most basic rights are often denied, it is difficult to look beyond the desire for such fundamental securities to pursue a broader vision. Yet this is precisely what we must do. While civil rights initiatives are a necessary part of this social movement, an element of our struggle that need not and should not be abandoned, they represent only one, partial approach to gaining freedom. In prioritizing civil rights strategies over other tactics, we risk abandoning necessary demands for change in favor of assimilation and token concessions. Vaid terms the contemporary situation of gays and lesbians, brought about by the movement's emphasis on civil rights, "virtual equality," which she describes as a condition that "simulates genuine civic equality but cannot transcend the simulation" (1995, 4).

The cases of Roberta Achtenberg and Grethe Cammermeyer provide unusually vivid illustrations of how civil rights initiatives can simultaneously advance and constrain the movement for gay and lesbian liberation. In both of these cases, a civil rights approach is the necessary avenue of response, because both women are fighting to advance within traditional institutions, seeking access to the rights and privileges these institutions grant to heterosexuals. Achtenberg, a politician, and Cammermeyer, a soldier, are not pursuing what we generally think of as "radical" change, or change that goes to the roots of the system. They are, in fact, wholly committed to the mainstream institutions they serve. They seek to better, rather than to undermine, these institutions through the eradication of discriminatory policies. So dedicated are they to the ultimate good of the institutions that they are willing to risk personal vulnerability and professional ruin, offering up their own futures as sacrifices to what they perceive as a greater good.

The juxtaposition of these two case studies illuminates the larger dynamics of gay and lesbian oppression that persist even in the presence of liberal perspectives. One of the clearest threads that runs through the discourse of both cases is the implicit and explicit insistence on "not telling" as a condition of liberal tolerance. For Grethe Cammermeyer, the act of telling was quite literal, as her single statement of identity represented the entirety of her misconduct. For Roberta Achtenberg, her introduction of her "beloved partner" provided the gateway to criticism of the countless ways she had "told." She had told through her professional activism (working as a lawyer for lesbian causes), her political activism (appearing at the San Francisco Gay and Lesbian Pride parade), and her personal life (choosing a woman as her life partner and deciding to have a child with her).

The distinction made in the rhetoric directed against Achtenberg—that she is not just a lesbian but a lesbian *activist*—parallels the distinction drawn in the military compromise between being a homosexual and being an *avowed* or admitted homosexual. The key in both instances is the insistence on silence and invisibility as the conditions of tolerance. When shame and societal condemnation can no longer be counted on to silence gays and lesbians—an internalized "don't tell" that was highly effective historically—other tools of oppression appear to reinforce invisibility and silence. One such tool has been a rhetoric that offers tolerance at a high price: continued "discretion." Such discretion translates into hiddenness and constant self-censorship, into keeping the "private" lives of gays and lesbians removed from view. The demand for this kind of trade-off in both of the cases examined here alerts us to the limits of pursuing legal solutions to oppression, warning us of the dangers we court by putting too much faith in such solutions. It should remind us, as well, of the need to develop a long-term vision that exceeds the horizons of civil rights gains alone.

## The Limits of Legal Strategies

Ruthann Robson, a lesbian attorney and legal scholar, reminds us that "the law is a limited remedy for our marginalization" (1990, 45). As this analysis shows, relying on legal discourse raises a number of concerns for the pursuit of gay and lesbian liberation. Participation in the legal system entails the adoption of legal categories and concepts, despite the fact that legal ideologies are often too narrow to describe or encompass gay and lesbian lives. The legal system classifies groups through a myopic focus on a single shared characteristic, emphasizing commonality at the expense of difference. The process through which such classification is accomplished has a number of consequences, few of which are beneficial to gay and lesbian advancement in the long term.

The legal arguments that emerge from a guiding civil rights agenda seek to protect gays and lesbians by fortifying the boundaries that divide human beings into distinct, inflexible classifications based on sexual orientation. Through their characteristic double gesture, such approaches champion equality by simultaneously highlighting the existence of a distinct group of "homosexuals" and veiling this group behind the cloak of "privacy," invisibility, and silence. The act of classification these initiatives undertake thereby reinforces a dominant belief system that wants to separate, clearly and finally, an identifiable group of insiders from an equally unambiguous group of "Others." The uncertainty and uneasiness that characterize American attitudes toward sexuality heighten and make more urgent this impulse to split "us" from "them." The fluidity of sexual categories and the instability of their membership, the impossibility of identifying "outsiders" with certainty, and the general anxiety around sex and sexuality in this culture all contribute to the firm resolve of dominant institutions to keep difference clearly in focus, and to keep those bearing the mark of difference at bay. Civil rights arguments strengthen distinctions between categories of "heterosexual" and "homosexual," in legal cases and public discourse, in the name of equality.

Classifying human beings into convenient legal categories has a number of troublesome consequences. To begin with, these categories fail to acknowledge either the differences between lesbians and gay men or the diversity within these groups. Yet these differences are as important as, and often more important than, the commonalities among those with a shared sexual orientation. In Chapter 1, I outlined the historical obscuring of lesbian specificity under the generalized terms *homosexual* or *gay*. This error of merging the category of "lesbians" into that of "gay men" is committed not only by opponents but also by the lesbian and gay rights movement itself, when it mistakes solidarity for sameness.

Where opponents and supporters fail to draw distinctions between gay men and lesbians, it is difficult to locate particular constructions of "the lesbian" or representations of lesbianism. This trouble itself reveals how civil rights initiatives produce a discourse that ignores the particularity of lesbian oppression, that is, the oppression of roughly half its constituents. A vast distance separates the work of the lesbian feminist theorists cited in Chapter 1 from the approaches of powerful segments of the gay and lesbian rights movement that emphasize civil rights strategies leading to assimilation. Too often in these portions of the movement, lesbians are viewed primarily as "gay women" or even "female gays," with no attempt to understand how the two components of these terms might interact. An infusion of lesbian feminist perspectives would enhance the sophistication and precision of a civil rights discourse that claims to represent both gay men *and* lesbians.

New approaches are also needed to address the issue of diversity *among* lesbians, which is largely overlooked by civil rights approaches. Differences of race, age, ethnicity, religion, class, physical ability, and other social distinctions may play a key role in the formation of sexual identities, sexual politics, and even sexual practice. As a result, notable differences exist among lesbians, and the same is true for gay men (Clarke 1983). Therefore, it may make little sense to ask or answer questions about the origins, identity, or conduct that characterizes "homosexuality." The false assumption is that one answer could apply to all those who label themselves or are labeled "gay" or "lesbian." As in the case of heterosexuals, such questions will inevitably have a multitude of answers, perhaps as many answers as there are gays and lesbians. Accounting for such differences requires conceptualizing a plurality of homosexualit*ies*—rather than a single, uniform homosexualit*y*—along with a multiplicity of heterosexualities (Epstein 1987; Phelan 1994).

By adopting legal and other categories to name ourselves, we also obscure the multiple differences *within* individuals that the systems themselves cannot accommodate. Classifications such as "gay" and "lesbian" claim to represent complex individuals by extracting one particular aspect of our behavior or identity, while blatantly ignoring all the rest. For some individuals, this single element might seem, subjectively, to be a dominant or even the dominant aspect of their experience or identity. For others, it will seem less important or even completely unimportant. In all cases, sexual orientation is misrepresented when it is discussed as though it exists in isolation; it is always intertwined with race, class, gender, age, religion, and numerous other variables (Herman 1994).

This reduction of complexity to a single category is not accidental. It is precisely the function of the law to achieve this oversimplification. "The representation in law does not reflect any 'whole' conception of the person. When individuals come before a court, they do not present themselves as they would in everyday life; instead, they come before the court in one of their roles." Within the framework of the legal system, "victims of discrimination struggle against their exclusion, not by asserting what they believe to be their true self-image, but by aspiring to the idealized victimization acknowledged within the law" (Bumiller 1988, 61–62). In this way, legal categories necessarily obscure the self-identities of legal supplicants, replacing them with identity categories that a patriarchal, heterosexist legal establishment imposes.

Instead of offering a mode of empowerment, a legal discourse that imposes the role of the victim may reinforce a lack of control that gays and lesbians already feel in so many aspects of our lives, reinscribing our status as powerless outsiders (Bumiller 1988). Such a discourse inaccurately portrays the position of gays and lesbians in relation to structures of power, denying the abundant and incontrovertible evidence that lesbians and gays are already present within all mainstream institutions at all levels, though often hidden. It promotes a view of lesbians and gays as a preexisting, identifiable class of outsiders rather than a group constituted through processes of exclusion and discrimination. Within this framework, heterosexuality remains the invisible and unchallenged norm, while the focus remains on the gay and lesbian "victims" who must appeal for the granting of our rights. In refusing to question the supposed "naturalness" of heterosexuality, this strategy fails to expose the unstable and provisional nature of sexual categories, underscoring instead the distinction between "us" and "them."

This failure is a crucial one because "there is a profound need to address the social construction of all sexualities and, in particular, heterosexuality. If we are to really assault the notion of the naturalness of sexuality, it is the 'unnaturalness' of heterosexuality that needs asserting and not the 'naturalness' of homosexuality" (Edwards 1994, 157). This rethinking of heterosexuality holds great promise yet has barely begun to be undertaken. We must begin to ask "questions [that] usefully shift the focus from lesbian identity to heterosexist social institutions," for "this shift has the signal virtue of avoiding the constructions of lesbianism that trap us" (Phelan 1993, 771). The language of the law and the structure of legal institutions are unable to bring about this shift of focus. The social construction of all sexual identities is ignored by privacy arguments and claims of immutability, so that these strategies offer at best limited solutions to the problems confronting gays and lesbians.

Our faith in legal avenues of change must also be tempered by an awareness of the substantial difference between the awarding of rights per se and the distribution of actual benefits (Herman 1994). While a growing number of institutions have added sexual orientation to their anti-discrimination statements, these same institutions have been much less willing to support this stated equality with material benefits. Few of these organizations formally recognize domestic partnerships, and many continue to deny to partners of gay or lesbian employees the health insurance and other benefits routinely granted to the spouses of heterosexual employees. This inequity is further magnified in the case of the federal government. According to the government's General Accounting Office, there are 1,049 federal statutes that confer rights, benefits, and privileges on individuals who have the legal right to marry—benefits that are denied across the board to gays and lesbians (Advocate Report 1997, 17).

Another limitation of legal approaches is that in court cases involving lesbian and gay rights, victories may impact primarily on those involved in the current or in subsequent legal action. Losses, in contrast, may have widespread impact even on those not involved in legal action. The denial of rights gives license to homophobia culture-wide. It legitimizes forms of discrimination that range from the relatively passive (e.g., the refusal of housing) to the violently aggressive. In contrast, the granting of rights, while certainly a cause for celebration, does not necessarily hold the promise of widespread dissemination. This is the case because when rights are granted to a specific plaintiff, it does not mean they will be available to all gays and lesbians. It means only that other gays and lesbians who are denied rights and wish to (and have the means to) pursue legal action may have a precedent on which to draw.

Moreover, many lesbians and gay men will be unable or unwilling to pursue legal action even if laws are enacted to protect them. Legal battles are prohibitively time-consuming and expensive, with costs that are psychological as well as financial. Fighting discrimination on the basis of sexual orientation necessitates coming out as a gay man or lesbian not only to family and friends but also to one's community and, in cases of widespread media attention, to the entire nation. As a result, gays and lesbians "may be too intimidated by virulent homophobia even to make use of their rights under such [anti-discrimination] laws since it would require coming out to do so" (Nava and Dawidoff 1994, 208–9). The risks involved in coming out are such that even if the legal battle can be won, the personal cost may ultimately be too high.

While noting the limitations of our successes, however, we must also recognize our potential for turning losses into triumphs. Community activism spurred by injustice can transform an apparent defeat into merely a temporary setback. Short-term losses can energize our movement, yielding unanticipated gains in the long run. In one example, an anti-gay resolution passed in 1993 by the commissioners of Cobb County, Georgia, declared that the "gay lifestyle" was "incompatible with the standards to which this community subscribes." As a result of the resolution, anti-discrimination activists joined together in that county for the first time, forming the Cobb Citizens Coalition. The group worked to rescind the resolution and attracted a great deal of national support for its efforts. It also sought to effect positive change in the community through educational and other outreach efforts. Both supporters and opponents of the resolution now agree that the resolution served as a springboard for anti-discrimination organization and activism that would not otherwise have occurred (Manuel 1997, F5).

In another case of turning defeat into victory, in 1992, Colorado voters passed an anti-gay initiative known as Amendment 2. The amendment banned all state and local laws protecting gays and lesbians from discrimination. Although this vote represented a clear and painful loss for gays and lesbians, it launched a flurry of gay and lesbian activism both in Colorado and across the country, attracting the support of many straight allies as well. A national boycott of Colorado tourism was organized, costing the state an estimated $40 million in convention business and drawing even greater national attention to and support for gay and lesbian rights. An appeal prevented the law's enforcement while the Supreme Court debated its constitutionality. Finally, in what has been called "the most significant legal victory ever for gays and lesbians in the United States," in May 1996 the Supreme Court declared Amendment 2 unconstitutional ("Civil Rights or Special Rights?" 1996).

Such complexities highlight the ways in which legal change and social change are distinct yet interrelated. Achieving either one without the other is insufficient for shedding our second-class status (Vaid 1995).[1] We must refuse, finally, to sacrifice advances in one area in order to make gains in the other. "We must enter the arena of public discourse without vanishing. Strategies of simple assimilation are unacceptable" (Phelan 1993, 779). Using the legal system as an instrument of equality demonstrates participation and belief in the authority of dominant institutions. It thereby reinforces the key role of the system in regulating the social order, inevitably strengthening the system itself (Smart 1989).[2] Moreover, it works toward the assimilation of an outside group whose identity is reshaped and rearticulated through the terms and concepts of that dominant institution. Although the law can bring about important changes, then, it cannot be a panacea for the problems of exclusion and oppression that gays and lesbians suffer. It can right only the wrongs that law itself creates or perpetuates (Bumiller 1988). Thus we see the continued existence of racism decades after the legal implementation of civil rights; thus widespread prejudice remains against groups based on gender, religion, national origin, and physical disability years after such groups were granted legal protections.

Disagreement persists between those gays and lesbians who believe "the real challenge is to change attitudes, not laws," and those who identify legal changes as "the first step toward changing hearts and minds" (Shapiro, Cook, and Krackov 1993, 48). Legal battles can positively influence social attitudes and behaviors. Those who proceed from a legal viewpoint thus argue that "*progressive* law reform signals to bigots, and to those who would discriminate, that such attitudes and behaviours are no longer acceptable" (Herman 1994, 4). However, the law has a limited range of influence, so that "even where there are few legal impediments to homosexuality, social mores may still constitute a very powerful force for intolerance" (Mendus 1989, 4). As a result, "even after law reform and antidiscrimination ordinances, a whole fabric of discrimination remains" (Altman 1982, 25).

Neither legal nor attitudinal change alone is sufficient to achieve liberation. If rights are granted but individuals are unable to exercise them because they fear violence or ostracism, then such rights are of little use. Conversely, if social attitudes change but rights are not granted, the situation will at best simply commodify gays and lesbians. In viewing us as "trendy" without offering any more deeply rooted or lasting guarantee of rights, such a context would neither reduce the prevalence of anti-gay violence nor combat other forms of discrimination. At worst, it could create a situation similar to that which Clinton produced when he promised to lift the military ban. Some gay and lesbian service members were lulled by his words into thinking it was safe to come out, and then were punished for having done so. For all these reasons, "the gay movement must be concerned not just with specific legal and electoral battles, but also with the far broader and more amorphous ways in which homophobia is maintained through a complex structure of institutions, values, and often unconscious prejudices" (Altman 1982, 130–31).

In evaluating the extent and the limits of legal change, we are reminded as well of the geographical boundaries that circumscribe our legal initiatives. Although the lesbian and gay rights movement in the United States has focused almost exclusively on the concerns of American gays and lesbians, the arguments we make within our national borders will inevitably impact on lesbians and gays internationally as well. It is especially crucial to keep this global perspective in mind when making arguments about the nature and origins of homosexuality. In particular, arguments that support a biological basis for homosexuality may help protect gays and lesbians in the U.S. based on this country's equal protection laws. However, while these claims will undoubtedly influence perceptions and treatment of lesbians and gays in other countries, any legal protections we gain through such contentions will end at our national borders (Schüklenk and Ristow 1996). It takes only a cursory knowledge of history to envision the actions that some countries might take against those who are perceived to have an inherent, genetic deficiency that makes them inferior beings. Thus claims about the biological basis of homosexuality may endanger gays and lesbians in other countries even as they extend the rights of American gays and lesbians.

A final danger of employing legal categories is the risk of confusing the terms and concepts that are legally or politically expedient with the terms and concepts that provide a fuller picture of gay and lesbian life. "Because the dominant culture is infiltrated by legal concepts, we also use legalism as part of our common sense. . . . We use legal concepts without thinking" (Robson 1992, 19). The danger in adopting these terms as our own is that we are enticed into "substitut[ing] legal categories and concepts for our lesbian ones" (Robson 1992, 17–18). When these vital distinctions are lost, we easily become constrained by our use of dominant categories in our own self-explanations. Indeed, even with vigilance some such effect is inevitable, for "dominant frameworks of meaning cannot be harnessed by social movements without those frameworks in turn shaping and reconstituting actors and communities" (Herman 1994, 6). Despite the possibilities that may lie in the legal system and other existing institutions, these institutions are unlikely to provide us with useful or enlightening means of understanding ourselves. We must recognize the limitations of these frameworks for naming ourselves, defining our experiences, and representing our lives.

## RESISTING THE MAINSTREAM

The cases investigated in this book reveal how arguments for privacy uphold the second-class status of gays and lesbians. The insistence on keeping lesbian and gay expression and affection hidden can produce only inequality, unless we implement a policy that enforces on everyone's personal life equal "closetedness." There would be little joy in such a repressive society. It would have to prevent any displays—symbolic, verbal, or nonverbal—of personal feelings or affection in any public forum: workplaces, airports, restaurants, movie theaters, sidewalks, even front porches or yards. It would effectively impose on everyone the kinds of constraints under which most lesbians and gays live now, an idea that evokes the climate of George Orwell's *1984*.

It is unlikely that anyone, of any sexual orientation, would advocate such restrictions if they were uniformly applied. An alternate and infinitely more reasonable solution would be to allow all individuals to make the kinds of statements and display the forms of affection that are today considered permissible and appropriate only for heterosexuals. I am not suggesting that we permit or encourage sexual displays that would now be considered lewd or indecent if heterosexuals performed them publicly. I am proposing that we permit or censor *equally* all displays of affection and statements of sexual identity by anyone, regardless of sexual orientation.

The privileges granted to heterosexual individuals and couples must either be revoked or distributed fairly to all. This is but one element of a larger strategy to dismantle compulsory heterosexuality in all its many forms (Rich 1986). It is unlikely, and possibly undesirable, that we could entirely do away with the institutions that create the social fabric—those of romantic partnership and family, structures of community, and systems of law and education, to name just a few. Instead of trying to envision a world without these, we might instead imagine ways to redefine these institutions in fundamental ways. In some cases, the problem lies primarily in recognizing and legitimizing new forms that are already taking shape—a question of ideology lagging behind practice. The title of Kath Weston's *Families We Choose* (1991), for example, coins a phrase that accurately describes the formation of many families today, and not only gay and lesbian families (see Collins 1991). The concept of domestic partnership, while theoretically based on the model of heterosexual marriage and often employed this way in civil rights arguments, represents in practice a tremendous range of committed relationships that patriarchal ideology does not account for. Some of these relationships between gay men or lesbians may look very much like the heterosexual model. Others resemble it very little or not at all. It is equally important to note that many of today's heterosexual relationships bear little resemblance to this alleged "norm."

If our goal is not simply to reproduce the structure of the nuclear family in our own communities, neither is it to replace one privileged family form with another. The term *family*, like the concept of a committed partnership between two adults, needs to be understood in much more varied and multifaceted ways than it has been in the past. The fact that there is no term that most gays and lesbians find appropriate to express the nature of their intimate relationships suggests that the recognition of these relationships has the potential to transform available understandings of relationships more broadly, for all kinds of people.[3] Nonetheless, we surrender the transformative potential inherent in these other ways of living and loving when we trade pride in ourselves and our own ways of being for provisional tolerance from the mainstream.

It is the cost of this limited acceptance, as the cases of Achtenberg and Cammermeyer illustrate, that we must keep in the forefront of our consciousness. If we do not, it will exact its price from us unaware. The very language of the military ban, its label as a "compromise," alerts us to its failings. Constitutional rights are not available for negotiation or compromise. They can be neither partial nor conditional, for when compromised, they no longer represent the full freedoms guaranteed to all of us. We must therefore always be dissatisfied with acceptance at the price of assimilation, or with any partial granting of institutional access that demands the sacrifice of other basic rights. This is not to say there will not be compromises and half steps along the way or that we should reject all but total liberation. Undoubtedly, change will occur only incrementally. The notion of a total Marxist-style revolution neither is realistic nor, possibly, is it even in our best interest. But we must not be misled into believing that provisional tolerance is authentic acceptance or that the denial of difference makes difference disappear.

As much as we might wish it were otherwise, assimilation offers no protection against the most terrible manifestations of prejudice and discrimination—a lesson we take from the assimilated Jews in Nazi Germany. We can be "model" citizens, hide or deny our difference, and silence ourselves. Still, the stereotypes that incite hatred and violence against us will persist and resurface at the moment we ask for too much or seem to have acquired too much power or privilege. The myth, and consequent danger, of a civil rights approach is the belief that if we ask "nicely" enough, show that we can "behave" well enough, and demonstrate obedience within the framework of compulsory heterosexuality, then we will be accepted as "normal" people who simply have unusual bed partners. The potential for even such provisional acceptance can be tempting. For those of us forced to live with rejection, "the notion that homosexuality has been mainstreamed is an illusion we yearn to believe because we are so tired of being vilified, loathed, and marginalized. We want to be accepted and loved" (Vaid 1995, 5).

Nevertheless, this is a temptation to be resisted. We must resist it not only because of the psychic damage involved in hiding our loves, restricting our lives, and silencing our voices; we must also reject it for more pragmatic reasons. Despite its apparent promise, this assimilationist approach will not make us safe. Disappearance does not erase difference, nor does it substantially alter its consequences. Try as we might to "blend in" and be like "everyone else," even those of us who can succeed are never assured of safety. As long as our difference can be targeted, discovered, and punished, we will not be safe. Just as important, the apparent blending in of some of us only accentuates the difference of others who cannot or choose not to blend in. We abandon this group when we make assimilation our aim (Vaid 1995).

Those of us who most closely resemble the mainstream seemingly have the most to gain from assimilation, but we are also at the greatest risk for developing a false sense of security. Assimilation entices us to sacrifice our own brilliantly different "colors" in exchange for the perceived safety of main-stream acceptance. However, our fragmentation and self-denial are too high a price to pay for such conditional and tenuous "acceptance." Our best efforts to "blend in" must always remain illusory and fleeting. At any time, we may be plucked out of the complacency of perceived assimilation by those whose perspective on difference sees not complex human beings but only isolated elements of identity. When these elements are perceived as fearful and threat-ening, they are despised and therefore targeted for destruction.

## THE POWER OF OPENNESS AND THE PROTECTION OF SPEECH

Another issue this book raises is the need to protect lesbian and gay self-ex-pression. Visibility and voice are often sacrificed in civil rights strategies through their designation as prohibited conduct. This leaves dominant hier-archies of power and privilege intact. The trade-off demanded by the dom-inant ideology is the granting of rights only on the condition that other de-mands are withdrawn. For rights to be awarded, the more disruptive chal-lenges raised by political voice and visibility must be quieted. "Sex and gender outsiders—gay men, transsexuals, lesbians, bisexuals—are constantly invited to lose their voices, or suffer the consequences (job loss, baseball bats) of using them." Consequently, "'don't tell' is more than a U.S. military pol-icy; it remains U.S. public policy, formally and informally, on sex and gender nonconformity" (Gamson 1996, 80).

At stake here is not only the self-identity of lesbians and gay men as such but also the ability to tell our stories and share our lives. The ability to speak of oneself in one's own terms, to tell the story of one's life, marks the dif-ference between existence and nonexistence, community and isolation, pride and shame. Both our self-images and the images others have of us de-pend on our freedom to share our stories. The importance of stories in changing others' attitudes cannot be overestimated, for "our stories hold the power of persuasion. We must counter disinformation with the truth of our lives" (Vaid 1993, 28). Ensuring that such speech is protected must remain a primary goal of the lesbian and gay rights movement, for "openness has enormous power in the politics of personal relationships," an arena that legal initiatives cannot reliably access or influence (Kopkind 1993, 8). This is why individual acts of coming out as lesbian or gay have always comprised a key strategy of the movement. Despite their ambiguities, such acts are still rec-ognized as one of the most effective means of increasing support for gay and lesbian rights. They facilitate an understanding of gays and lesbians as multifaceted human beings instead of one-dimensional sexual creatures. For these and other reasons, "the first need for our politics is the guarantee that [our words and voices] will be heard" (Phelan 1993, 779).

What can we do to create space for these stories and an audience for these voices? We must begin by critically examining our own individual filters, the lenses through which we perceive and classify difference and the ways in which we talk about difference. We must recognize, perhaps with some surprise, that although we may not be politicians or lawyers, the language we choose and the thoughts we express may have a tremendous influence on those around us. Our choice of language speaks volumes to our children and families, our friends and coworkers, and all the various communities of which we are a part. We need to be aware of how the public discourse around us shapes our own attitudes and beliefs and how the expression of our opinions influences the attitudes of others. We need to make choices about how we represent ourselves and each other, rather than uncritically adopting the ready-made categories and distinctions our culture imposes.

Ultimately, all sexuality and sexual orientations need to be understood as falling along a continuum of possibilities, rather than as a set of categories by which to divide and label human beings (see Kinsey, Pomeroy, and Martin 1948; Institute for Sex Research 1953; Snitow, Stansell, and Thompson 1986). The idea that identities are socially constructed is not an abstract theory divorced from the everyday world. On the contrary, varying understandings of identity permeate all of our lives. They influence the degree of freedom we have in our choices of whom we can become and whom we can love. The act of coming out often implies choosing a category, rejecting one label or box only to adopt another. To foster a liberatory vision, this concept might be better understood as an ongoing process, a becoming, or a "coming into oneself." In such a reinterpretation, rather than selecting from among preexisting, ready-made categories, we would refuse the system of categorization for the purposes of self-understanding. Coming out would then denote a process of transition and growth accessible to anyone, not only gays and lesbians. It would be a process of learning to trust our own voices and listen to our own hearts. Instead of a transition that closes one off from loving half the world, coming into oneself means opening oneself to loving those whom we were formerly forbidden to love. It represents an expansion, not a reduction, of possibilities.

Allowing individuals to name themselves is a tremendously empowering act that has applications to a variety of concrete settings. When we label people, we narrow their possibilities, presenting them with a limited selection of categories from which to choose. To a degree, this is a necessary process. Labels lend order and predictability to our world. They allow us to recognize and ally ourselves with others who share our self-identification, fostering personal as well as political empowerment. Nevertheless, the labels and categories our culture provides are neither natural nor sacred. They are constructions of language and the other institutions that organize our society, from education to religion to law. They are not universal, either across cultures or across history. Thus these labels must be presented and used with considerable care and mindfulness, when used at all. When we extend them to others as possibilities, we must exercise particular tentativeness, attentive to the ways in which the complexity of individuals exceeds the bounds of any given category. The need for such caution extends to all who are entrusted with educating others about difference: teachers, counselors, religious leaders, and parents, to name but a few. How we learn to think and talk about difference, whether our own or someone else's, leaves an indelible impression on how we perceive ourselves in relation to the world around us.

Our responsibility extends beyond reconsidering our own uses of the labels and stereotypes that reduce the richness of individual variation to a meager set of options. We must also actively resist and challenge the reductive definitions and misleading representations that others perpetuate. This act requires a courageous willingness to speak out against bigotry and hatred. The word *courage* is derived from the Latin word *cor*, meaning "heart." It is in the brave act of standing up for ourselves and for other oppressed groups that we truly act with heart. In the debates surrounding Achtenberg and Cammermeyer, opponents disseminated a litany of destructive and demeaning stereotypes of gays and lesbians. While supporters denounced such negative images, they often failed to advance alternative, diverse representations of lesbians and gays. The support we see in these cases amounts most often to tolerance of difference, but few seem willing to embrace difference actively. Instead, they are silenced by the fear of familiar accusations: of "flaunting" sexuality, of ramming it down others' throats, of advocating a "homosexual lifestyle." Such phrases coerce us all into invisibility and silence by suggesting that if only we would behave correctly, if only we would be appropriately quiet, discreet, and private, we would somehow win the favor of the mainstream and be granted our rights. This is the premise that underlies an assimilationist agenda. It encourages us to believe that, indeed, our silence *will* protect us.

Such a belief is but another weapon in the armory of our oppressors. As we have seen repeatedly, no matter what we do or refrain from doing, no matter how discreet we attempt to be, nothing less than absolute silence and complete closetedness is acceptable to those who condemn us. As a result, accusations of "flaunting it" will occur in response to any kind of honesty about ourselves, any verbal or physical expression that can be interpreted as conveying who we are. We know, as well, from the experiences of other minority groups that attempting to win favor from those in power through "good behavior" or patience has never been a successful strategy for attaining equality or liberation.

We must refuse to be cowed into silence and invisibility by such accusations. Such a response will gain us nothing, despite what our opponents would have us believe. We need to abandon the belief that silence, discretion, and patience will eventually win us our rights. Instead, we must speak up, come out, and present our society with alternatives to the narrow, stereotypical, hypersexual images of gays and lesbians that still dominate public discourse and the public imagination. We need to be advocates, to "flaunt it." We need to counter forcefully the destructive portrayals that reduce us to sex, that deny the complexity of our lives, that ignore the diversity within our movement, and that force us into a single mold that is male, white, and middle-class.

In providing alternatives, we must offer not one but many, so as not to repeat the mistake of homogenizing our movement. We need to offer a multitude of different perspectives and different representations of lesbians and gays. This means that in our own movement, we need to promote diverse expression and actively pursue diverse representation. We must not depend on a few celebrities to come out for all of us or permit a small number of high-profile professionals to provide our primary representations. As many of us as possible, from all of our varied lesbian and gay communities, need to come out so that we may be seen in all of our diversity and our wholeness. We need to come out in different forums, so that we can be seen for "all of who we are" (Beck 1982, xxx). We need to present ourselves as parents, grandparents, daughters, sons, teachers, clergy, and workers in every field; as rich and poor, young and old, able-bodied and disabled; as women and men of different religions, races, and nationalities. We must refuse to collaborate in or to promote stereotypes of others in our movement or of other minority groups. In bolstering and perpetuating stereotypes, we demean not only others but also ourselves.

We must, finally, demand to be seen and to be heard, not only erasing the picture that hatred has painted of us but providing our own, more accurate and more complete portrait of ourselves and the world that we hope to create. Far from the ugly, threatening image our opponents advance, lesbian and gay visions of the future have much practical and moral value for the rest of the world. Their components include the freedom of self-expression, new-found respect for families of all configurations, encouragement to listen to our hearts and trust where they lead, an escape from the constraints of those labels and boxes that confine or suffocate individual minds and spirits, and the right to love whomever we choose without penalty or fear.

This is not some monstrous "gay agenda" that attacks families, children, religion, and morality. However, that is what our opponents would have the public believe, *must* have them believe in order to perpetuate hatred and fear. The way to counter these predominant images is not to remain silent or hidden but to make our own visions come alive by speaking honestly of ourselves, our lives, and the transformations we hope to achieve. This is our duty regardless of our own sexual orientation, regardless of the breadth of our sphere of influence. Every one of us must participate in this effort, in every possible forum, at every possible opportunity, wherever we can do so without unduly risking our safety or sacrificing those things we must have to survive. In creating this alternative image, a portrait forever in process, the artistic vision of each of us is not only welcome but vital. When we all speak and act, when we create a vivid and colorful mosaic with the stories of our lives, only then will those around us begin to see us and hear us as we are, and as we can be.

## CONCLUSION

Clearly, resolving the issue of how best to pursue liberation is beyond the scope of any single study, calling for broader and more varied perspectives than can be provided by any one individual. These are issues for gays and lesbians and our communities to ponder and for legal scholars and activists to debate. They are questions that must concern all of us who advocate an end to homophobia, sexism, racism, and other forms of oppression. They must inevitably be of concern to those who count a lesbian or gay man among their family or friends. They must, finally, concern all of us who work with or care about young people, those who are at the greatest risk from the perilous effects of oppression. This includes not only gay and lesbian youth themselves but also the legions of young people who are questioning and uncertain. Among this generation, the ravages of homophobia may become the roots of unmanageable, ultimately insurmountable self-hatred and fear.

These young people stand as reminders to us, in their innocence and, often, their despair, of what we might otherwise overlook in analyzing the movement. What is at fault is not the behavior or "conduct" of lesbians and gay men, any more than desperation is the fault of these youth. It is not activism, speech, or self-identification that creates the "problem" of homosexuality. What does create the problem is the enforcement of rigid sex-role stereotypes and the condemnation and labeling of those who do not conform to them. The "symptoms" of such nonconformity will vary. They may lie in the gender of one's sexual or affectional partner. But they may lie as well in how one dresses or wears one's hair, in one's organizational membership or participation in certain "suspect" events, in the restaurants or bars one frequents, in one's fondness for or aversion to sports, or even in one's choice of friends. The attitude supporting this rigid enforcement views heterosexual love and heterosexual behavior as natural and normal, while any alternative is deviant and perverse. It is an attitude whose dual components, heterosexism and homophobia, are instilled in all of us and enforced with all the strength that our society's most powerful institutions—the government, military, schools, religion, law, and many others—can muster.

Individually and collectively, we need to accept responsibility for "outing" homophobia and heterosexism wherever we find it. We must shift the burden of justification and accountability from those who seek an equitable application of constitutional principles to those who would deny it. We need to banish formulations that blame the victims for the problem and vigorously reject proposed solutions that compromise our basic rights and freedoms. We must identify bigotry and hatred, not lesbian and gay self-expression or activism, as the villains, models of unacceptable conduct that requires regulation and expulsion. We must expose prejudice and discrimination as the true examples of offensive and reprehensible acts. Finally, we must identify the instilling of hatred and fear of difference as the real dangers that threaten to corrupt our children's hearts and minds.

The critique of civil rights presented in this analysis is not intended to advocate the abandonment of legal avenues for change. On the contrary, I support the assertion that

> lesbians need to fight for civil rights legislation. These rights are part of our collective empowerment. We need to fight for them even when the terms of legal discourse do not square with our understandings of ourselves (which is to say, most of the time). We need to do this quite simply because without the safety afforded by these minimal guarantees we will never get to change anything else. (Phelan 1994, 126)

Nevertheless, a civil rights approach is ultimately inadequate for achieving genuine social change because it can do little to undermine the existing classifications that dominant institutions have assigned to us. Rights-based arguments have the effect of reforming the existing system rather than creating a new vision, making them a necessary but not sufficient element for a liberatory agenda. Because a movement for liberation requires a broader vision than legal initiatives alone can achieve, "rights look more attractive when we consider them as one moment in oppositional politics rather than the whole and only goal" (Phelan 1994, 125).

The emphasis on legal strategies may explain what some have identified as the lack of a coherent or overall vision of transformation within the mainstream of the lesbian and gay rights movement, in particular among official, nationally organized gay and lesbian rights groups. The absence of a vision may be both a reason for and a consequence of the predominance of civil rights strategies. If influential sectors of our movement lack a vision, they can do little else but reform the existing system. Likewise, if reform is their primary goal, there is little need to expend energy on imagining what deeper social change might look like. Relying on the established legal system and its categories contributes to reform at the cost of a more expansive vision. Similarly, focusing on homosexuality as different without challenging heterosexuality as the unmarked norm preserves a view of the world in which gays and lesbians can be seen only as minorities and as victims. This viewpoint conceals the pride and empowerment that also characterize gay and lesbian lives and reduces the complexity of who we are to a single element out of the many that comprise our identities. As a result of the limits that civil rights approaches have imposed on self-expression, "our biggest challenge remains communication of who we are, of what it means to be gay, of what the society will look like when we achieve the full equality we seek" (Vaid 1993, 28).

If we seek to change attitudes, if we seek to eliminate gay bashing and other forms of violence against gays and lesbians, if we seek to do away with subtle forms of prejudice and discrimination that often escape the reach of the law, if we seek to create a genuinely safe environment for lesbians and gays to come out to their parents and families, if we seek to prevent lesbian and gay youth from being thrown out on the streets, if we seek to protect such youth from the hopelessness and fear that often lead to death by their own hands—if we wish to bring into being this kind of world, then we must pursue a more profound form of social change. We must make accessible a vast variety of representations of gay and lesbian individuals, relationships, families, and communities—representations created by lesbians and gays for ourselves, for heterosexuals, and for our youth. "The importance of educating the public, young heterosexuals, and all segments of the population in the truth about homosexual lives and our aspirations for equality cannot be overstated. Straight people still believe dangerous and mistaken myths about homosexuals. Our exclusive focus on legal, legislative, and administrative policy reform helps end blatantly discriminatory practices, but it leaves these myths intact." In contrast, "by engaging homophobia in the cultural spheres, we challenge such myths where they originate and where they are perpetuated" (Vaid 1995, 25).

For this reason, cultural visibility—the dissemination of the widest possible range of our voices, our faces, and our life stories—must be made available, even ubiquitous, in a culture that today often seems only too ready to relegate gays and lesbians anew to the invisibility of the closet. To achieve the visibility we desire, gays and lesbians must be represented and be able to represent ourselves openly and proudly, in all arenas, in every aspect of national life—from the media to the government to the military—as well as in our own families, schools, workplaces, religious institutions, and local communities. We must be able to reeducate our society to recognize that our families *are* families, that our relationships *are* relationships, that love and not merely sex lies at the heart of who we are. "Until the goodness and worth of our relationships can be perceived, we will continue as second-class citizens" (Becker 1995, 149). Only when we can be seen and heard in our genuine diversity, rather than through the stereotypes inflicted on us by a repressive, dominant ideology, will such an awareness inscribe itself widely in our culture.

Mary Newcombe asks, "What is a lesbian vision?" She answers as follows: "It is first a voice. We have been silent (and silenced) for too long. We must affirm our identities and speak the truths of our lives or we will continue to suffer the invisibility that has permitted the development of a legal system that does not even acknowledge our existence" (1991, 7). Ultimately, legal and nonlegal goals must be intertwined, yielding a vision of a future in which we all share the freedom of self-expression. The project of creating this future must be the responsibility of all of us who, like Roberta Achtenberg and Grethe Cammermeyer, share a dream of another kind of society—a society where difference is valued and embraced and where minds and attitudes are broadened by the peaceful coexistence of different kinds of relationships, families, households, and communities. In such a vision, invisibility and silence can play no part. It is painful and even absurd to suggest that a group exclude itself from its own liberatory vision, that it should organize on behalf of its own rights only to disappear again as a condition of its legal advances. Nor should such a vision accept the silencing of those who create it. As anyone who has tried to maintain such a silence knows all too well, doing so fosters a feeling not of safety but rather of constant fear and dread. Silence is inevitably accompanied by the terror of discovery. No liberatory vision can, or should, accommodate the psychic space and energy that such a fear entails.

Instead, in such a vision, legal equality will represent only one component of a new kind of openness that today most lesbians and gays can only imagine. This vision, our vision, will foresee and incorporate many ways of loving, many ways of being a man or a woman—ways that do not depend on the constraints of "appropriately" gendered roles of sexual conquest and submission. Finally, such a vision will not suppress but will celebrate same-sex desire and emotion. It will embrace and rejoice in that which is central to our existence as human beings and crucial to the fulfillment of our human potential: the ability to love.

# NOTES

1. Mark Blasius cites a 1989 study commissioned by the U.S. Department of Health and Human Services which reports that "gay youth are two to three times more likely to attempt suicide than heterosexual youth, and up to 30% of those teenagers who do commit suicide are gay or lesbians" (1994, 37n. 18). A second study, published in the journal *Pediatrics* in June 1991, reports that "30 percent of gay youth attempt suicide near the age of fifteen and . . . almost one-half of gay and lesbian teens interviewed said they had attempted suicide more than once" (Blasius 1994, 37–38n. 18).

NOTES TO CHAPTER I

1. The military appealed Cammermeyer's reinstatement while she remained an active member of the Washington State National Guard. She transferred to inactive status in May 1996. Finally, with Cammermeyer nearing retirement, the military ceased its efforts to discharge her. However, it continued its legal fight to erase from the books the judicial decision that reinstated her and declared the ban unconstitutional. In October 1996, a federal appeals court declined to issue any ruling on the case, declaring it moot because Cammermeyer had been reinstated and the rules under which she was discharged had been superseded by the "Don't Ask, Don't Tell" policy ("No Ruling" 1996, 41).

2. When referring to the social movement for lesbian and gay civil rights, I use variants of the phrase "lesbian and gay rights movement" or "lesbian/gay rights movement" rather than the more common "gay rights movement." I believe that the disappearance of lesbians under the ostensibly nongendered term *gay* is one of the problems afflicting the movement, as I discuss throughout this book. Although it may appear unwieldy, the longer phrase will seem less so as we become more familiar with its use, and I believe its accuracy and inclusiveness are well worth the sacrifice of brevity.

3. Deborah K. King coins the term *multiple jeopardy* to convey the impact of multiple forms of discrimination on women of color. She explains, "Most applica-

162 NOTES TO CHAPTER ONE

tions of the concepts of double and triple jeopardy have been overly simplistic in assuming that the relationships among the various discriminations are merely additive." In contrast, "multiple jeopardy" refers "not only to several, simultaneous oppressions but to the multiplicative relationships among them as well" (1988, 47).

4. Only two books by speech communication scholars have focused on discourse by or about gays and lesbians. James Chesebro's edited collection titled *Gayspeak*, published in 1981, is currently out of print. More recently, R. Jeffrey Ringer edited a 1994 compilation titled *Queer Words, Queer Images*, which examines representations of gays and lesbians in a variety of contexts. To date, however, no book has taken a rhetorical approach in examining lesbian and gay civil rights discourse. Nor has any book analyzed public speech by or about lesbians, separate from that by or about gay men or homosexuality in general. Moreover, only one article in a mainstream journal of rhetorical studies has focused specifically on lesbian, nonfictional discourse (see Kurs and Cathcart 1983).

5. In the area of literary studies, see Castle 1993, Faderman 1994, Griffin 1993a, Hoogland 1997, Jay and Glasgow 1990, Meese 1992, Munt 1992, Palmer 1993, Pollack and Knight 1993, Roof 1991, Wolfe and Penelope 1993, and Zimmerman 1993. Examples of such work in cultural studies include Doan 1994, Griffin 1993b, Hart 1994, Stein 1993, Traub 1991, Weiss 1993, and Wilton 1995. In the field of history, see Ainley 1995, Brown 1986, Faderman 1981, Faderman 1991, and the Lesbian History Group 1989. For lesbian feminist readings in psychology, see the Boston Lesbian Psychologies Collective 1987, Brown 1989, Brown 1992, and Kitzinger and Perkins 1993.

6. Institutional forms of oppression are certainly not the only consequence of increased visibility, however. Too frequently, the alternative is violence: "Where the discipline of remaining 'in the closet' to enforce the norms of heterosexism breaks down, homophobic individuals (with or without recourse to institutional support) restore disciplinary power through force or violence" (Blasius 1994, 33). The incidence of gay bashing and other hate crimes directed against gays and lesbians gives brutal testament to the accuracy of this claim. According to the U.S. Justice Department, there were 2,395 acts of anti-gay violence reported nationally in 1995. The figure rose to 2,529 incidents in 1996 (Vozzella 1997). These numbers do not include numerous incidents that were undoubtedly never reported.

7. I am indebted to Tricia Lootens for her contributions to my thinking on this point.

8. Some writers have recently argued, however, that Stonewall is better understood as a "galvanising symbol [sic]" than as an accurate historical marker of the birth of the gay rights movement (Plummer 1995, 90). Kenneth Plummer disputes the characterization of Stonewall as the "first" radical action by lesbians and gays, noting that by the time the riots occurred, more advanced traditions of gay and lesbian radicalism on the West Coast and in parts of Europe were already well established.

Supporting this interpretation, Urvashi Vaid writes, "Stonewall was neither the worst example of police brutality against gay people in New York, nor was it the first time that gay people had fought back" (1995, 55).

9. *Heterosexism* may be defined as "that ideological structure that assumes heterosexuality as the norm and homosexuality as deviant and, indeed, despicable" (Altman 1982, 111).

10. This exclusion parallels privileged gays' and lesbians' disregard of other forms of oppression. Examples include the lack of acknowledgment by many white gays and lesbians of the problems of gays and lesbians of color and the ignorance of many middle-class gays and lesbians about the issues facing those who are working-class or poor.

11. Although Blasius offers the contrasting view that "sexism and heterosexism are *discrete* forms of domination," he, too, concedes that "lesbians and gay men are affected by and often act to eliminate both of them" (1994, 29n. 13).

12. I use the term *choice* here in a broad sense, and not to address the issue of whether lesbianism is a choice or a biological imperative. While lesbians may or may not have a "choice" about whom we are sexually attracted to, we are faced with choices every day. Circumscribed by the threat of homophobia and discrimination, we must choose daily whether to acknowledge or act on our sense of sexual identity and attraction.

13. Monique Wittig clarifies this point when she writes, "Although women are very visible as sexual beings, as social beings they are totally invisible" (1992, 8).

14. This is a characteristic of class as well as gender oppression. It is true not only for women who run households, for example, but also for workers who clean office buildings or university classrooms at night. Such work frequently goes unnoticed by those who most benefit from it.

15. An exception may be found in Mary Daly's book titled *Websters' First New Intergalactic Wickedary of the English Language* (1987). However, the lengths to which Daly must go in order to escape the patriarchal and heterosexist trappings of language demonstrate precisely how ingrained in language such biases are. I thank Pam Lannutti for drawing my attention to this example.

16. This would not be true in a climate in which heterosexuality is not presumed. For example, coming out as gay or lesbian to other participants at a lesbian and gay pride march or a women's music festival has little impact. In such contexts, it is heterosexuals who must decide whether to "come out" to counter a presumption of homosexuality.

17. Ruthann Robson offers an example of the risks involved in adopting legal concepts. In seeking domestic partner benefits, she explains, "we may argue in a court of law that a lover is equivalent to a spouse . . . our lover is expressed and limited to the legal terms set under the rule of law—heterosexual marriage." However, she continues, "In making this argument, we might lose our own definition of our

lover. If we refuse to argue this way, based on the belief that our lover is nothing like a wife or husband, we might preserve our lesbianism but probably lose the benefits" (1992, 12).

18. Despite the claims of queer theory to be inclusive and to transcend restrictive categories, it has often been criticized for its high level of abstraction that erases lesbian experience and specificity, particularly the experiences of lesbians of color (Anzaldúa 1991, 251). It has also been faulted for its insistence on subsuming all lesbians under the generic, undefinable, ultimately male-centered designation "queer," thereby erasing gender distinctions between lesbians and gay men.

19. I have placed the term *pro-gay* in quotation marks because it implies a degree of affirmation that not all supporters of gay and lesbian rights share. A "pro-gay" position advocates equal rights for all citizens regardless of sexual orientation. Some individuals who personally condemn homosexuality nevertheless support such a position, believing that sexual orientation should not be the basis for discrimination.

NOTES TO CHAPTER 2

1. The Senate Committee on Banking, Housing, and Urban Affairs was responsible for voting on Achtenberg's nomination initially and submitting their recommendation to the entire Senate. The Committee's vote took place on May 5, 1993. The nomination passed by a vote of fourteen to four.

2. This quote from Helms appeared in the *Washington Times* on May 6, 1993. The reporter wrote that Helms "said he will try to block the nomination . . . 'Because she's a damn lesbian. I'm not going to put a lesbian in a position like that.'" Helms added, "If you want to call me a bigot, fine" (Moss 1993, A3). During the debate, Helms was asked whether the quote was accurate. He responded, "It does not sound like me, but I may have said it" (*Congressional Record*, May 19–24, 1993, S6101).

3. An article in the *San Francisco Chronicle* further supports this claim with the contention that "a core group of about 10 conservative senators is fighting against Achtenberg, basing their opposition on everything from her sexual orientation to her liberal views on civil rights. Some hope to use the fight to embarrass President Clinton" (Lynch and Lochhead 1993, A6).

4. In an interesting side note, Senator Sam Nunn, the most prominent Senate critic of efforts to lift the ban, voted in favor of Achtenberg's nomination.

5. Ruthann Robson explains that "race is the paradigm suspect class because of the historical development of the equality doctrine" (1992, 82).

6. For an excellent lesbian feminist analysis of *Hardwick* and the limitations of the sexual privacy argument, see Robson 1992, especially 65–67.

7. All unspecified page references preceded by an "S" refer to the text of the *Congressional Record*, May 19–24, 1993.

8. I am grateful to Anne Layton for her reflections on prejudice that are incorporated here.

9. As the *California Journal* of July 1, 1993, notes:

The Supreme Court is not the only institution in Washington that is obsessed with precedent. The painfully cautious politicians in Congress prefer to stick with the tried-and-true whenever possible. But once they have been coaxed or coerced into doing something new, that becomes a precedent they follow just as comfortably. Thus, the next gay or lesbian nominee for a senior position may merely be "another Achtenberg" to the habit-bound creatures of the Senate. ("Achtenberg Confirmation" 1993)

This assessment, in fact, was quickly borne out. As the *San Jose Mercury News* subsequently reported, openly gay patent lawyer Bruce Lehman was easily confirmed by the Senate only a month later, "without a peep from Helms" (Shepard 1994, A2).

10. That Achtenberg is viewed by her opponents as a representative of gays and lesbians is not in doubt; Helms refers to her as "the showpiece of the homosexual movement in the United States" (S6352).

11. Such comparisons, however, raise a complicated set of issues for those belonging to both racial and sexual minorities.

12. In repeating this comparison, however, I do not mean to imply that race or sex, any more than sexual orientation, should be accepted as a biological or "natural" category; the critique of biology suggested here applies equally to often undisputed categories such as race and sex (Fuss 1989; Winant 1990). Nevertheless, it is precisely the virtually unchallenged status of these categories as natural that legitimizes claims to the "naturalness" of a particular sexual orientation.

13. This quote is later found to have been misattributed and, as Senator Don Riegle subsequently points out, in fact is taken from a letter to the editor in that same paper, and not from an editorial. In an angry response to this misattribution, the *Chronicle* printed an editorial on May 20 in which it explicitly endorsed Achtenberg's nomination (S6177).

14. Only two other senators, both Achtenberg supporters, use the word *lesbian* at all. Senator Dianne Feinstein and Senator Edward Kennedy each use it once, but neither instance undermines the negative connotation attributed by Helms. Feinstein argues that because "Roberta Achtenberg is a lesbian, she is being subjected on the floor of the Senate to a barrage of unseemly, nasty, and untrue allegations" (S6201). Kennedy likewise comments, "We have heard considerable discussion about the fact that Roberta is a lesbian. I admire her willingness to be open about who she is. But it is her skills and not her sexual orientation that is at issue here" (S6220).

15. Frye's metaphor of oppression as a birdcage is helpful in examining the limitations of a metaphor that takes a line as the representative barrier and crossing as the means of escape. She writes:

Consider a birdcage. If you look very closely at just one wire in the cage, you cannot see the other wires. If your conception of what is before you is determined by this myopic focus, you could look at that one wire, up and down the length of it, and be unable to see why a bird would not just fly around the wire any time it wanted to go somewhere. . . . It is only when you step back, stop looking at the wires one by one, microscopically, and take a macroscopic view of the whole cage, that you can see why the bird does not go anywhere. . . . It is perfectly *obvious* that the bird is surrounded by a network of systematically related barriers, no one of which would be the least hindrance to its flight, but which, by their relations to each other, are as confining as the solid walls of a dungeon. (1983, 4–5)

16. In a striking example of the pervasiveness of masculinity as an underlying norm, Murkowski illustrates this point with the need to wear a necktie—the quintessential apparel of the heterosexual male. Murkowski argues, "Many of the people who work here wear a necktie to work every day. Wearing a tie does not make a person any smarter, any better or more qualified. It is a matter of conformity." If someone does not conform in this way, he continues, "if it is a member of my staff, I might say, hey, maybe we ought to get rid of this person. That's the situation in the case of this nominee" (S6169). The equation here of heterosexual male fashion with conformity is perhaps as revealing as any direct discussion of difference and the interlocking barriers limiting the access of minority groups to political power. The nonmale, nonheterosexual is linked here with offensive nonconformity, with being "out of line."

17. Domenici, who is highly critical of Achtenberg on several counts, nevertheless says he will vote for her nomination because "while my doubts are great . . . this nominee comes very close to the point but does not *cross the line* at which I would vote to deny the President a nominee of his choice" (S6355; emphasis mine).

18. The bombing of an Atlanta bar called the Otherside Lounge on February 21, 1997, illustrates one danger of obscuring these connections. The media reported that the lounge is a "gay bar," when, in fact, it is primarily a lesbian bar. The distinction is particularly important because this incident was preceded by another bombing, at an Atlanta abortion clinic. Only by realizing that this was primarily a women's bar could the police and the public recognize the possibility that the attacks might be related and that the targets might have been women (Colbert 1997).

19. The *San Francisco Chronicle* later reported that "the Boy Scouts issue was brought up so often that some tourists sitting in the Senate visitors gallery became confused as to whether they were hearing debate on the Scouts or a HUD nomination" (Lynch 1993, A6).

20. Not coincidentally, during this discussion a number of senators opposing Achtenberg's nomination stood up to announce that they had been Boy Scouts or that their sons were Boy Scouts (S6206; S6215; S6221; S6355). Not coincidental, either, is the similarity between the symbolic position of the Boy Scouts and that of the U.S. military. Even the Boy Scout slogan "Be Prepared" suggests a kind of military readiness that informs the spending patterns of our national budget. In this way, the antagonism set up between gays and the Boy Scouts evokes the controversy, already heated at this time, surrounding gays and lesbians in the military. This antag-

onism may represent a displacement of the military issue that calls on the emotions already aroused by this difficult debate.

Clues to this parallel are the repetition of the argument that the Scouts prohibit "*announced* or *avowed* homosexuals" from becoming either scoutmasters or scouts (S6212; emphasis mine) and a reference to Achtenberg as "candidly and unapologetically lesbian" (S6353). Although it is never stated, the implication is that those who do not disclose their sexuality are not necessarily excluded from the Boy Scouts. Such a stance parallels the "Don't Ask, Don't Tell" policy that was being suggested (and was later adopted) in response to protests over the exclusion of gays and lesbians from the military.

21. Nevertheless, this challenge to biological motherhood is extreme even for anti-gay discourse. More typical is the example of a *Washington Times* article in which a photograph of Achtenberg's family identifies "Roberta Achtenberg, her lover, Mary Morgan, and Judge Morgan's son" (Price 1993, A1).

NOTES TO CHAPTER 3

1. As used in the Department of Defense policy, the term *homosexual* is defined as "a person who engages in, desires to engage in, or intends to engage in homosexual acts." The phrase "homosexual acts" refers to "bodily contact, actively undertaken or passively permitted, between members of the same sex for the purpose of satisfying sexual desires" (*Policy Hearings* 1993, 30).

2. Although initiated thirty years prior to the military board hearing, Cammermeyer's years of service total twenty-seven because she was separated from the military for three years after the birth of her first child in 1968. Military regulations at the time prohibited women with children under age sixteen from serving in the armed forces. However, this regulation changed in 1972, and Cammermeyer returned to her military career (Cammermeyer 1994).

3. After disclosing her sexual orientation, Cammermeyer continued to serve in her position as chief nurse of the Washington State National Guard for more than three years, pending her military board hearing.

4. For a complete, autobiographical account of Cammermeyer's life and the events leading up to her discharge, see Cammermeyer 1994.

5. However, Cammermeyer's case was neither the first nor the only challenge to the ban. Thus the significance of this military "victory" was undoubtedly mitigated by the fact that despite the stated policy, several openly gay service members were still in uniform as a result of civil court decisions. Perry Watkins, for example, was a gay man who repeatedly told his superior officers of his homosexuality yet was allowed to serve for seventeen years. He was eventually discharged by the military but subsequently reinstated by a civil court, which ruled that it was unfair to dismiss a soldier whom the military had known all along was gay.

6. The willingness of many gay activists to rally around the issue of gay and lesbian rights in the military, despite their misgivings, was not universally shared. In one

example, a group calling itself QUASH (Queers United Against Straight-acting Homosexuals) posted a display of queer guerrilla art that referred disparagingly to the "'military takeover' of our movement" (Deitcher 1995, 137). For a discussion of the ambivalence many gays and lesbians felt about this issue, see Deitcher 1995, especially 176–77.

7. Some writers have argued that the preoccupation with access to the military "reveals a gay political agenda that is not merely moderate but conservative" (Smith 1993, 14). A contrasting view suggests that disagreement about the military issue may be a function of class differences (Cruikshank 1994). The military has long been a primary source of employment for working-class men and women, and thus the military ban disproportionately impacts on and concerns working-class gays and lesbians.

8. By emphasizing the symbolic importance of this debate, I do not wish to minimize its material consequences for enormous numbers of gays and lesbians. Although there is no way to calculate precisely how many gays and lesbians currently serve in the military, the testimony of Dr. Lawrence Korb, former assistant secretary for defense under Ronald Reagan, offers some suggestion of the magnitude of the issue. Korb cites a military report estimating that as much as 10 percent of the armed forces may be gay or lesbian. He notes that "even at five percent that's 100,000 people on active duty. . . . Since only roughly 1,400 are being discharged each year, there's another roughly 99,000 in there" (Department of the Army 1991, 53).

9. That this belief still persists among some military leaders is evident in the testimony of Master Chief David Borne, who compares the claim that the ban discriminates against gays to the claim that a child molester is "discriminated against" by not being allowed to work in a day-care center (*Policy Hearings* 1993, 607).

10. Even opponents of lifting the ban were finally forced to concede the folly of such a position. One such example is Charles Moskos, Jr., who, despite identifying many problems that would result from lifting the ban, asserts that "the argument that homosexuals are susceptible to blackmail is illogical. (If there were no ban, a gay service member could not be manipulated by the threat of exposure.) No evidence exists that homosexuals, under present rules, have been greater security risks than anyone else" (1994, 63).

11. However, this determinative link between statement and action is not attributed equally to other groups. As argued in Judge Thomas S. Zilly's decision, for example, simply stating that one is an alcoholic or drug abuser is not sufficient cause for punitive action or dismissal. Instead, any action on the part of the military "requires actual evidence of substance abuse or that the individual's status impairs his or her ability to function in the military" (*Cammermeyer v. Aspin* 1994, 30n. 13).

12. In terms of practical consequences, since the policy was implemented in 1994, the number of discharges for homosexuality has actually increased by 42 percent. In 1996, the number of separations reached its highest level since 1987, with 850 people discharged ("Could It Be a Witch-Hunt?" 1997, 15). Such numbers can-

not account for those gays and lesbians who are harassed, given poor evaluations, or forced out of the military by other means because of their sexual orientation (Lehring 1996).

Yet even these numbers do not tell nearly the whole story of the cost, in dollars as well as in human lives, of maintaining the military ban. A report from the General Accounting Office in 1992 disclosed that from 1980 to 1991, it cost the military $494 million to train people who were subsequently discharged under the anti-gay policy. Although the cost of the military's investigations into homosexual allegations for that same period are not known, the report estimated that in 1990 alone, the cost was greater than $2.5 million (Cammermeyer 1994, 293). Randy Shilts estimates that "in the past decade, the cost of investigations and the dollars spent replacing gay personnel easily amount to hundreds of millions" (1993, 4). Still more costly is the toll the policy takes on human lives, as lives and careers are ruined; some men and women commit suicide when the fear of discovery becomes too much to live with (Shilts 1993).

13. There is only one other provision in the UCMJ under which such behaviors may be prosecuted. Article 134 is a General Article that reads:

Though not specifically mentioned in this chapter, all disorders and neglects to the prejudice of good order and discipline in the armed forces, all conduct of a nature to bring discredit upon the armed forces, and crimes and offenses not capital, of which persons subject to this chapter may be guilty, shall be taken cognizance of by a general, special, or summary court-martial, according to the nature and degree of the offense, and shall be punished at the discretion of that court.

14. Of the twenty-one states with sodomy laws, only six (Arkansas, Kansas, Maryland, Missouri, Oklahoma, and Texas) outlaw homosexual but not heterosexual sodomy. The remaining fifteen (Alabama, Arizona, Florida, Georgia, Idaho, Louisiana, Massachusetts, Michigan, Mississippi, Minnesota, North Carolina, Rhode Island, South Carolina, Utah, and Virginia) prohibit noncoital sex between any sexual partners (Price 1997).

15. A more complete definition is supplied by the RAND Report, an independent study commissioned by the Clinton administration in 1993 (Otjen 1994, 204). It reads as follows: "It is unnatural carnal copulation for a person to take into that person's mouth or anus the sexual organ of another person or of an animal, or to place that person's sexual organ in the mouth or anus of another person or of an animal or to have carnal copulation in any opening of the body except the sexual parts with another person or to have carnal copulation with an animal."

16. In a fascinating comparison, Cammermeyer's lawyers quote in their brief the 1942 report of the General Board on the issue of integrating African Americans into the navy. The lawyers insert the term *heterosexual* where *white* appears in the original and *homosexual* where *another race* appears. The board stated:

Enlistment for general service implies that the individual may be sent anywhere—to any ship or station where he is needed. Men on board ship live in

# 170 NOTES TO CHAPTER THREE

particularly close association; in their messes, one man sits beside another; their hammocks or bunks are close together; in their common tasks they work side by side; and in particular tasks such as those of a gun's crew, they form a closely knit, highly coordinated team. *How many white men [heterosexuals]* would choose, of their own accord, that their closest associates in sleeping quarters, at mess, and in a gun's crew should be *of another race [homosexual]*? How many would accept such conditions, if required to do so, without resentment and just as a matter of course? The General Board believes that the answer is "Few, if any," and further believes that if the issue were forced, there would be a lowering of contentment, teamwork and discipline in the service. (Memo in Support 1994, 44)

17. Joan Acker explains the nature of a gendered organization: "To say that an organization is gendered means that advantage and disadvantage, exploitation and control, action and emotion, meaning and identity, are patterned through and in terms of a distinction between male and female, masculine and feminine" (1990, 146).

18. As Defense Department general counsel Gorelick testified at the hearings, "The courts have . . . rejected the notion that a status-based policy is appropriate." This precedent alerted the government as early as 1981 that "if we did have a status-based as opposed to a conduct-based rule, that it would be vulnerable in the courts" (*Policy Hearings* 1993, 777).

19. Despite his opening disclaimers, Thurmond later rebukes two gay service members who testify before the committee, saying, "Your lifestyle is not normal. It is not normal for a man to want to be with a man or a woman with a woman" (*Policy Hearings* 1993, 567). He refers to homosexuality as "abnormal" (688) and a "handicap" (689), and he asks all the gay service members who testify on one panel if they have ever considered seeking "psychiatric or medical help" to "correct" their situation (688).

20. Defenders of the ban claim that there is an escape clause for those who have made such a statement. Built into the policy is a "rebuttable presumption" provision which states that when one has made such a statement, the presumption is that it is true, but the individual may "rebut" this presumption by proving otherwise, that is, proving "that he or she does not engage in homosexual acts and does not have a propensity or intent to do so" (*Policy Hearings* 1993, 702–3; see also 713). The only proof that would suffice would have to establish that the individual was drunk or otherwise mentally incapacitated at the time of the statement and did not know what he or she was saying, and that the statement simply was not true. Although this clause is made much of during the hearings, Defense Department representatives concede that while this rebuttable presumption was also incorporated into the old policy, it has never successfully been used to clear a service member from the charge of homosexuality.

21. Although technically the military recognizes three categories of sexual ori-

entation—heterosexuality, homosexuality, and bisexuality—for all practical purposes, bisexuality drops out of the discussion and leaves only the binary opposition. The reasons for this exclusion of bisexuality, which characterizes discussions of sexual orientation in many other forums as well, are too complex to address within the scope of this study. Nevertheless, it is probably safe to surmise that because bisexuality confounds the comfortable division of "them" and "us" that homophobia upholds, it is easier to ignore than to confront the ambiguity of bisexual status or conduct. For perspectives on bisexuality, see Beemyn and Eliason 1996; Hall and Pramaggiore 1996; Rose, Stevens, and the Off Pink Collective 1996; Tucker 1995; Eadie 1993; and George 1993.

22. Cammermeyer's formal statement to Agent Troutman reads, in part: "I am a Lesbian. Lesbianism is an orientation I have, emotional in nature, towards women. It does not imply sexual activity. . . . I want the Government to see me as a human being, not a woman who has sex with other wom[e]n. My sexual preference is irrelevant" (Memo in Support 1994, 9).

23. The obscuring of lesbians behind inaccurate stereotypes of gay men is prevalent elsewhere in the testimony of the Senate hearing. For example, in an article written by a retired Marine Corps colonel and submitted for the record by Senator Conrad Burns, the author argues that "homosexual conduct in the society does not present a convincing example from which to conclude that open homosexuals can conduct themselves, in general, with the restraint necessary to avoid serious disruption in efficiency and combat effectiveness" (*Policy Hearings* 1993, 503). He bases this assertion in part on comparisons of the number of sex partners of gay men versus that of heterosexual men. (Intriguingly, the numbers for gay men come from studies done in the late 1970s and early 1980s, while the numbers for heterosexual men come from studies completed in 1989 and 1990.) He also cites statistics for the rates of sexually transmitted diseases, alcoholism, and attempted suicide among gay men. The only claim he makes about lesbians is that "between 25 percent and 50 percent of homosexual men and women are alcoholics." However, even this "finding" is cited from an article titled "Alcoholics Anonymous and Gay American *Men*" (*Policy Hearings* 1993, 503; emphasis mine). Despite the obvious omissions here, he draws the sweeping conclusion that "open homosexual behavior is not correctable to the standards of good order and discipline established by all the Armed Forces and that such individuals do not seem good candidates for successful military service."

In another example, Senator Murkowski voices his opposition to lifting the ban based on the risk of AIDS (*Policy Hearings* 1993, 469). The argument itself is erroneous because, as Senator John Kerry observes, the disease is increasing faster in the heterosexual community than it is in the homosexual community (*Policy Hearings* 1993, 489). Moreover, the position is unconvincing given the military's policy of testing all military personnel for HIV every six months. Just as important, however, is the fact that such an argument excludes lesbians from the class of "gays" entirely, for lesbians have a lower rate of infection than gay men or heterosexual men or women and much less risk of contracting the disease through sexual contact than does any other sexually active group (Editors of the *Harvard Law Review* 1990, 19). Senator Kerry reflects that if the military's goal is to eliminate the problem of HIV infection in its ranks, "I do not know what you do, go to an all-lesbian army or something" (*Policy Hearings* 1993, 489).

24. In an apparent, if failed, attempt to correct the accuracy of his statement, Thurmond then added, "Or [heterosexuals] do not admit they do. Homosexuals do admit they practice sodomy."

25. The misinterpretation of sodomy statutes to suggest their specificity to homosexuality has been pervasive in legal arguments at even the highest levels (Halley 1991). One of the most blatant examples of this error appears in *Bowers v. Hardwick*, in which the state of Georgia "justified its facially neutral statute based on its 'interest in prosecuting homosexual activity'" (Editors of the *Harvard Law Review* 1990, 21). The Supreme Court itself magnified the mistake when "the plurality opinion in Bowers restrict[ed] itself to reviewing the constitutionality of the Georgia statute as applied to homosexual sodomy *even though the gender of Hardwick's partner was never stated in the original complaint*, the only official record of the incident" (Currah 1995, 67–68).

26. This view echoes the homophobic application of Christian charity: love the sinner, hate the sin. The Catholic Church, for example, holds the position that "because of homosexuality's involuntary nature, it cannot of itself be morally culpable (although homosexual *acts* still are)" (Sullivan 1993, 26).

27. Although the appropriateness of the sodomy statute is itself highly arguable, debate on this issue is beyond the scope of my discussion.

28. An interesting side note concerns the considerable slippage that occurs between the categories of "speech" and "conduct," an ambiguity that regularly functions to protect and maintain patriarchal power. Most frequently, as in this case, this slippage is an effect of linking categories of speech and conduct through the medium of sex and manipulating the definition of sexual acts as speech or as conduct, depending on dominant interests. Perhaps the most notable example is that of pornography, which is defined as speech and protected as such under the First Amendment, even though pornography clearly involves conduct: violent sexual acts involving pain, injury, or even death, carried out through coercion or physical force, are regularly performed on women's bodies to produce pornography (Dworkin and MacKinnon 1988). Yet, despite the startlingly broad definition of what may be protected as "speech" in this context, the military maintains that in the absence of any activity whatsoever, a verbal statement of homosexual identity is itself an instance not of speech but of conduct and, as such, is not subject to First Amendment protection.

29. I thank Celeste Condit for drawing my attention to the origins of this distinction in Greek thought.

30. A simple example is the use of E-mail for "private" discussions, perhaps of illegal activities. Whereas phone tapping is subject to legal restrictions and reading someone else's mail is a felony, E-mail is a publicly accessible medium (records of E-mail sent and received are kept by systems operators and can be readily accessed by legal authorities) that most of us nevertheless use freely, as though it were private and protected.

31. Senator Warner points out the enormity of the expectations such a policy places on gay and lesbian service members: "You are asking homosexuals to take an oath of celibacy, mental and physical, for the balance of their terms of active duty. I think that is unrealistic, unfair, and discriminatory. It is not a step forward, it is a step back" (*Policy Hearings* 1993, 736).

32. One explanation for this hypocrisy is that "the military establishment, schools, churches all understand the importance of the closet in maintaining institutional order. That is why the services never cared a damn about gays who did not proclaim their identity, by word or deed. It is why school superintendents have lived for centuries with lesbian and gay teachers, but panic when anyone comes out. It's why churches countenance lesbian nuns and gay priests and ministers as long as they lie about themselves" (Kopkind 1993, 577).

## NOTES TO CHAPTER 4

1. For a thorough analysis of the connections between legal reform and attitude change, see Cuklanz 1996.

2. More specifically, "while some law reforms may indeed benefit some women, it is certain that all law reforms empower law" (Smart 1989, 161).

3. The term *partner* is sometimes used, for lack of a better word, to describe each member of a committed relationship between two gay men or lesbians. Yet it is often rejected as sounding too formal and impersonal, as though one were referring to a business associate. *Lover* is sometimes used, but many couples find it too personal or misrepresentative of what is valued in the relationship. Some lesbians and gay men use the term *mate*, and others prefer *spouse*, especially if they have participated in a commitment ceremony. Still others, with or without a degree of irony, use *husband* or *wife*.

# BIBLIOGRAPHY

The Achtenberg confirmation. 1993. *California Journal,* July 1.

Acker, J. 1990. Hierarchies, jobs, bodies: A theory of gendered organizations. *Gender and Society* 4, 2: 139–58.

Adam, B. D. 1994. Anatomy of a panic: State voyeurism, gender politics, and the cult of Americanism. In *Gays and lesbians in the military: Issues, concerns, and contrasts,* edited by W. J. Scott and S. C. Stanley, 103–18. Hawthorne, N.Y.: Aldine de Gruyter.

Advocate report. 1997. *The Advocate* (April 1): 17.

Ainley, R. 1995. *What is she like? Lesbian identities from the 1950s to the 1990s.* London: Cassell.

Altman, D. 1982. *The homosexualization of America, the Americanization of the homosexual.* New York: St. Martin's Press.

Alyson, S. 1993. *The Alyson almanac: 1994–95 edition.* Boston: Alyson Publications.

Anzaldúa, G. 1990a. Bridge, drawbridge, sandbar or island: Lesbians of-color *hacienda alianzas.* In *Bridges of power: Women's multicultural alliances,* edited by L. Albrecht and R. M. Brewer, 216–31. Philadelphia: New Society Publishers.

———. 1990b. Haciendo caras, una entrada. In *Making face, making soul, haciendo caras: Creative and critical perspectives by feminists of color,* edited by G. Anzaldúa, xv–xxviii. San Francisco: Aunt Lute Books.

———. 1991. To(o) queer the writer—*loca, escritora y chicana.* In *InVersions: Writing by dykes, queers and lesbians,* edited by B. Warland, 249–63. Vancouver: Press Gang Publishers.

Beck, E. T. 1982. Why is this book different from all other books? In *Nice Jewish girls: A lesbian anthology,* edited by E. T. Beck, xiii–xxxvi. Trumansburg, N.Y.: Crossing Press.

Becker, M. 1995. Becoming visible. *National Journal of Sexual Orientation Law* 1, 2: 147–50. Internet: http://sunsite.unc.edu/gaylaw.

Beemyn, B., and M. Eliason. 1996. *Queer studies: A lesbian, gay, bisexual, and transgender anthology.* New York: New York University Press.

Belenky, M. F., B. M. Clinchy, N. R. Goldberger, and J. M. Tarule. 1986. *Women's ways of knowing: The development of self, voice, and mind.* New York: Basic Books.

Benecke, M. M., and K. S. Dodge. 1996. Military women: Casualties of the armed forces' war on lesbians and gay men. In *Gay rights, military wrongs: Political perspectives on lesbians and gays in the military*, edited by C. A. Rimmerman, 71–108. New York: Garland.

Bennett, P. 1982. Dyke in academe (II). In *Lesbian studies: Present and future*, edited by M. Cruikshank, 3–8. New York: Feminist Press.

———. 1993. Gender as performance: Shakespearean ambiguity and the lesbian reader. In *Sexual practice, textual theory: Lesbian cultural criticism*, edited by S. J. Wolfe and J. Penelope, 94–109. Cambridge, Mass.: Blackwell.

Bérubé, A. 1990. *Coming out under fire: The history of gay men and women in World War Two*. New York: Free Press.

Blasius, M. 1994. *Gay and lesbian politics: Sexuality and the emergence of a new ethic*. Philadelphia: Temple University Press.

Blumstein, P., and P. Schwartz. 1983. *American couples: Money, work, sex*. New York: Morrow.

Boston Lesbian Psychologies Collective. 1987. *Lesbian psychologies: Explorations and challenges*. Urbana: University of Illinois Press.

Boswell, J. 1993. Battle-worn. *New Republic* (May 10): 15–18.

Brown, J. C. 1986. *Immodest acts: The life of a lesbian nun in Renaissance Italy*. New York: Oxford University Press.

Brown, K. 1993. Our damn lesbian. *Deneuve* 3 (September-October): 22–24, 56.

Brown, L. S. 1989. New voices, new visions: Toward a lesbian/gay paradigm for psychology. *Psychology of Women Quarterly* 13: 455–58.

———. 1992. While waiting for the revolution: The case for a lesbian feminist psychotherapy. *Feminism and Psychology* 2 (June): 239–53.

Brummett, B. 1979. A pentadic analysis of ideologies in two gay rights controversies. *Central States Speech Journal* 30: 250–61.

Bull, C. 1994. Choosing up sides. *The Advocate* (July 12): 29–30.

Bumiller, K. 1988. *The civil rights society: The social construction of victims*. Baltimore: Johns Hopkins University Press.

Bunch, C. 1987. *Passionate politics: Feminist theory in action*. New York: St. Martin's Press.

Burrelli, D. F. 1994. An overview of the debate on homosexuals in the U.S. military. In *Gays and lesbians in the military: Issues, concerns, and contrasts*, edited by W. J. Scott and S. C. Stanley, 17–31. Hawthorne, N.Y.: Aldine de Gruyter.

Butler, J. 1990. *Gender trouble: Feminism and the subversion of identity*. New York: Routledge.

———. 1993. Imitation and gender insubordination. In *The lesbian and gay studies reader*, edited by H. Abelove, M. A. Barale, and D. M. Halperin, 307–20. New York: Routledge.

Cammermeyer, M. 1994. *Serving in silence*. New York: Penguin Books.

*Cammermeyer v. Aspin*, 1994. 850 F. Supp. 910 (W.D. Wa.).

Campbell, K. K. 1989. *Man cannot speak for her: A critical study of early feminist rhetoric*. Vol. 1. New York: Praeger.

Castle, T. 1993. *The apparitional lesbian: Female homosexuality and modern culture*. New York: Columbia University Press.

Cerullo, M. 1990. Hope and terror: The paradox of gay and lesbian politics in the 90s. *Radical America* 24 (July–September): 10–16.

Chesebro, J. W. 1981. *Gayspeak: Gay male and lesbian communication*. New York: Pilgrim Press.

Civil rights or special rights? 1996. CNN Interactive, May 21. Internet: http://www.cnn.com/US/9605/21/gay.reax/index.html.

Clarke, C. 1983. Lesbianism: An act of resistance. In *This bridge called my back: Writings by radical women of color*, edited by C. Moraga and G. Anzaldúa, 128–37. New York: Kitchen Table: Women of Color Press.

Clausen, J. 1997. *Beyond gay or straight: Understanding sexual orientation*. Philadelphia: Chelsea House Publishers.

Cohen, D. 1993. Notes on a Grecian yearn: Pederasty in Thebes and Sparta. *New York Times*, March 31, A23.

Cohen, E. 1993. *Talk on the Wilde side: Toward a genealogy of a discourse on male sexualities*. New York: Routledge.

Colbert, C. 1997. Lesbians targeted in latest Atlanta bombing. New America News Service, March 5.

Collins, P. H. 1991. *Black feminist thought: Knowledge, consciousness, and the politics of empowerment*. New York: Routledge.

Could it be a witch-hunt? 1997. *The Advocate* (April 1): 15.

Cruikshank, M. 1994. Gay and lesbian liberation: An overview. In *Gays and lesbians in the military: Issues, concerns, and contrasts*, edited by W. J. Scott and S. C. Stanley, 3–16. Hawthorne, N.Y.: Aldine de Gruyter.

Cuklanz, L. M. 1996. *Rape on trial: How the mass media construct legal reform and social change*. Philadelphia: University of Pennsylvania Press.

Currah, P. 1995. Searching for immutability: Homosexuality, race and rights discourse. In *A simple matter of justice? Theorizing lesbian and gay politics*, edited by A. R. Wilson, 51–90. London: Cassell.

Daly, M. 1987. *Websters' first new intergalactic wickedary of the English language*. Boston: Beacon Press.

Deitcher, D. 1995. Law and desire. In *The question of equality: Lesbian and gay politics in America since Stonewall*, edited by D. Deitcher, 135–81. New York: Scribner's.

de Lauretis, T. 1993. Sexual indifference and lesbian representation. In *The lesbian and gay studies reader*, edited by H. Abelove, M. A. Barale, and D. M. Halperin, 141–58. New York: Routledge.

Department of the Army. 1991. *Transcript of proceedings: Federal recognition board hearing for Margarethe Cammermeyer*. Camp Murray, Tacoma, Washington. July 15.

Doan, L., ed. 1994. *The lesbian postmodern*. New York: Columbia University Press.

Douglas, C. A. 1990. *Love and politics: Radical feminist and lesbian theories*. San Francisco: ism press.

Dworkin, A., and C. A. MacKinnon. 1988. *Pornography and civil rights: A new day for women's equality*. Minneapolis: Organizing Against Pornography.

Eadie, J. 1993. Activating bisexuality: Towards a bi/sexual politics. In *Activating theory: Lesbian, gay, bisexual politics*, edited by J. Bristow and A. R. Wilson, 139–70. London: Lawrence & Wishart.

Editors of the *Harvard Law Review*. 1990. *Sexual orientation and the law*. Cambridge: Harvard University Press.

Edwards, T. 1994. *Erotics and politics: Gay male sexuality, masculinity and feminism*. London: Routledge.

Epstein, S. 1987. Gay politics, ethnic identity: The limits of social construction. *Socialist Review* 1, 3–4: 9–54.

Faderman, L. 1981. *Surpassing the love of men: Romantic friendship and love between women from the Renaissance to the present*. New York: Morrow.

———. 1991. *Odd girls and twilight lovers: A history of lesbian life in twentieth century America*. New York: Columbia University Press.

———, comp. and ed. 1994. *Chloe plus Olivia: An anthology of lesbian literature from the seventeenth century to the present*. New York: Viking.

Fajer, M. A. 1992. Can two real men eat quiche together? Storytelling, gender-role stereotypes, and legal protection for lesbians and gay men. *University of Miami Law Review* 46, 3: 511–655.

———. 1996. *Bowers v. Hardwick, Romer v. Evans*, and the meaning of anti-discrimination legislation. *National Journal of Sexual Orientation Law* 2, 2: 207–15. Internet: http://sunsite.unc.edu/gaylaw/fajer.pag.

Fejes, F., and K. Petrich. 1993. Invisibility, homophobia, and heterosexism: Lesbians, gays and the media. *Critical Studies in Mass Communication* 10: 395–422.

Flores, L. A. 1994. *Shifting visions: Intersections of rhetorical and Chicana feminist theory in the analysis of mass media*. Ph.D. diss., University of Georgia, Athens.

Foss, S. K. 1996. *Rhetorical criticism: Exploration and practice*. 2d ed. Prospect Heights, Ill.: Waveland Press.

Foucault, M. 1978. *The history of sexuality*, vol. 1: *An introduction*. New York: Vintage Books.

Franken, B. 1993. Roberta Achtenberg wins Senate approval for HUD post. CNN, May 25, transcript 368-1.

Frye, M. 1983. *The politics of reality: Essays in feminist theory*. Freedom, Calif.: Crossing Press.

Fure, T. 1992. Something blue. On *Postcards from paradise*, by C. Williamson and T. Fure. Lunafish Music (BMI). Oakland, Calif.: Olivia Records.

Fuss, D. 1989. *Essentially speaking*. New York: Routledge.

Gallagher, J. 1992. GAO: Military spent $500 million discharging gays. *The Advocate* (July 30): 21.

Gamson, J. 1996. Do ask, do tell. *Utne Reader* 73 (January-February): 78–83.

George, S. 1993. *Women and bisexuality*. London: Scarlet Press.

Gilligan, C. 1982. *In a different voice: Psychological theory and women's development*. Cambridge: Harvard University Press.

Gomez, J. 1995. Out of the past. *The question of equality: Lesbian and gay politics in America since Stonewall*, edited by D. Deitcher, 17–66. New York: Scribner's.

Grahn, J. 1984. *Another mother tongue: Gay words, gay worlds*. Boston: Beacon Press.

Griffin, G. 1993a. *Heavenly love? Lesbian images in twentieth-century women's writing*. Manchester, N.Y.: Manchester University Press.

————, ed. 1993b. *Outwrite: Lesbianism and popular culture*. Boulder, Colo.: Pluto Press.

Hall, D. E., and M. Pramaggiore, eds. 1996. *Representing bisexualities: Subjects and cultures of fluid desire*. New York: New York University Press.

Halley, J. E. 1989. The politics of the closet: Towards equal protection for gay, lesbian, and bisexual identity. *UCLA Law Review* 36: 915–76.

————. 1991. Misreading sodomy: A critique of the classification of "homosexuals" in federal equal protection law. In *Body guards: The cultural politics of gender ambiguity*, edited by J. Epstein and K. Straub, 351–77. New York: Routledge.

————. 1993. Reasoning about sodomy: Act and identity in and after *Bowers v. Hardwick. Virginia Law Review* 79: 1721–50.

Hart, L. 1994. *Fatal women: Lesbian sexuality and the mark of aggression*. Princeton: Princeton University Press.

Herman, D. 1994. *Rights of passage: Struggles for lesbian and gay legal equality*. Toronto: University of Toronto Press.

Hollibaugh, A. 1993. We can get there from here. *The Nation* 257 (July 5): 26–31.

Hoogland, R. C. 1997. *Lesbian configurations*. New York: Columbia University Press.

hooks, bell. 1989. *Talking back: Thinking feminist, thinking black*. Boston: South End Press.

Horner, D. H., Jr., and M. T. Anderson. 1994. Integration of homosexuals into the armed forces: Racial and gender integration as a point of departure. In *Gays and lesbians in the military: Issues, concerns, and contrasts*, edited by W. J. Scott and S. C. Stanley, 247–60. Hawthorne, N.Y.: Aldine de Gruyter.

Institute for Sex Research. 1953. *Sexual behavior in the human female*. Philadelphia: Saunders.

Jay, K., and J. Glasgow. 1990. *Lesbians texts and contexts: Radical revisions*. New York: New York University Press.

Kasindorf, J. R. 1993. Lesbian chic: The bold, brave new world of gay women. *New York Magazine* 26 (May 10): 30–37.

Kaye/Kantrowitz, M. 1992. *The issue is power*. San Francisco: Aunt Lute Books.

Keller, E. F. 1985. *Reflections on gender and science*. New Haven: Yale University Press.

Kerby, A. P. 1991. *Narrative and the self*. Bloomington: Indiana University Press.

King, D. K. 1988. Multiple jeopardy, multiple consciousness: The context of a Black feminist ideology. *Signs* 14, 1: 42–72.

King, J. D., and J. W. Riddlesperger, Jr. 1991. Senate confirmation of appointments to the cabinet and executive office of the president. *Social Science Journal* 28, 2: 189–202.

Kinsey, A. C., W. B. Pomeroy, and C. E. Martin. 1948. *Sexual behavior in the human male.* Philadelphia: Saunders.

Kitzinger, C., and R. Perkins. 1993. *Changing our minds: Lesbian feminism and psychology.* New York: New York University Press.

Koedt, A. 1973. Lesbianism and feminism. In *Radical Feminism,* edited by A. Koedt, E. Levine, and A. Rapone, 246–58. New York: Quadrangle Books.

Kopkind, A. 1993. The gay movement. *The Nation* 256 (May 3): 577.

Koppel, T. 1994. Interview with Tracy Thorne. *ABC News Nightline,* July 14.

Korb, L. 1994. Evolving perspectives on the military's policy on homosexuals: A personal note. In *Gays and lesbians in the military: Issues, concerns, and contrasts,* edited by W. J. Scott and S. C. Stanley, 219–29. Hawthorne, N.Y.: Aldine de Gruyter.

Krauss, C. 1993. Housing nominee is attacked. *New York Times,* May 21, A12.

Kurs, K., and R. S. Cathcart. 1983. The feminist movement: Lesbian-feminism as confrontation. *Women's Studies in Communication* 6: 12–23.

Lehring, G. L. 1996. Constructing the *"other"* soldier: Gay identity's military threat. In *Gay rights, military wrongs: Political perspectives on lesbians and gays in the military,* edited by C. A. Rimmerman, 269–93. New York: Garland.

Lesbian History Group. 1989. *Not a passing phase: Reclaiming lesbians in history 1840–1985.* London: Women's Press.

Lesbians, long overlooked, are central to debate on military ban. 1993. *New York Times,* May 4, A23.

Lever, J. 1995. Lesbian sex survey. *The Advocate* (August 22): 22–30.

Lorde, A. 1984. *Sister outsider.* Freedom, Calif.: Crossing Press.

Lugones, M. 1990. Playfulness, "world"-travelling, and loving perception. In *Making face, making soul, haciendo caras: Creative and critical perspectives by feminists of color,* edited by G. Anzaldúa, 390–402. San Francisco: Aunt Lute Books.

Lynch, A. 1993. Achtenberg rebuts critics—says she's religious, not mean. *San Francisco Chronicle,* May 27, A6.

Lynch, A., and C. Lochhead. 1993. Fiery Achtenberg Senate debate expected next week. *San Francisco Chronicle,* May 15, A6.

Lynch, L. 1990. Cruising the libraries. In *Lesbian texts and contexts: Radical revisions,* edited by K. Jay and J. Glasgow, 39–48. New York: New York University Press.

Manuel, M. 1997. Cobb group refocuses as furor on gays abates. *Atlanta Journal/Constitution,* March 16, F5.

Martin, J. L. 1987. The impact of AIDS on gay male sexual behavior patterns in New York City. *American Journal of Public Health* 77, 5: 578–81.

Meese, E. A. 1992. *(Sem)Erotics: Theorizing lesbian: Writing.* New York: New York University Press.

Memo in support of plaintiff's motion for summary judgment. 1994. *Cammermeyer v. Aspin,* 850 F. Supp. 910 (W.D. Wa.).

Mendus, S. 1989. *Toleration and the limits of liberalism*. Atlantic Highlands, N.J.: Humanities Press International.

Mennis, B. 1982. Repeating history. In *Nice Jewish girls: A lesbian anthology*, edited by E. T. Beck, 89–96. Trumansburg, N.Y.: Crossing Press.

Miles, S. 1995. Roberta's run. *Out* (September): 68–71, 116–21.

Miller, L. L. 1994. Fighting for a just cause: Soldiers' views on gays in the military. In *Gays and lesbians in the military: Issues, concerns, and contrasts*, edited by W. J. Scott and S. C. Stanley, 69–85. Hawthorne, N.Y.: Aldine de Gruyter.

Minh-ha, T. T. 1990. Not you/like you: Post-colonial women and the interlocking questions of identity and difference. In *Making face, making soul, haciendo caras: Creative and critical perspectives by feminists of color*, edited by G. Anzaldúa, 371–75. San Francisco: Aunt Lute Books.

Mohr, R. D. 1994. *A more perfect union: Why straight America must stand up for gay rights*. Boston: Beacon Press.

Moraga, C. 1983. La güera. In *This bridge called my back: Writings by radical women of color*, edited by C. Moraga and G. Anzaldúa, 27–34. New York: Kitchen Table: Women of Color Press.

Moskos, C., Jr. 1994. From citizens' army to social laboratory. In *Gays and lesbians in the military: Issues, concerns, and contrasts*, edited by W. J. Scott and S. C. Stanley, 53–65. Hawthorne, N.Y.: Aldine de Gruyter.

Moss, J. J. 1993. Achtenberg's name sent to Senate; Helms awaits. *Washington Times*, May 6, A3.

————. 1997. Losing the war. *The Advocate* (April 15): 22–30.

Munt, S. 1992. *New lesbian criticism: Literary and cultural readings*. New York: Columbia University Press.

Nava, M., and R. Dawidoff. 1994. *Created equal: Why gay rights matter to America*. New York: St. Martin's Press.

Newcombe, M. 1991. Introduction: A lesbian vision. *UCLA Women's Law Journal* 1: 7–9.

————. 1996. Telephone conversation with author. February 12.

*Nominations of Kenneth D. Brody, Roberta Achtenberg, and Nicolas P. Retsinas: Hearing before the Committee on Banking, Housing, and Urban Affairs*. 1993. U.S. Senate, 103d Cong. 1st sess. April 29.

No ruling on defunct Cammermeyer case. 1996. *Front Page* 17 (October 11): 41.

Osburn, C. D., and M. M. Benecke. 1996. Conduct unbecoming continues: The first year under "Don't Ask, Don't Tell, Don't Pursue." In *Gay rights, military wrongs: Political perspectives on lesbians and gays in the military*, edited by C. A. Rimmerman, 249–68. New York: Garland.

Otjen, General J. P. 1994. Deposition. *Cammermeyer v. Aspin*, 850 F. Supp. 910 (W.D. Wa.).

Palmer, P. 1993. *Contemporary lesbian writing: Dreams, desire, difference*. Buckingham, England: Open University Press.

Pharr, S. 1988. *Homophobia, a weapon of sexism.* Inverness, Calif.: Chardon Press.

Phelan, S. 1993. (Be)Coming out: Lesbian identity and politics. *Signs* 18, 4: 765–90.

———. 1994. *Getting specific: Postmodern lesbian politics.* Minneapolis: University of Minnesota Press.

———. 1995. The space of justice: Lesbians and democratic politics. In *A simple matter of justice? Theorizing lesbian and gay politics*, edited by A. R. Wilson, 193–220. London: Cassell.

Pheterson, G. 1990. Alliances between women: Overcoming internalized oppression and internalized domination. In *Bridges of power: Women's multicultural alliances*, edited by L. Albrecht and R. M. Brewer, 34–48. Philadelphia: New Society Publishers.

Plaintiff's memo in opposition to defendant's motion for judgment on the pleadings. 1994. *Cammermeyer v. Aspin*, 850 F. Supp. 910 (W.D. Wa.).

Plaintiff's reply memo in support of plaintiff's motion for summary judgment. 1994. *Cammermeyer v. Aspin*, 850 F. Supp. 910 (W.D. Wa.).

Plaskow, J. 1994. Lesbian and gay rights: Asking the right questions. *Tikkun* 9, 2: 31–32.

Plummer, K. 1995. *Telling sexual stories: Power, change and social worlds.* London: Routledge.

*Policy concerning homosexuality in the armed forces: Hearings before the Committee on Armed Services.* 1993. 103d Cong. 2d sess.

Pollack, S., and D. D. Knight, eds. 1993. *Contemporary lesbian writers of the United States: A bio-bibliographical critical sourcebook.* Westport, Conn.: Greenwood Press.

Ponse, B. 1978. *Identities in the lesbian world: The social construction of self.* Westport, Conn.: Greenwood Press.

Price, D. 1997. Colonial-era anti-sodomy laws now simply reflect discrimination. *Detriot News,* July 11, E2.

Price, J. 1993. Strident activism steps on toes; video raises questions of HUD nominee's values. *Washington Times,* May 24, A1.

Rebolledo, T. D. 1990. The politics of poetics: Or, what am I, a critic, doing in this text anyhow? In *Making face, making soul, haciendo caras: Creative and critical perspectives by feminists of color*, edited by G. Anzaldúa, 346–55. San Francisco: Aunt Lute Books.

Reuters. 1993. Lesbian politician selected for top government post, report says. January 27.

Rich, A. 1979. *On lies, secrets, and silence: Selected prose 1966–1978.* New York: Norton.

———. 1986. *Blood, bread, and poetry: Selected prose 1979–1985.* New York: Norton.

Ringer, R. J., ed. 1994. *Queer words, queer images: Communication and the construction of homosexuality.* New York: New York University Press.

Robb, S. 1993. About face. *Crossroads* (April): 10–12.

Robson, R. 1990. Discourses of discrimination and lesbians as (out)laws. *Radical America* 24, 4: 39–47.

————. 1992. *Lesbian (out)law: Survival under the rule of law*. Ithaca, N.Y.: Firebrand Books.

Rolison, G. L., and T. K. Nakayama. 1994. Defensive discourse: Blacks and gays in the military. In *Gays and lesbians in the military: Issues, concerns, and contrasts*, edited by W. J. Scott and S. C. Stanley, 121–33. Hawthorne, N.Y.: Aldine de Gruyter.

Roof, J. 1991. *A lure of knowledge: Lesbian sexuality and theory*. New York: Columbia University Press.

Rose, S., C. Stevens, and the Off Pink Collective, eds. 1996. *Bisexual horizons: Politics, histories, lives*. London: Lawrence & Wishart.

Sandoval, C. 1982. Comment on Krieger's "Lesbian identity and community: Recent social science literature." In *The lesbian issue: Essays from Signs*, edited by E. B. Freedman, B. C. Gelpi, S. L. Johnson, and K. M. Weston, 241–45. Chicago: University of Chicago Press.

Satter, S. 1993. Achtenberg's honest about her sexuality, and she's punished. *San Francisco Examiner*, May 25, 15A.

Schüklenk, U., and M. Ristow. 1996. Inquiring into sex. *The Lancet* 347 (January 27): 266–67.

Scott, W. J., and S. C. Stanley. 1994. Introduction: Sexual orientation and military service. In *Gays and lesbians in the military: Issues, concerns, and contrasts*, edited by W. J. Scott and S. C. Stanley, xi-xx. Hawthorne, N.Y.: Aldine de Gruyter.

Sedgwick, E. K. 1990. *Epistemology of the closet*. Berkeley: University of California Press.

————. 1993. *Tendencies*. Durham: Duke University Press.

Segrest, M. 1995. Visibility and backlash. In *The question of equality: Lesbian and gay politics in America since Stonewall*, edited by D. Deitcher, 84–122. New York: Scribner's.

Shapiro, J. P., G. G. Cook, and A. Krackov. 1993. Straight talk about gays. *U.S. News and World Report* 115 (July 5): 42–48.

Shepard, A. C. 1994. Where she lives. *San Jose Mercury News*, March 27. Newsbank, PEO 7: G14-8: A4. Microfiche.

Shilts, R. 1993. *Conduct unbecoming: Gays and lesbians in the U.S. military: Vietnam to the Persian Gulf*. New York: St. Martin's Press.

Shotter, J., and K. J. Gergen. 1989. Preface and introduction. In *Texts of identity*, edited by J. Shotter and K. J. Gergen, ix-xi. Newbury Park, Cailf.: Sage Publications.

Showalter, E. 1985. Introduction: The feminist critical revolution. In *The new feminist criticism: Essays on women, literature, and theory*, edited by E. Showalter, 3–17. New York: Pantheon Books.

Smart, C. 1989. *Feminism and the power of law*. New York: Routledge.

Smith, B. 1993. Where's the revolution? *The Nation* 257 (July 5): 12–16.

Snitow, A., C. Stansell, and S. Thompson. 1986. Afterword to "Compulsory heterosexuality and lesbian existence." In *Blood, bread, and poetry: Selected prose 1979–1985*, by A. Rich, 68–75. New York: Norton.

Stanback, M. H. 1985. Language and black woman's place: Evidence from the black middle class. In *For alma mater: Theory and practice in feminist scholarship*, edited by P. A. Treichler, C. Kramarae, and B. Stafford, 177–93. Urbana: University of Illinois Press.

Stiehm, J. H. 1994. The military ban on homosexuals and the cyclops effect. In *Gays and lesbians in the military: Issues, concerns, and contrasts*, edited by W. J. Scott and S. C. Stanley, 149–62. Hawthorne, N.Y. : Aldine de Gruyter.

Stein, A., ed. 1993. *Sisters, sexperts, queers: Beyond the lesbian nation*. New York: Plume.

Stoddard, T. 1993. Man and woman of the year. *The Advocate* (December 28): 45–50.

Sullivan, A. 1993. The politics of homosexuality. *New Republic* (May 10): 24–37.

Taylor, J. 1995. Is there a lesbian in this text? Sarton, performance and multicultural pedagogy. *Text and Performance Quarterly* 15,4: 282–300.

Traub, V. 1991. The ambiguities of "lesbian" viewing pleasure: The (dis)articulations of *Black Widow*. In *Body guards: The cultural politics of gender ambiguity*, edited by J. Epstein and K. Straub, 305–28. New York: Routledge.

Trebilcot, J. 1994. *Dyke ideas: Process, politics, daily life*. Albany: State University of New York Press.

Tucker, N., ed. 1995. *Bisexual politics: Theories, queries, and visions*. New York: Haworth Press.

Vaid, U. 1993. After identity. *New Republic*, May 10, 28.

———. 1995. *Virtual equality: The mainstreaming of gay and lesbian liberation*. New York: Doubleday Anchor Books.

Vozzella, L. 1997. Home-grown crime scarier than serial killers, gays say. *Fort Worth Star-Telegram*, August 6, 1.

Weiss, A. 1993. *Vampires and violets: Lesbians in film*. New York: Penguin Books.

Weston, K. 1991. *Families we choose: Lesbians, gays, kinship*. New York: Columbia University Press.

Wiegman, R. 1994. Introduction: Mapping the lesbian postmodern. In *The lesbian postmodern*, edited by L. Doan, 1–20. New York: Columbia University Press.

Wilson, A. R. 1995. Introduction. In *A simple matter of justice? Theorizing lesbian and gay politics*, edited by A. R. Wilson, 1–9. London: Cassell.

Wilton, T., ed. 1995. *Immortal, invisible: Lesbians and the moving image*. London and New York: Routledge.

Winant, H. 1990. Postmodern racial politics in the United States: Difference and inequality. *Socialist Review* 20, 1: 121–47.

Wittig, M. 1992. *The straight mind and other essays*. Boston: Beacon Press.

———. 1993. One is not born a woman. In *The lesbian and gay studies reader*, edited by H. Abelove, M. A. Barale, and D. M. Halperin, 103–9. New York: Routledge.

Wolfe, S. J., and J. Penelope. 1993. Sexual identity/textual politics: Lesbian {de/com}positions. In *Sexual practice, textual theory: Lesbian cultural criticism*, edited by S. J. Wolfe and J. Penelope, 1–24. Cambridge, Mass.: Blackwell.

Wolinsky, M., and K. Sherrill. 1993. Introduction. In *Gays and the military: Joseph Stef-*

*fan versus the United States*, edited by M. Wolinsky and K. Sherrill, xiii–xxii. Princeton: Princeton University Press.

Wolkoff, G. 1993. Achtenberg charges anti-Semitism. *Jewish Bulletin of Northern California* 142 (May 28): 1, 41.

Zaeske, S. 1995. The "promiscuous audience" controversy and the emergence of the early woman's rights movement. *Quarterly Journal of Speech* 81: 191–207.

Zimmerman, B. 1982. The politics of transliteration: Lesbian personal narratives. In *The lesbian issue: Essays from Signs*, edited by E. B. Freedman, B. C. Gelpi, S. L. Johnson, and K. M. Weston, 251–70. Chicago: University of Chicago Press.

———. 1992. Lesbians like this and that: Some notes on lesbian criticism for the nineties. In *New lesbian criticism: Literary and cultural readings*, ed. S. Munt, 1–15. New York: Columbia University Press.

———. 1993. What has never been: An overview of lesbian feminist criticism. In *Sexual practice, textual theory: Lesbian cultural criticism*, edited by S. J. Wolfe and J. Penelope, 33–54. Cambridge, Mass.: Blackwell.

# INDEX

Achtenberg, Roberta, 9, 17, 18, 30, 44, 85, 86, 139, 154, 159, 167n. 20; accused of intolerance, 68, 70; activism of, 45, 53–55, 57, 59–60, 71, 74, 75, 78, 87, 110, 141–142; anti-Semitic attack on, 67; as Clinton supporter, 75, 86; compared with Carol Moseley-Braun, 50, 58; conflict with Boy Scouts, 69–72; distinguished from lesbian/gay community, 58, 60, 87; family of, 54, 66, 71–72, 74, 76, 141–142, 167n. 21; Jewish identity of, 9, 67, 73; participation in pride parade, 53, 54; politics of, 74–75; portrayed as mainstream, 48, 52, 58, 79, 87; privilege of, 9–10; as religious, 73; representative status of, 10, 18, 35, 43, 48, 68, 70, 79, 87, 165n. 10

Achtenberg nomination, 1, 164n. 1; Banking Committee hearing, 1, 39, 43, 61, 65, 67, 69, 76, 164n. 1; and civil rights strategies, 41–43, 46, 47–59, 73, 74–78; compared with Cammermeyer case, 87–88, 101; opposition to, 1, 39–40, 41, 52–57, 64–65, 66–73, 74, 76, 78, 79–80, 87, 125, 154, 164n. 3, 165n. 10; as precedent, 43, 45, 56, 65, 165n. 9; as progressive, 42–43, 48, 49, 51, 61; support for, 40, 42–43, 46, 48–49, 50–52, 56, 57–61, 68–73, 74, 75, 87, 165n. 14

Activism, 74, 80, 110, 141–142, 157; attacks on, 45, 53–55, 57, 59–60, 65, 71, 78, 87; as means of empowerment, 133–134; spurred by defeat, 146–147

ACT UP (AIDS Coalition To Unleash Power), 29, 73, 74

Affectional orientation, 117, 123–124, 171 n. 22. See also Sexual orientation

Affirmative action, 19

African American women. See Women of color

Agnos, Mayor Art, 60

AIDS, 74, 78, 101, 117, 119, 123; and gay bathhouses, 55, 70; military concerns about, 171–172 n. 23

Amendment 2 (Colorado), 11, 44, 146–147

American Civil Liberties Union (ACLU), 107, 112

American Psychiatric Association, 92

Anti-discrimination laws. See Equal protection laws

Anti-gay rhetoric, 35–36; views of homosexuality in, 50

Anti-gay violence, 12, 21, 31–32, 91, 148, 152, 162 n. 6

Anti-Semitism, 67

Army, 98, 106, 107

Aspin, Les, 97

Assimilation, 18–19, 23, 61, 154; consequences of, 47–48, 141, 147, 151–152; as goal of lesbian and gay rights movement, 8, 15, 140, 143; "white light" metaphor for, 46–47

Bathhouses, gay, 55, 69, 71, 78; as representative of homosexuality, 63, 70, 77

Bisexuality, 8, 66, 93, 171 n. 21

Black and White Men Together, 8

*Bowers v. Hardwick*, 100, 115, 164 n. 6, 172 n. 25; misapplication of, 111–112; prohibition of conduct in, 41, 48, 116

Boxer, Sen. Barbara, 51, 56, 57, 60, 68, 72

Boy Scouts, 53, 54, 69–71, 72, 73, 101; parallel to military, 166–167 n. 20

Brown, Dr. Laura, 116

Brown, Rita Mae, 66, 139

Bush, George, 72

# ABOUT THE AUTHOR

Diane Helene Miller received her B.A. in English and Sociology from Trinity University, her M.A. in Rhetoric from the University of California at Berkeley, and her Ph.D. in Speech Communication with a Graduate Certificate in Women's Studies from the University of Georgia. She is a recipient of the Berkeley Fellowship, the AAUW Athenian Award for Outstanding Scholarship, and the Chris Kramerae Outstanding Dissertation Award presented by the Organization for the Study of Communication, Language, and Gender.

Dr. Miller has taught courses in women's studies, argumentation and composition, rhetorical criticism, and public speaking. She has served as a Residence Halls Area Coordinator at Trinity University and is the former director of the Writing and Communication Center at East Tennessee State University. She now lives in Athens, Georgia. This is her first book